Everyday

Mathematics®

The University of Chicago School Mathematics Project

Assessment Handbook

Grade **1**

Mc Graw Hill **Wright Group**

The McGraw·Hill Companies

The University of Chicago School Mathematics Project (UCSMP)

Max Bell, Director, UCSMP Elementary Materials Component;
   Director, *Everyday Mathematics* First Edition
James McBride, Director, *Everyday Mathematics* Second Edition
Andy Isaacs, Director, *Everyday Mathematics* Third Edition
Amy Dillard, Associate Director, *Everyday Mathematics* Third Edition

Authors
Jean Bell, William M. Carroll, Amy Dillard, Kathleen Pitvorec

Teacher in Residence
Soundarya Radhakrishnan

Photo Credits
©Ralph A. Clevenger/Corbis, cover, *center;* ©Getty Images, cover, *bottom left;* ©Tom & Dee Ann McCarthy/Corbis, cover, *right.*

Permissions
The quotes on pages 4, 5, 8, and 35 are reprinted with permission from *Knowing What Students Know: The Science and Design of Educational Assessment* © 2001 by the National Academy of Sciences, courtesy of the National Academies Press, Washington, D.C.

Contributors
Lynn Dubiel, Laura Heil, Kate Murphy, Myra Vasilarakos; Huong Banh, Mary Ellen Dairyko, Sharon Draznin, Nancy Hanvey, Laurie Leff, Fran Moore, Denise Porter, Herb Price, Joyce Timmons, Jenny Waters, Lana Winnet, Lisa Winters

---

www.WrightGroup.com

Printed in the United States of America.

Send all inquiries to:
Wright Group/McGraw-Hill
P.O. Box 812960
Chicago, IL 60681

ISBN 0-07-604543-9

11 12 13 14 HSO 12 11 10

The McGraw-Hill Companies

Contents

Philosophy of Assessment in *Everyday Mathematics*

Introduction

Too often, school assessment tends to provide only scattered snapshots of student achievement rather than continuous records of growth. In *Everyday Mathematics,* assessment is like a motion picture, revealing the development of each child's mathematical understanding over time while also giving the teacher useful feedback about the instructional needs of individual children and the class.

For assessment to be useful to teachers, children, parents, and others, the *Everyday Mathematics* authors believe that...

◆ Teachers need to have a variety of assessment tools and techniques to choose from so children can demonstrate what they know in a variety of ways and teachers can have reliable information from multiple sources.

◆ Children should be included in the assessment process. Self assessment and reflection are skills children will develop over time if they are encouraged.

◆ Assessment and instruction should be closely aligned. Assessment should assist teachers in making instructional decisions concerning individual children and the class.

◆ Assessment should focus on all important outcomes, not only on outcomes that are easy to measure.

◆ A good assessment program makes instruction easier.

◆ The best assessment plans are developed by teachers working collaboratively within their schools and districts.

Everyday Mathematics offers many opportunities for assessing children's knowledge and skills. This handbook describes the *Everyday Mathematics* assessment resources and serves as a guide for navigating through those resources and helping you design and implement a balanced classroom assessment plan.

Balanced Assessment

When planning a balanced assessment, begin by asking several basic questions:

◆ *What are the purposes of assessment?*

◆ *What are the contexts for assessment?*

◆ *What are the sources of evidence for assessment?*

◆ *What content is assessed?*

What Are the Purposes of Assessment?

The purposes of assessment serve three main functions: to support learning, to measure achievement, and to evaluate programs. Each purpose is integral to achieving a balanced assessment plan.

Formative assessment supports learning by providing information about children's current knowledge and abilities so you can plan future instruction more effectively. Formative assessment encourages children to identify their areas of weakness or strength so they can focus their efforts more precisely.

Summative assessment measures student growth and achievement. A summative assessment might be designed, for example, to determine whether children have learned certain material by the end of a fixed period of study.

Program evaluation means judging how well a program is working. A school district, for example, may want to identify schools with especially strong mathematics programs so their successes can be replicated in other schools with weaker programs. Program evaluation makes this possible.

Assessment tools and techniques often serve more than one purpose. Assessments built into a curriculum might give teachers information they can use to plan future instruction more effectively or prepare progress reports. District administrators might use this information to allocate professional development resources.

Purposes of Assessment

Formative Assessment	Summative Assessment	Program Evaluation
◆ Used to plan instruction ◆ Helps students to reflect on their progress	◆ Used to measure student growth and achievement ◆ Helps determine if students have learned content	◆ Used to evaluate overall success of the math program

What Are the Contexts for Assessment?

Assessment occurs in a variety of contexts.

- **Ongoing assessment** involves gathering information from children's everyday work. These assessments can take place at the same time as regular classroom instruction.
- **Periodic assessment** consists of formal assessments that are built in to a curriculum, such as an end-of-unit Progress Check.
- **External assessment** is independent of the curriculum. An example of an external assessment is a standardized test.

Everyday Mathematics supports all three contexts for assessment, and it provides tools and materials for ongoing and periodic assessments that you can use to create a balanced assessment plan.

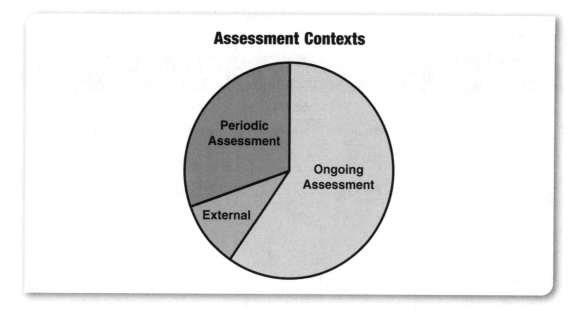

The sizes of the sections of the circle in the figure above are meant to be suggestive, but the exact proportions of ongoing, periodic, and external assessments will vary depending on your grade level, the time of year, state and district mandates, and many other factors.

What Are the Sources of Evidence for Assessment?

> *Assessment is a process of reasoning from evidence.*
>
> (Pellegrino, Chudowsky, and Glaser 2001, 36)

The evidence for assessing what children know is indirect because we cannot know exactly what they are thinking. Evidence about children's knowledge and capabilities comes from observing children while they are actively engaged and from analyzing the products of their work. Whatever conclusions we may make about children's thinking must be based on **observations** or **products.**

The table below shows the different contexts for assessment and the sources of evidence used for each context. Specific assessment tasks in *Everyday Mathematics* are included. Use this table as a guide in designing your balanced assessment plan.

Sources of Evidence and Assessment Contexts

		Assessment Contexts		
		Ongoing Assessment	**Periodic Assessment**	**External Assessment**
Sources of Evidence	**Observation**	◆ Informing Instruction notes ◆ Recognizing Student Achievement notes for • Mental Math and Reflexes ◆ "Kid watching"	◆ Progress Check Oral/Slate Assessments	◆ Classroom observations by resource teachers or other outside experts
	Product	◆ Recognizing Student Achievement notes for • Journal pages • Exit Slips • Games record sheets • Math Boxes ◆ Writing/Reasoning prompts ◆ Portfolio opportunities	◆ Mid-Year and End-of-Year written assessments ◆ Progress Check Written Assessments ◆ Student Self Assessments ◆ Open Response problems	◆ Standardized tests mandated by the school district or the state

Each context for assessment (ongoing, periodic, or external) can yield evidence through observations or products.

◆ Observing children as they are doing their daily work can provide a great deal of information about their understandings, skills, and dispositions; this kind of ongoing observational assessment may be considered "kid watching."

◆ A written assessment that is included as part of a curriculum is an example of a periodic product assessment.

◆ A classroom visit by an outside expert who will observe particular children is an example of an external assessment using observational evidence.

What Content Is Assessed?

In recent years, national organizations and most states have issued detailed sets of learning goals and standards, which provide useful guidance about what content is important to learn and, therefore, important to assess. Aligning assessment, curriculum, and instruction with standards and goals increases coherence in the system and produces better outcomes. To help teachers understand the structure of *Everyday Mathematics* and therefore better understand what to assess, the authors developed Program Goals, which are organized by content strand and carefully articulated across the grades. Below are the six content strands and their related Program Goals.

Everyday Mathematics Program Goals

Number and Numeration
- Understand the meanings, uses, and representations of numbers
- Understand equivalent names for numbers
- Understand common numerical relations

Operations and Computation
- Compute accurately
- Make reasonable estimates
- Understand meanings of operations

Data and Chance
- Select and create appropriate graphical representations of collected or given data
- Analyze and interpret data
- Understand and apply basic concepts of probability

Measurement and Reference Frames
- Understand the systems and processes of measurement; use appropriate techniques, tools, units, and formulas in making measurements
- Use and understand reference frames

Geometry
- Investigate characteristics and properties of two- and three-dimensional geometric shapes
- Apply transformations and symmetry in geometric situations

Patterns, Functions, and Algebra
- Understand patterns and functions
- Use algebraic notation to represent and analyze situations and structures

Program Goals are threads that weave the curriculum together across grades. "Compute accurately," for example, is a Program Goal. Children in *Everyday Mathematics* are expected to compute accurately. The expectations for a student achieving this goal in Grade 2 are obviously different from what is expected from a student in Grade 6. For this reason, the Program Goals are further refined through Grade-Level Goals.

Grade-Level Goals are guideposts along trajectories of learning that span multiple years. They are the big ideas at each grade level; they do not capture all of the content covered. The Grade-Level Goals describe how *Everyday Mathematics* builds mastery over time—first through informal exposure, later through more formal instruction, and finally through application. Because the Grade-Level Goals are cumulative, it is essential for students to experience the complete curriculum at each grade level. The example below shows the development of Grade-Level Goals for addition and subtraction procedures.

Grade K	Use manipulatives, number lines, and mental arithmetic to solve problems involving the addition and subtraction of single-digit whole numbers.
Grade 1	Use manipulatives, number grids, tally marks, mental arithmetic, and calculators to solve problems involving the addition and subtraction of 1-digit whole numbers with 1- or 2-digit whole numbers; calculate and compare the values of combinations of coins.
Grade 2	Use manipulatives, number grids, tally marks, mental arithmetic, paper & pencil, and calculators to solve problems involving the addition and subtraction of 2-digit whole numbers; describe the strategies used; calculate and compare values of coin and bill combinations.
Grade 3	Use manipulatives, mental arithmetic, paper-and-pencil algorithms, and calculators to solve problems involving the addition and subtraction of whole numbers and decimals in a money context; describe the strategies used and explain how they work.
Grade 4	Use manipulatives, mental arithmetic, paper-and-pencil algorithms, and calculators to solve problems involving the addition and subtraction of whole numbers and decimals through hundredths; describe the strategies used and explain how they work.
Grade 5	Use mental arithmetic, paper-and-pencil algorithms, and calculators to solve problems involving the addition and subtraction of whole numbers, decimals, and signed numbers; describe the strategies used and explain how they work.
Grade 6	Use mental arithmetic, paper-and-pencil algorithms, and calculators to solve problems involving the addition and subtraction of whole numbers, decimals, and signed numbers; describe the strategies used and explain how they work.

All assessment opportunities in *Everyday Mathematics* are linked to specific Grade-Level Goals. The curriculum is designed so that the vast majority of students will reach the Grade-Level Goals for a given grade upon completion of that grade and as a result will be well prepared to succeed in higher levels of mathematics. The complete list of Program Goals and Grade-Level Goals begins on page 37 of this handbook.

Creating a Balanced Assessment Plan

In *Everyday Mathematics,* assessment is primarily designed to help you

◆ learn about children's current knowledge and abilities so you can plan future instruction more effectively—formative assessment; and

◆ measure children's progress toward and achievement of Grade-Level Goals—summative assessment.

Although there is no one right assessment plan for all classrooms, all assessment plans should provide a balance of assessment sources from different contexts. See the chart on page 4 of this handbook for specific assessment tasks in *Everyday Mathematics* that support the different sources and contexts.

Planning Tips

Do not try to use all the assessment resources at once. Instead, devise a manageable, balanced plan. Choose those tools and techniques that best match your teaching style and your children's needs.

Consider the following guidelines:

◆ Start small.
◆ Incorporate assessment into your daily class routine.
◆ Set up an easy and efficient record-keeping system.
◆ Personalize and adapt the plan as the year progresses.

Your assessment plan should be designed to answer these questions:

◆ How is the class doing?
◆ How are individual children doing?
◆ How do I need to adjust instruction to meet children's needs?
◆ How can I communicate to children, parents, and others about the progress being made?

The following sections of this handbook provide further details about the tools and techniques you can use to develop a balanced assessment plan. Using these tools, you can support student learning, improve your instruction, measure student growth and achievement, and make the most of your experience with *Everyday Mathematics.*

Ongoing Assessment

> *No single test score can be considered a definitive measure of a student's competence. Multiple measures enhance the validity and fairness of the inferences drawn by giving students various ways and opportunities to demonstrate their competence.*
>
> (Pellegrino, Chudowsky, and Glaser 2001, 253)

An integral part of a balanced assessment plan involves gathering information from children's everyday work. Opportunities for collecting ongoing assessment in the form of observations and products are highlighted in *Everyday Mathematics* through Informing Instruction and Recognizing Student Achievement notes.

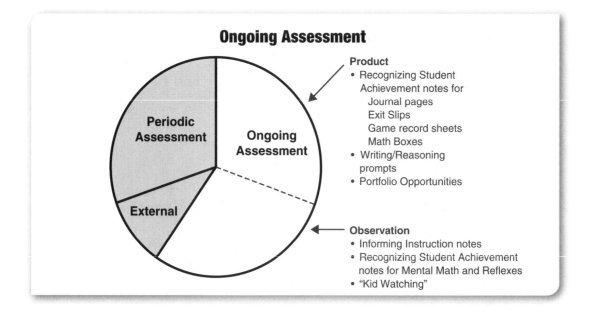

Ongoing Assessment—Informing Instruction

Informing Instruction notes are designed to help you anticipate and recognize common errors and misconceptions in children's thinking and alert you to multiple solution strategies or unique insights that children may offer. These notes suggest how to use observations of children's work to effectively adapt instruction.

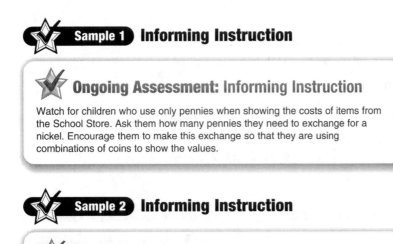

Sample 1 Informing Instruction

✔ Ongoing Assessment: Informing Instruction

Watch for children who use only pennies when showing the costs of items from the School Store. Ask them how many pennies they need to exchange for a nickel. Encourage them to make this exchange so that they are using combinations of coins to show the values.

Sample 2 Informing Instruction

✔ Ongoing Assessment: Informing Instruction

Watch for children who confuse "counting up or down" on the number grid with moving up and down on the page. Remind children to use the color-coded return sweeps to guide their movements.

Ongoing Assessment— Recognizing Student Achievement

Each lesson in *Everyday Mathematics* contains a Recognizing Student Achievement note. These notes highlight specific tasks that teachers can use for assessment to monitor children's progress toward Grade-Level Goals.

These tasks include:

◆ Journal pages (written problems—sometimes including explanations)
◆ Mental Math and Reflexes (oral or slate)
◆ Exit Slips (explanations of strategies and understanding)
◆ *Everyday Mathematics* games (record sheets or follow-up sheets)
◆ Math Boxes (written practice problems)

Each Recognizing Student Achievement note identifies the task to gather information from, the concept or skill to be assessed, and the expectations for a child who is *making adequate progress* toward meeting the specific Grade-Level Goal.

 Sample 1 **Recognizing Student Achievement**
Math Journal 1

> **Ongoing Assessment:**
> **Recognizing Student Achievement**
>
> Journal
> Page 89
> Problem 1
>
> Use **journal page 89, Problem 1** to assess children's ability to compare numbers through hundreds using < and >. Children are making adequate progress if they are able to correctly answer Problem 1. Some children may be able to answer all of the problems on the page correctly.
>
> [Patterns, Functions, and Algebra Goal 2]

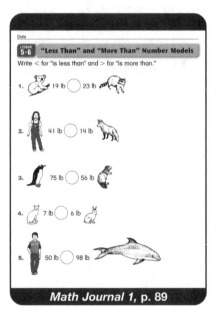

Math Journal 1, p. 89

Sample 2 Recognizing Student Achievement
Mental Math and Reflexes

Ongoing Assessment:
Recognizing Student Achievement

Mental Math
and
Reflexes

Use **Mental Math and Reflexes** to assess children's ability to skip count by 2s. Children are making adequate progress if they are able to count by 2s from a multiple of 10. Some children may be able to count by 2s from any even number.

[Number and Numeration Goal 1]

Mental Math and Reflexes ★

First, count up and back by 2s, starting at multiples of 10. Then start at even numbers that are not multiples of 10.

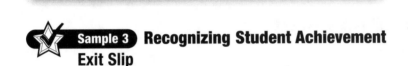 **Sample 3** Recognizing Student Achievement
Exit Slip

Ongoing Assessment:
Recognizing Student Achievement

Exit Slip

On an **Exit Slip** (*Math Masters,* page 305), have each child draw at least two cycles of a pattern he or she made. Use the Exit Slip to assess children's ability to create and extend patterns. Children are making adequate progress if they draw two cycles of a repeating pattern. Some children may be able to draw more than two cycles.

[Patterns, Functions and Algebra Goal 1]

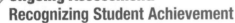

Math Masters, p. 305

⭐ Sample 4 Recognizing Student Achievement
Game Record Sheet

⭐ Ongoing Assessment:
Recognizing Student Achievement

Math Masters
Page 344 ⭐

Use **Math Masters, page 344** to assess children's understanding of finding sums of 1-digit numbers. Children are making adequate progress if they correctly count the dots on the dice to find the sum. Some children may be able to find sums without counting the dots.

[Operations and Computation Goal 2]

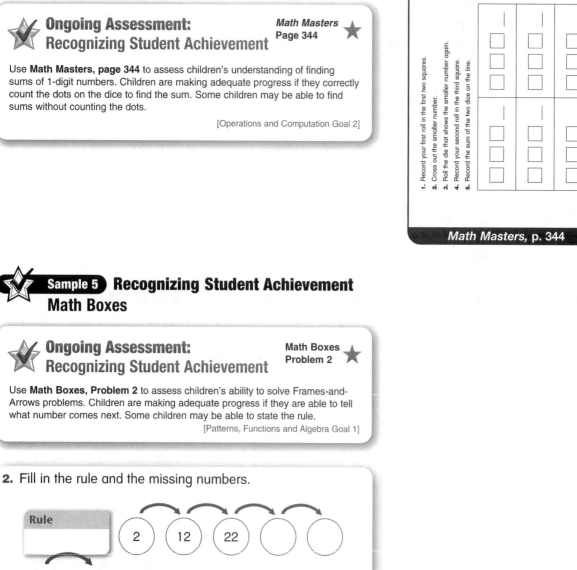

Math Masters, p. 344

⭐ Sample 5 Recognizing Student Achievement
Math Boxes

⭐ Ongoing Assessment:
Recognizing Student Achievement

Math Boxes
Problem 2 ⭐

Use **Math Boxes, Problem 2** to assess children's ability to solve Frames-and-Arrows problems. Children are making adequate progress if they are able to tell what number comes next. Some children may be able to state the rule.

[Patterns, Functions and Algebra Goal 1]

2. Fill in the rule and the missing numbers.

Rule

(2) (12) (22) ( ) ( )

The Recognizing Student Achievement tasks were chosen with the expectation that the majority of children will be successful with them. Children who are *making adequate progress* as defined by a Recognizing Student Achievement task are on a trajectory to meet the corresponding Grade-Level Goal. Based on student progress toward Grade-Level Goals, you may choose to use Readiness activities or Enrichment activities to modify your instructional plan to meet an individual child's needs. See the chart on the next page for how to understand and use the results of the Recognizing Student Achievement tasks.

Using the Results of the Recognizing Student Achievement Tasks

Children complete Recognizing Student Achievement task.

| Children demonstrate a sophisticated and well-articulated understanding of the concepts and skills in the task. | Children are making adequate progress. | Children are progressing toward meeting the criteria for adequate progress. | Children do not demonstrate an understanding of the concepts and skills in the task. |

Consider doing related Enrichment activities when the concept or skill is revisited.

Consider doing related Readiness activities before the concept or skill is revisited. Play games that review related skills and concepts. Revisit related Explorations.

Sample   **Recognizing Student Achievement**

The following example illustrates how to implement further Enrichment or Readiness for a given Recognizing Student Achievement task.

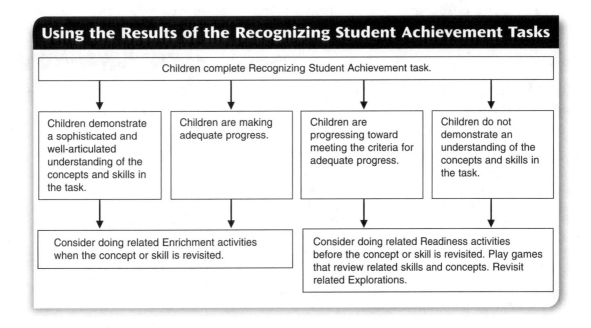

Ongoing Assessment:
Recognizing Student Achievement

Journal Page 30 ★

Use **journal page 30** to assess children's ability to distinguish between even and odd numbers. Children are making adequate progress if they are able to correctly count the boxes and the stars. Some children will have success distinguishing between even and odd numbers even at this early stage.

[Number and Numeration Goal 5]

Math Journal 1, p. 30

 **Sample** **Enrichment**

If children are *making adequate progress,* consider using Enrichment activities in this lesson, if applicable, or related lessons.

ENRICHMENT   INDEPENDENT ACTIVITY

▶ **Finding Even and Odd Numbers in Skip Counts**   15–30 Min

(Math Masters, p. 54)

To further explore even and odd numbers in skip counts, have children complete *Math Masters,* page 54. Have children look at the different skip-counting patterns marked with shapes. Encourage them to generalize rules about the even and odd numbers generated when skip counting by different numbers. Ask: *If you count by an even number, do you always land on even numbers?* Yes *If you count by an odd number, do you always land on odd numbers?* No; you alternate between even and odd numbers.

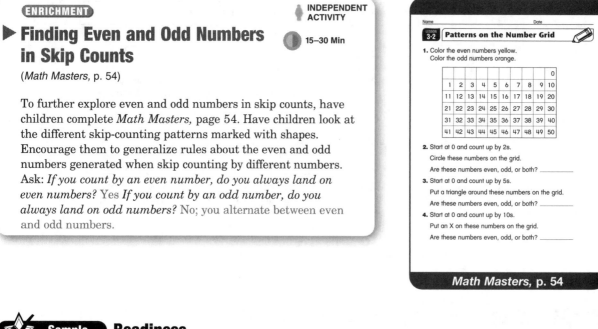

Math Masters, p. 54

 **Sample** **Readiness**

If children are *not making adequate progress,* consider using the Readiness activities before teaching related lessons.

READINESS   SMALL-GROUP ACTIVITY

▶ **Exploring Domino-Dot Patterns**   5–15 Min

(Math Masters, p. 64)

To explore even and odd numbers using a visual model, have children look for patterns in dice dots on *Math Masters,* page 64. When children have finished the page, have them discuss any patterns they see in the sets of dots that are even and the sets of dots that are odd. The odd number patterns always have a dot in the middle. The even number patterns never have a dot in the middle.

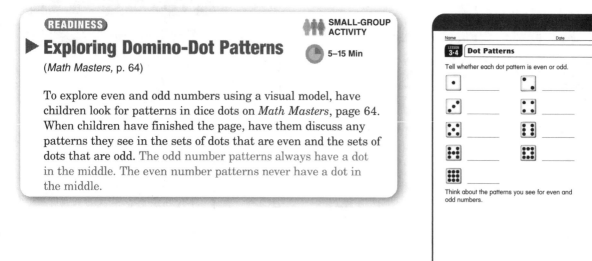

Math Masters, p. 64

Writing/Reasoning Prompts for Math Boxes

Most units contain suggestions for prompts to use with Math Boxes problems. Use these prompts in a number of ways: (1) Collect children's responses to these prompts on Exit Slips. (2) Request that children keep a math notebook where they record their answers to Math Message problems, Exit Slip prompts, and Writing/Reasoning prompts for Math Boxes problems. (3) Have children record responses on Math Log or Exit Slip masters and then add them to their portfolio collections.

 **Sample 1** Writing/Reasoning Prompt

Portfolio Ideas | **Writing/Reasoning** Have children draw, write, or verbalize an answer to the following question: *What is a rectangle?* A reasonable answer should describe a shape with 4 sides and 4 corners.

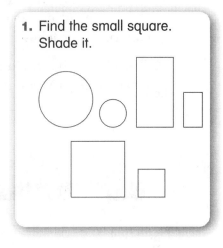

1. Find the small square. Shade it.

 **Sample 2** Writing/Reasoning Prompt

Portfolio Ideas | **Writing/Reasoning** Have children draw, write, or verbalize an answer to the following question: *How do you know which is the winning number in* Top-It? A reasonable answer should include a pictorial representation of the two numbers of reference to a number line. Sample answer: Because if you count when you say 1, 2, 3, 4, 5, 6, 7, 8; the seven is before the eight.

1. Circle the winning card in *Top-It.*

    18   17

Portfolios

Portfolios are a versatile tool for student assessment. They help children reflect on their mathematical growth and help you understand and document that growth. Portfolios are part of a balanced assessment plan in that they:

◆ emphasize progress over time;

◆ involve children more directly in the assessment process as they participate in selecting work and explaining what the work demonstrates; and

◆ document strengths and weaknesses in a child's mathematical development.

 is the symbol used to indicate opportunities to collect children's work for portfolios. Several portfolio opportunities are highlighted in each unit, but in addition to highlighted opportunities, you and your children can choose from the variety of work in daily lessons to add to children's portfolios.

Consider asking children to write about their selected works. Two optional masters, Good Work! and My Work, are provided for this.

Name	Date	Time
Good Work!		

:) I have chosen this work for my portfolio because

AH, p. 257

Name	Date	Time
My Work		

This work shows that I can _____

I am still learning to _____

258

Name	Date	Time
My Work		

This work shows that I can _____

I am still learning to _____

AH, p. 258

See pages 251–259 in this book for additional masters that you might ask children to complete periodically and incorporate into their portfolios. *For example:*

- Math Log A
- Math Log B
- Math Log C

- About My Math Class A
- About My Math Class B

You may also ask parents to complete a Parent Reflection page (*Assessment Handbook,* page 250) for inclusion in children's portfolios.

Math Log A

Name ___ Date ___ Time ___

What did you learn in mathematics this week?

AH, p. 254

Math Log C

Name ___ Date ___ Time ___

Work Box

Tell how you solved this problem.

256

Math Log C

Name ___ Date ___ Time ___

Work Box

Tell how you solved this problem.

AH, p. 256

About My Math Class A

Name ___ Date ___ Time ___

Draw a face or write the words that show how you feel.

Good   OK   Not so good

| 1. This is how I feel about math: | 2. This is how I feel about working with a partner or in a group: | 3. This is how I feel about working by myself: |
| 4. This is how I feel about solving number stories: | 5. This is how I feel about doing Home Links with my family: | 6. This is how I feel about finding new ways to solve problems: |

Circle **yes, sometimes,** or **no.**

7. I like to figure things out. I am curious.

yes   sometimes   no

8. I keep trying even when I don't understand something right away.

yes   sometimes   no

AH, p. 252

About My Math Class B

Name ___ Date ___ Time ___

Circle the word that best describes how you feel.

1. I enjoy mathematics class.   **yes   sometimes   no**
2. I like to work with a partner or in a group.   **yes   sometimes   no**
3. I like to work by myself.   **yes   sometimes   no**
4. I like to solve problems in mathematics.   **yes   sometimes   no**
5. I enjoy doing Home Links with my family.   **yes   sometimes   no**
6. In mathematics, I am good at ___
7. One thing I like about mathematics is ___
8. One thing I find difficult in mathematics is ___

AH, p. 253

Periodic Assessment

Periodic assessments are another key component of a balanced assessment plan. Progress Check lessons and Mid-Year and End-of-Year written assessments require children to complete a variety of tasks, including short answer questions, open response problems, and reflection questions. These tasks provide you and your children with the opportunity to regularly review and reflect upon their progress—in areas that were recently introduced as well as in areas that involve long-term retention and mastery.

The figure below lists the various periodic assessment tasks provided in *Everyday Mathematics*.

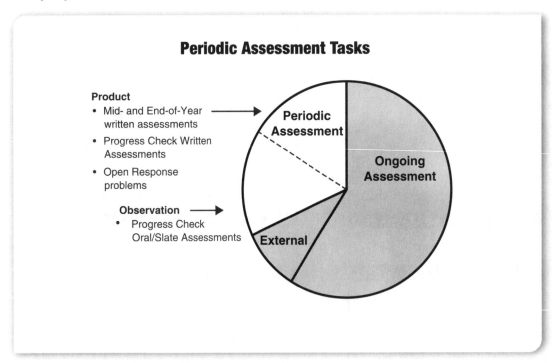

Periodic Assessment Tasks

Product
- Mid- and End-of-Year written assessments
- Progress Check Written Assessments
- Open Response problems

Observation
- Progress Check Oral/Slate Assessments

Periodic Assessment

Ongoing Assessment

External

Written Assessments

Experts in assessment distinguish between summative and formative purposes of assessment. Summative assessment measures student growth and achievment so you can determine whether children have learned certain material. Formative assessment provides information about children's current knowledge and abilities so you can plan future instruction more effectively.

Accordingly, all *Everyday Mathematics* periodic written assessments include two parts:

◆ Part A is designed for summative purposes. The questions provide teachers with information on how children are progressing toward Grade-Level Goals. The questions can be used in the same way as Recognizing Student Achievement notes. Children *making adequate progress* toward Grade-Level Goals should do fairly well on this section.

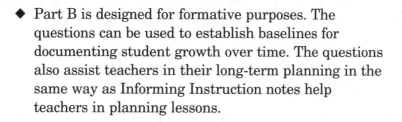

◆ Part B is designed for formative purposes. The questions can be used to establish baselines for documenting student growth over time. The questions also assist teachers in their long-term planning in the same way as Informing Instruction notes help teachers in planning lessons.

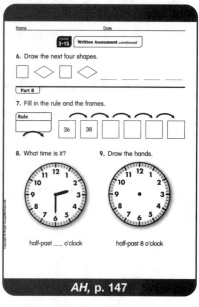

Mid-Year and End-of-Year Written Assessments

To provide a snapshot of how children are progressing toward a broader range of Grade-Level Goals, the program includes two comprehensive written assessments at each grade level—Mid-Year written assessment and End-of-Year written assessment. These written assessments include summative and formative components that cover important concepts and skills presented throughout the year. The Mid-Year and End-of-Year written assessments provide additional information that you may wish to include in developing your balanced assessment plan.

Progress Check Written Assessments

Each Progress Check lesson includes a Written Assessment incorporating tasks that address content from lessons in the current and previous units. The Grade-Level Goals addressed in the Written Assessment are listed at the beginning of the lesson. These assessments provide information for evaluating student progress and planning for future instruction.

Written Assessments are one way children demonstrate what they know. Maximize opportunities for children to show the breadth of their knowledge on these assessments by adapting questions as appropriate. Beginning on page 51 in the unit-specific section of this handbook, there are suggested modifications for the Written Assessments that will allow you to tailor questions and get a more accurate picture of what children know.

Oral and Slate Assessment

Each Progress Check lesson features an Oral and Slate Assessment that includes problems similar to those in Mental Math and Reflexes, which appears in each lesson. You may choose to manage the collection of information from these problems differently than you do with the daily practice. For example, you may give the problems to small groups of children at a time or have children record their answers on paper rather than on slates.

Student Self Assessment

Each Progress Check lesson includes a Self Assessment master that children complete. These Self Assessments are part of a balanced assessment plan as they allow:

◆ children to reflect on their progress, strengths, and weaknesses;

◆ teachers to gain insights into how children perceive their progress; and

◆ teachers and children to plan how to address weaknesses.

The Self Assessment engages children in evaluating their competency with the concepts and skills addressed in the unit. For each skill or concept, children check a box to indicate one of the following:

◆ I can do this by myself. I can explain how to do this.

◆ I can do this by myself.

◆ I can do this with help.

If children feel as though they need help or do not understand, consider talking with them about how they may learn more about the concept or skill. Look to related Readiness activities in Part 3 of lessons and to games for ideas about further developing children's understanding.

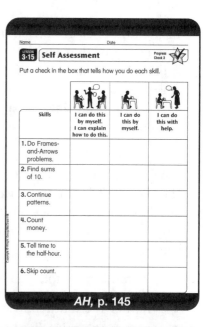

AH, p. 145

Open Response Tasks

Each Progress Check lesson includes an Open Response task linked to one or more Grade-Level Goals emphasized in the unit. These Open Response assessment tasks can provide additional balance in an assessment plan as they allow children to:

◆ become more aware of their problem-solving processes as they communicate their understanding, for example, through words, pictures, or diagrams;

◆ apply a variety of strategies to solve the longer tasks;

◆ further demonstrate their knowledge and understanding through application of skills and concepts in meaningful contexts; and

◆ be successful on a variety of levels.

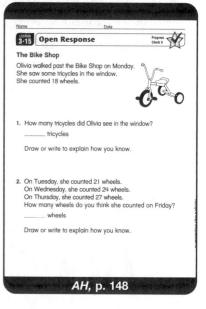

AH, p. 148

The Open Response tasks have been selected with the following points in mind:

◆ The problem context makes sense to children.
◆ The skill level of the problem is appropriate for children.
◆ The problem involves mathematics in which children have a foundation.
◆ The mathematics of the problem is important to the grade level. The problem addresses one or more Grade-Level Goals for the grade.
◆ The problem has connections to the real world that children have experience with.
◆ The problem may not be a multistep problem, but the solution strategy involves several steps.
◆ The problem may have more than one correct solution.

In the unit-specific section of this handbook that begins on page 51, each Open Response task has suggested implementation strategies, a sample task-specific rubric, and annotated children's samples demonstrating the expectations described in the rubric. The unit-specific section also includes suggestions for adapting the Open Response task to meet the needs of a diverse group of children.

The sample rubrics are on a 4-point scale. The top two scores (4 points and 3 points) are designated for student work that demonstrates success with the task. The bottom two scores (2 points and 1 point) are designated for student work that does not demonstrate success with the task; 0 points are reserved for situations where children have made no effort to understand or solve the problem.

In general, the sample rubrics focus on assessing the following items:

◆ whether the mathematics children use is correct;
◆ whether the solution strategy makes sense, is reasonable, addresses the problem, and may lead to a successful solution;
◆ whether the explanation of the strategy is clear and easy to follow; and
◆ whether the solution is correct (or correct except for minor errors).

The Bike Shop Rubric

4 Answers both parts correctly. Clearly explains his or her solution strategy. Recognizes the pattern of adding three for each day for Problem 2 and explains how to use the pattern to solve the problem.

3 Answers both parts correctly. Explains his or her solution strategy, but the explanation might be unclear or incomplete. It might not mention the pattern, but there is evidence that he or she recognizes the pattern of adding three for each day.

2 Understands that this is a counting problem, but might make errors or be unable to apply a strategy to solve the problem.

1 Attempts to solve the problem, but demonstrates little understanding of the problem.

0 Does not attempt to understand or solve the problem.

You may want to work with other teachers from your grade level to apply the *Everyday Mathematics* rubric to your children's work or to create rubrics for scoring these tasks. Consider the expectations of standardized tests in your area when creating or applying a rubric and modify this sample rubric as appropriate. For more child involvement, consider having children participate in developing a list of expectations for a Level-4 paper.

External Assessment

Outside tests, which are one example of external assessment, are generally tests given at the school, district, or state level, or are nationally standardized tests. Most teachers are familiar with the standardized tests that have multiple-choice responses. The frustrating aspect of this type of test is that it analyzes a narrow range of mathematical thinking and does not assess the depth and breadth of the mathematical knowledge that should be attained in a well-implemented *Everyday Mathematics* classroom.

Everyday Mathematics can help your children function more effectively in testing environments. For example, some Math Boxes problems have been tailored to help prepare children for the formats of an outside test. Even without such preparation, *Everyday Mathematics* students generally do just as well on the computation sections of standardized tests. However, they do much better on concepts and problem-solving sections than children in traditional programs.

More recently, some district and state tests have included performance assessments or open-ended components. *Everyday Mathematics* presents varied mathematics tasks that prepare children for these testing situations: problems requiring children to explain their thinking, writing prompts designed to help children explore content more deeply, and richer Open Response tasks that may require an entire class period for children to solve. If you have a choice in your district, encourage the use of these performance-based or open-ended assessments. They better depict the depth of your children's understandings, as well as their abilities to communicate mathematically, solve problems, and reason.

Performance-based assessments developed at the school or district level probably provide the best opportunities to gather information about student achievement in local classrooms. Teams of teachers and administrators can develop assessments and rubrics that enhance the learning process rather than focus on narrow thinking used only in a small portion of mathematical activities. At some grade levels, these assessments can be used exclusively. When standardized testing is mandatory at a certain grade level, performance-based assessments can provide a better picture of the mathematical education occurring in the classroom than other types of standardized tests.

Record-Keeping

If you teach *Everyday Mathematics* as intended and use the techniques described in this book, you will soon have a vast amount of information about children's mathematical skills and understanding. This section of the handbook offers several tools to help you organize and record this information.

Class Checklists and Individual Profiles of Progress

Each lesson in *Everyday Mathematics* identifies a suggested ongoing assessment opportunity in the form of a Recognizing Student Achievement note. These notes highlight specific tasks from which teachers can collect student performance data to monitor and document children's progress toward meeting specific Grade-Level Goals. Each unit in *Everyday Mathematics* contains a Progress Check lesson with suggested periodic assessment tasks. A wealth of assessment information can be collected from these and other sources.

To help you keep track of children's progress in areas that are important to your school and district, checklists for individuals and for the class are provided beginning on page 200 of this handbook. There are Class Checklists for each unit and for each quarter. There are Individual Profiles of Progress for each unit. These checklists provide an organizational system for recording the information you collect to assess student progress on Grade-Level Goals.

The unit checklists include places to record information gathered from the Recognizing Student Achievement notes and from the Progress Check lesson in the unit. The checklists identify the related Grade-Level Goal for each Recognizing Student Achievement task. There is an additional column in which you can add your comments or other notes. To simplify data entry, these checklists are organized according to lesson number.

The quarterly checklists include places to record information gathered throughout the quarter from the Recognizing Student Achievement tasks. To simplify the process of aggregating data in meaningful ways, these checklists are organized according to mathematical strand.

You may prefer using the Class Checklists (on the right) to gather and organize information, transferring selected information to the Individual Profiles of Progress sheet for each child's portfolio or for use during parent conferences.

AH, p. 202

Checklist Flow Chart

```
Ongoing Observational
Assessment              ----------OR---------->

Ongoing Product
Assessment              ----->     Class          ----->   Individual
                                   Checklists              Profiles of
Periodic Observational  ----->                             Progress
Assessment

Periodic Product
Assessment              ----------OR---------->
```

The Individual Profiles of Progress, Class Checklists, and Quarterly Checklists can be found in the Assessment Masters beginning on page 200 of this handbook. Blank checklists have been provided as well.

Options for Recording Data on Checklists

There are several different record-keeping schemes for checklists. Two such schemes are described below.

Option 1

Because Recognizing Student Achievement suggestions include descriptions of the expectations for *making adequate progress,* consider recording this information on a checklist using the following:

A	Child is making adequate progress toward Grade-Level Goal.
N	Child is not making adequate progress toward Grade-Level Goal.

Or

✓	Child is making adequate progress toward Grade-Level Goal.
—	Child is not making adequate progress toward Grade-Level Goal.

Option 2

As the teacher, you can decide how you define what is *making adequate progress* and what is not. For example, if you use a 4-point rubric like the sample below, you may decide to define 3 or 4 points as *making adequate progress* and 1 or 2 points as *not making adequate progress.*

4 points	Child is making adequate progress. Child solves the problem correctly and demonstrates a sophisticated and well-articulated understanding of the concept or skill being assessed.
3 points	Child is making adequate progress. Child solves the problem correctly with only minor errors and demonstrates a developmentally appropriate understanding of the concept or skill being assessed.
2 points	Child is not making adequate progress. Child appears to understand some components of the problem and attempts to solve the problem. Child demonstrates an understanding of the concept or skill being assessed that is marginally short of what is expected.
1 point	Child is not making adequate progress. Child appears to not understand the problem but makes some attempt to solve it. Child demonstrates an understanding of the concept or skill being assessed that is significantly short of what is expected.
0 points	Child does not attempt to solve the problem.

Assessment Management System

Introduction

The *Everyday Mathematics* Assessment Management System is an electronic tool that assists educators in monitoring and documenting children's progress toward meeting *Everyday Mathematics* Grade-Level Goals.

Record-Keeping

You can use the tool to enter student performance information for the following *Everyday Mathematics* assessments:

◆ Ongoing Assessment: Recognizing Student Achievement
◆ Progress Check: Oral and Slate
◆ Progress Check: Written Assessment
◆ Progress Check: Open Response
◆ Mid-Year Assessment
◆ End-of-Year Assessment

You can also easily complement the assessments provided in *Everyday Mathematics* by adding student performance data from tasks you design or from the many other tasks in the *Everyday Mathematics* curriculum.

Features

The *Assessment Management System* includes many features for supporting your balanced assessment plan. *For example:*

◆ All the suggested *Everyday Mathematics* assessment tasks are built into the system. Clicking a lesson number will bring you directly to the corresponding assessment task.
◆ As long as you assign a Grade-Level Goal to the assessment task, any other tasks that you create or that you use from the curriculum are incorporated into the system.
◆ A variety of data-entry options allow you to record general student performance, detailed-scoring information, and text comments for each of your children. You can determine the level of specificity that best suits your assessment needs.

When you track student progress on a Recognizing Student Achievement task, you can view a description of the task and the corresponding Grade-Level Goal.

Everyday Mathematics Assessment

Options   Help   Glossary   Log Out

Class: 3rd Period Level 3

Unit Unit 2   Lesson 4

2•4   Recognizing Student Achievement

Use an **Exit Slip** (*Math Masters*, page 398) to assess children's ability to write number models. Children are making adequate progress if they are able to write a number model for this story: *Two alligators laid eggs. One clutch had 60 eggs; the other had 33 eggs. How many eggs were there in all?* Some children might include a unit box or a parts-and-total diagram. [**Patterns, Functions, and Algebra Goal 2**]

- Set Up Class
- Set Up Assessment
- Tracking Progress
- Recognizing Student Achievement
- Progress Check
- Teacher Assessment
- Mid/End Year Assessment
- Student Reports
- Class Reports

Student	making adequate progress	not making adequate progress	not assessed		Date Assessed
Sellect All	●	○	○		4/20/05
Andrew Malick	○	●	○	Detailed Scoring ✓	4/20/05
Barry Aiton	●	○	○	Detailed Scoring ✓	4/20/05
Chantal Daniels	●	○	○	Detailed Scoring	4/20/05
Dean Jones	●	○	○	Detailed Scoring	4/20/05

You can assess the entire class as *making adequate progress, not making adequate progress,* or *not assessed* by using the buttons in the Select All row.

Additionally, you can also assess individual students as *making adequate progress, not making adequate progress*, or *not assessed*.

You can further document individual student performance by clicking the Detailed Scoring link. When you click this link, you can assign a score for an individual student based on a 4-point rubric as well as record notes for that student.

Student Reports

Once you have entered student assessment data, the *Assessment Management System* provides you with a variety of ways to sort and organize the information. *For example:*

◆ Class and individual reports show student performance data on specific assessment tasks.

◆ Class and individual reports show student performance data sorted by content strand, Program Goal, or Grade-Level Goal.

◆ Class and individual reports are based on time frames that you create, which allows you to tailor the reports to correspond with your district's marking periods.

These reports can then be viewed electronically or printed for distribution.

Monitor Student Progress

Everyday Mathematics was designed so the vast majority of children will reach the Grade-Level Goals for a given grade upon completion of that grade. Each assessment task provides a snapshot of a child's progress toward the corresponding Grade-Level Goal. Taken together, these snapshots form a moving picture that can help teachers assess whether a child is on a trajectory or path to meet the Grade-Level Goal.

The *Assessment Management System* is a valuable tool for managing the tremendous flow of information about student performance. By viewing the reports, you can determine whether or not children have successfully accomplished what is expected of them up to that point in the curriculum. Furthermore, reports display future assessment tasks for a given Grade-Level Goal. This function allows you to see additional assessment opportunities coming up so you can monitor student progress toward specific goals.

Grading Assistance

While grading is not the primary goal of the *Assessment Management System,* the tool can assist you in assigning grades. The *Assessment Management System* allows you to sort and view student performance on assessment tasks by content strand, Program Goal, and Grade-Level Goal so that you can keep documented evidence of the performance. Additionally, the *Assessment Management System* allows you to monitor student progress on many types of assessment tasks, including those that you create so your evidence for assessment is based on multiple sources. These records of student performance, combined with the careful observations you make about your children's work, will help you assign fair and accurate grades.

Online User Instructions and Help

For assistance with the *Assessment Management System* and specific feature instructions, click the Help link at the top of any screen within the tool. Text and animated instructions have been included to help you smoothly incorporate the *Assessment Management System* into your balanced assessment plan.

Frequently Asked Questions

1. **Do the Grade-Level Goals summarize all the concepts and skills that are covered each year?**

   No; Although the Grade-Level Goals reflect the core of the curriculum at each grade level, they are not comprehensive. They do not capture all the content that is addressed each year. Nor are they a list of activities that are completed each year. Some grade-level content supports future Grade-Level Goals that are not articulated at the given grade level.

2. **With all these Grade-Level Goals, how will I know when I'm simply exposing children to a concept or skill?**

   The *Everyday Mathematics* curriculum aims for student proficiency with concepts and skills through repeated exposures over several years. The *Teacher's Lesson Guide* alerts teachers to content that is being introduced for the first time through Links to the Future notes. These notes provide specific references to future Grade-Level Goals and help teachers understand introductory activities at their grade levels in the context of the entire K–6 curriculum.

   All the content in *Everyday Mathematics* is important, whether it's being experienced for the first or the fifth time. The *Everyday Mathematics* curriculum is similar to an intricately woven rug, with many threads that appear and reappear to form complex patterns. Different children will progress at different rates, so multiple exposures to important content are critical for accommodating individual differences. The program was created so it is consistent with how children learn mathematics. It builds understanding over a period of time, first through informal exposure and later through more formal and directed instruction. For children to succeed, they need the opportunity to experience all that the curriculum has to offer in every grade.

3. **There are a lot of lessons in my grade-level materials. Do I have to finish all of them? For example, I teach second grade. Automaticity with ×0, ×1, ×2, ×5, and ×10 facts is not a Grade-Level Goal until third grade. Can't I just skip all of the second-grade lessons that cover multiplication facts?**

Everyday Mathematics was created to be consistent with how children actually learn mathematics, building understanding over time, first through informal exposure and later through more formal instruction. Because the Grade-Level Goals are cumulative, it is essential for children to experience the complete curriculum at each grade level. Children in *Second Grade Everyday Mathematics,* for example, participate in many hands-on activities designed to develop an understanding of multiplication. This makes it possible for children to achieve multiplication goals in third grade.

4. **Do I need to keep track of progress on Program Goals?**

Program Goals are the threads that weave the content together across grade levels and form the skeleton of the curriculum. The Program Goals are further refined through the Grade-Level Goals. *Everyday Mathematics* provides a variety of tools you can use to assess student progress on the Grade-Level Goals throughout the year. Because every Grade-Level Goal is related to a Program Goal, you are gathering information at this less-specific level as well. This allows great flexibility in reporting to parents. Depending on how your district requires you to aggregate data, you can look broadly at strands, more closely at Program Goals, or specifically at Grade-Level Goals using the suggested assessments in *Everyday Mathematics.*

5. **What do the authors mean by "adequate progress"?**

Children who are making adequate progress as defined by a Recognizing Student Achievement note are on a trajectory to meet the Grade-Level Goal. Such children have successfully accomplished what is expected up to that point in the curriculum. If children continue to progress as expected, then they will demonstrate proficiency with the Grade-Level Goal upon completion of the year.

The performance expectations described in the Recognizing Student Achievement notes for any given Grade-Level Goal progress developmentally throughout the year. The level of performance that is expected in October is not the same as what is expected in April. The term *adequate progress* describes the level of competency that the majority of children can be expected to have at a particular time. The authors of *Everyday Mathematics* chose the Recognizing Student Achievement tasks with the expectation that the majority of children would be successful with them, which is in line with the expectation that the vast majority of children will successfully reach the Grade-Level Goals for their grade level.

6. **Do children have to complete all the Recognizing Student Achievement tasks before I can know whether they are making adequate progress?**

Each lesson in *Everyday Mathematics* contains a Recognizing Student Achievement note. These notes highlight specific tasks from which teachers can collect student performance data to monitor and document children's progress toward meeting specific Grade-Level Goals. Each Recognizing Student Achievement note addresses part of a Grade-Level Goal. The suggested assessment tasks build a complete picture over time for each Grade-Level Goal. If children perform well on one or two Recognizing Student Achievement tasks for a goal, that may not provide enough information about the goal in its entirety. Teachers are the experts in their classrooms. If you choose to not do some of the Recognizing Student Achievement tasks, consider collecting similar information from tasks you designate to assemble a complete picture for each Grade-Level Goal.

7. **Can I use only Math Boxes to collect assessment information? They seem to have all the skills in them.**

Everyday Mathematics includes a variety of assessment tasks to ensure that all children have sufficient opportunities to demonstrate what they know. Some children best demonstrate their knowledge through pencil-and-paper tasks, some through performance tasks, and some through explanations and demonstrations. The assessment tasks in the program have been chosen to accommodate a range of learners. Using only one tool might limit what you are able to learn about your children.

8. **I understand that *Everyday Mathematics* provides a Recognizing Student Achievement task for every lesson. May I choose my own instead of or in addition to the ones designated by the curriculum? If I don't think the results of a particular Recognizing Student Achievement task accurately reflect what a child knows, what should I do?**

The Recognizing Student Achievement tasks and Progress Check questions occur at carefully chosen points, based on the opportunities for distributed practice that occur throughout the program. Assessment tasks were also designed to vary the ways in which children are assessed for each Grade-Level Goal.

The *Everyday Mathematics* authors respect teachers as professionals and expect that teachers will use their professional judgment when assessing children. If a particular Recognizing Student Achievement task does not adequately assess student achievement, the teacher may choose to disregard it. The *Everyday Mathematics* authors also anticipate that children's performances on tasks that are not identified in Recognizing Student Achievement notes will often provide useful information regarding their progress toward a particular Grade-Level Goal. Teachers should feel free to link such tasks to appropriate Grade-Level Goals and include them in their assessment stories.

9. **I understand the different record-keeping options that were presented in this handbook. My district, however, evaluates children by assigning traditional letter grades. How should I evaluate student performance?**

Because local assessment systems are based on local norms and values, it would be impossible to design a system that would apply universally. But the authors of *Everyday Mathematics* recognize that many teachers are required by their districts to give traditional grades. And although it is impossible to design a single grading system that will work for everyone, there are some broad principles to follow:

◆ Grades should be fair and based on evidence that can be documented.
◆ Evidence for grading should come from multiple sources.
◆ Grades should be based on content that is important. They should not be based only on the content that is most easily assessed.
◆ The grading system should be aligned with both state and local standards and with the curriculum.

10. **Suppose a child makes adequate progress on the majority of Recognizing Student Achievement tasks and Progress Check questions for a given Grade-Level Goal throughout the year. At the end of the year how likely is it that the child will have achieved the Grade-Level Goal?**

The Recognizing Student Achievement and Progress Check tasks supply a great deal of data on which teachers can base inferences about children's achievement of Grade-Level Goals. In the case of a consistent pattern of adequate progress on assessment tasks for a given Grade-Level Goal, one can reasonably conclude that the child has in fact achieved the given goal. As with any assessment, however, inferences based on positive performance are more straightforward than those based on negative performance. That is, if a child performs well, the most straightforward conclusion is that the child has probably mastered the material; whereas if a child performs poorly, there are many possible explanations, only one of which is a lack of mastery.

Teachers should also recognize that inferences about what children know should always be considered provisional because the inferences are fallible, based as they are on incomplete information, and because children are constantly growing and changing.

According to *Knowing What Students Know*:

> *. . . by its very nature, assessment is imprecise to some degree. Assessment results are estimates, based on samples of knowledge and performance drawn from the much larger universe of everything a person knows and can do. . . . Assessment is a process of reasoning from evidence. Because one cannot directly perceive students' mental processes, one must rely on less direct methods to make judgments about what they know.*
>
> (Pellegrino, Chudowsky, and Glaser 2001, 36)
>
> *An assessment is a tool designed to observe students' behavior and produce data that can be used to draw reasonable inferences about what students know.*
>
> (Pellegrino, Chudowsky, and Glaser 2001, 42)

Recommended Reading

Black, Paul, and Dylan Wiliam. "Assessment and Classroom Learning." *Assessment in Education* (March, 1998): 7–74.

_____. "Inside the Black Box: Raising Standards Through Classroom Assessment." *Phi Delta Kappan* 80, no. 2 (October, 1998): 139–149.

Bryant, Brian R., and Teddy Maddox. "Using Alternative Assessment Techniques to Plan and Evaluate Mathematics." *LD Forum 21,* no. 2 (winter, 1996): 24–33.

Eisner, Elliot W. "The Uses and Limits of Performance Assessment." *Phi Delta Kappan* 80, no. 9 (May, 1999): 658–661.

Kulm, Gerald. *Mathematics Assessment: What Works in the Classroom.* San Francisco: Jossey-Bass Publishers, 1994.

National Council of Teachers of Mathematics (NCTM). *Curriculum and Evaluation Standards for School Mathematics.* Reston, Va.: NCTM, 1989.

_____. *Assessment Standards for School Mathematics.* Reston, Va.: NCTM, 1995.

_____. *Principles and Standards for School Mathematics.* Reston, Va.: NCTM, 2000.

National Research Council. Committee on the Foundations of Assessment. Pellegrino, James W., Naomi Chudowsky, and Robert Glaser, eds. *Knowing What Students Know: The Science and Design of Educational Assessment.* Washington, D.C.: National Academy Press, 2001.

National Research Council, Mathematical Sciences Education Board. *Measuring What Counts: A Conceptual Guide for Mathematics Assessment.* Washington, D.C.: National Academy Press, 1993.

Pearson, Bethyl, and Cathy Berghoff. "London Bridge Is Not Falling Down: It's Supporting Alternative Assessment." *TESOL Journal* 5, no. 4 (summer, 1996): 28–31.

Shepard, Lorrie A. "Using Assessment to Improve Learning." *Educational Leadership* 52, no. 5 (February, 1995): 38–43.

Stenmark, Jean Kerr, ed. *Mathematics Assessment: Myths, Models, Good Questions, and Practical Suggestions.* Reston, Va.: National Council of Teachers of Mathematics, 1991.

Stiggens, Richard J. *Student-Centered Classroom Assessment.* Englewood Cliffs, N.J.: Prentice-Hall, 1997.

Webb, N. L., and A. F. Coxford, eds. *Assessment in the Mathematics Classroom: 1993 Yearbook.* Reston, Va.: National Council of Teachers of Mathematics, 1993.

http://everydaymath.uchicago.edu/

Everyday Mathematics GOALS

The following tables list the Grade-Level Goals organized by Content Strand and Program Goal.

Everyday Mathematics®

Content Strand: NUMBER AND NUMERATION

Program Goal: Understand the Meanings, Uses, and Representations of Numbers

Content	Kindergarten	First Grade	Second Grade	Third Grade	Fourth Grade	Fifth Grade	Sixth Grade
Rote counting	**Goal 1.** Count on by 1s to 100; count on by 2s, 5s, and 10s and count back by 1s with number grids, number lines, and calculators.	**Goal 1.** Count on by 1s, 2s, 5s, and 10s past 100 and back by 1s from any number less than 100 with and without number grids, number lines, and calculators.	**Goal 1.** Count on by 1s, 2s, 5s, 10s, 25s, and 100s past 1,000 and back by 1s from any number less than 1,000 with and without number grids, number lines, and calculators.				
Rational counting	**Goal 2.** Count 20 or more objects; estimate the number of objects in a collection.	**Goal 2.** Count collections of objects accurately and reliably; estimate the number of objects in a collection.					
Place value and notation	**Goal 3.** Model numbers with manipulatives; use manipulatives to exchange 1s for 10s and 10s for 100s; recognize that digits can be used and combined to read and write numbers; read numbers up to 30.	**Goal 3.** Read, write, and model with manipulatives whole numbers up to 1,000; identify places in such numbers and the values of the digits in those places.	**Goal 2.** Read, write, and model with manipulatives whole numbers up to 10,000; identify places in such numbers and the values of the digits in those places; read and write money amounts in dollars-and-cents notation.	**Goal 1.** Read and write whole numbers up to 1,000,000; read, write, and model with manipulatives decimals through hundredths; identify places in such numbers and the values of the digits in those places; translate between whole numbers and decimals represented in words, in base-10 notation, and with manipulatives.	**Goal 1.** Read and write whole numbers up to 1,000,000,000 and decimals through thousandths; identify places in such numbers and the values of the digits in those places; translate between whole numbers and decimals represented in words and in base-10 notation.	**Goal 1.** Read and write whole numbers and decimals; identify places in such numbers and the values of the digits in those places; use expanded notation to represent whole numbers and decimals.	**Goal 1.** Read and write whole numbers and decimals; identify places in such numbers and the values of the digits in those places; use expanded notation, number-and-word notation, exponential notation, and scientific notation to represent whole numbers and decimals.

Everyday Mathematics®

Content Strand: NUMBER AND NUMERATION *cont.*

Program Goal: Understand the Meanings, Uses, and Representations of Numbers *cont.*

Content	Kindergarten	First Grade	Second Grade	Third Grade	Fourth Grade	Fifth Grade	Sixth Grade
Meanings and uses of fractions	**Goal 4.** Use manipulatives to model half of a region or a collection; describe the model.	**Goal 4.** Use manipulatives and drawings to model halves, thirds, and fourths of a region or a collection; describe the model.	**Goal 3.** Use manipulatives and drawings to model fractions as equal parts of a region or a collection; describe the models and name the fractions.	**Goal 2.** Read, write, and model fractions; solve problems involving fractional parts of a region or a collection; describe strategies used.	**Goal 2.** Read, write, and model fractions; solve problems involving fractional parts of a region or a collection; describe and explain strategies used; given a fractional part of a region or a collection, identify the unit whole.	**Goal 2.** Solve problems involving percents and discounts; describe and explain strategies used; identify the unit whole in situations involving fractions.	**Goal 2.** Solve problems involving percents and discounts; explain strategies used; identify the unit whole in situations involving fractions, decimals, and percents.
Number theory		**Goal 5.** Use manipulatives to identify and model odd and even numbers.	**Goal 4.** Recognize numbers as odd or even.	**Goal 3.** Find multiples of 2, 5, and 10.	**Goal 3.** Find multiples of whole numbers less than 10; find whole-number factors of numbers.	**Goal 3.** Identify prime and composite numbers; factor numbers; find prime factorizations.	**Goal 3.** Use GCFs, LCMs, and divisibility rules to manipulate fractions.

Program Goal: Understand Equivalent Names for Numbers

Content	Kindergarten	First Grade	Second Grade	Third Grade	Fourth Grade	Fifth Grade	Sixth Grade
Equivalent names for whole numbers	**Goal 5.** Use manipulatives, drawings, and numerical expressions involving addition and subtraction of 1-digit numbers to give equivalent names for whole numbers up to 20.	**Goal 6.** Use manipulatives, drawings, tally marks, and numerical expressions involving addition and subtraction of 1- or 2-digit numbers to give equivalent names for whole numbers up to 100.	**Goal 5.** Use tally marks, arrays, and numerical expressions involving addition and subtraction to give equivalent names for whole numbers.	**Goal 4.** Use numerical expressions involving one or more of the basic four arithmetic operations to give equivalent names for whole numbers.	**Goal 4.** Use numerical expressions involving one or more of the basic four arithmetic operations and grouping symbols to give equivalent names for whole numbers.	**Goal 4.** Use numerical expressions involving one or more of the basic four arithmetic operations, grouping symbols, and exponents to give equivalent names for whole numbers; convert between base-10, exponential, and repeated-factor notations.	**Goal 4.** Apply the order of operations to numerical expressions to give equivalent names for rational numbers.

Everyday Mathematics®

Content Strand: NUMBER AND NUMERATION *cont.*

Program Goal: Understand Equivalent Names for Numbers *cont.*

Content	Kindergarten	First Grade	Second Grade	Third Grade	Fourth Grade	Fifth Grade	Sixth Grade
Equivalent names for fractions, decimals, and percents			**Goal 6.** Use manipulatives and drawings to model equivalent names for $\frac{1}{2}$.	**Goal 5.** Use manipulatives and drawings to find and represent equivalent names for fractions; use manipulatives to generate equivalent fractions.	**Goal 5.** Use numerical expressions to find and represent equivalent names for fractions and decimals; use and explain a multiplication rule to find equivalent fractions; rename fourths, fifths, tenths, and hundredths as decimals and percents.	**Goal 5.** Use numerical expressions to find and represent equivalent names for fractions, decimals, and percents; use and explain multiplication and division rules to find equivalent fractions and fractions in simplest form; convert between fractions and mixed numbers; convert between fractions, decimals, and percents.	**Goal 5.** Find equivalent fractions and fractions in simplest form by applying multiplication and division rules and concepts from number theory; convert between fractions, mixed numbers, decimals, and percents.

Program Goal: Understand Common Numerical Relations

Content	Kindergarten	First Grade	Second Grade	Third Grade	Fourth Grade	Fifth Grade	Sixth Grade
Comparing and ordering numbers	**Goal 6.** Compare and order whole numbers up to 20.	**Goal 7.** Compare and order whole numbers up to 1,000.	**Goal 7.** Compare and order whole numbers up to 10,000; use area models to compare fractions.	**Goal 6.** Compare and order whole numbers up to 1,000,000; use manipulatives to order decimals through hundredths; use area models and benchmark fractions to compare and order fractions.	**Goal 6.** Compare and order whole numbers up to 1,000,000,000 and decimals through thousandths; compare and order integers between -100 and 0; use area models, benchmark fractions, and analyses of numerators and denominators to compare and order fractions.	**Goal 6.** Compare and order rational numbers; use area models, benchmark fractions, and analyses of numerators and denominators to compare and order fractions and mixed numbers; describe strategies used to compare fractions and mixed numbers.	**Goal 6.** Choose and apply strategies for comparing and ordering rational numbers; explain those choices and strategies.

Everyday Mathematics®

Content Strand: OPERATIONS AND COMPUTATION

Program Goal: Compute Accurately

Content	Kindergarten	First Grade	Second Grade	Third Grade	Fourth Grade	Fifth Grade	Sixth Grade
Addition and subtraction facts		**Goal 1.** Demonstrate proficiency with +/− 0, +/− 1, doubles, and sum-equals-ten addition and subtraction facts such as 6 + 4 = 10 and 10 − 7 = 3.	**Goal 1.** Demonstrate automaticity with +/− 0, +/− 1, doubles, and sum-equals-ten facts, and proficiency with all addition and subtraction facts through 10 + 10.	**Goal 1.** Demonstrate automaticity with all addition and subtraction facts through 10 + 10; use basic facts to compute fact extensions such as 80 + 70.	**Goal 1.** Demonstrate automaticity with basic addition and subtraction facts and fact extensions.		
Addition and subtraction procedures	**Goal 1.** Use manipulatives, number lines, and mental arithmetic to solve problems involving the addition and subtraction of single-digit whole numbers.	**Goal 2.** Use manipulatives, number grids, tally marks, mental arithmetic, and calculators to solve problems involving the addition and subtraction of 1-digit whole numbers with 1- or 2-digit whole numbers; calculate and compare the values of combinations of coins.	**Goal 2.** Use manipulatives, number grids, tally marks, mental arithmetic, paper & pencil, and calculators to solve problems involving the addition and subtraction of 2-digit whole numbers; describe the strategies used; calculate and compare values of coin and bill combinations.	**Goal 2.** Use manipulatives, mental arithmetic, paper-and-pencil algorithms, and calculators to solve problems involving the addition and subtraction of whole numbers and decimals in a money context; describe the strategies used and explain how they work.	**Goal 2.** Use manipulatives, mental arithmetic, paper-and-pencil algorithms, and calculators to solve problems involving the addition and subtraction of whole numbers and decimals through hundredths; describe the strategies used and explain how they work.	**Goal 1.** Use mental arithmetic, paper-and-pencil algorithms, and calculators to solve problems involving the addition and subtraction of whole numbers, decimals, and signed numbers; describe the strategies used and explain how they work.	**Goal 1.** Use mental arithmetic, paper-and-pencil algorithms, and calculators to solve problems involving the addition and subtraction of whole numbers, decimals, and signed numbers; describe the strategies used and explain how they work.

Everyday Mathematics®

Content Strand: OPERATIONS AND COMPUTATION cont.

Program Goal: Compute Accurately cont.

Content	Kindergarten	First Grade	Second Grade	Third Grade	Fourth Grade	Fifth Grade	Sixth Grade
Multiplication and division facts				**Goal 3.** Demonstrate automaticity with ×0, ×1, ×2, ×5, and ×10 multiplication facts; use strategies to compute remaining facts up to 10 × 10.	**Goal 3.** Demonstrate automaticity with multiplication facts through 10 * 10 and proficiency with related division facts; use basic facts to compute fact extensions such as 30 * 60.	**Goal 2.** Demonstrate automaticity with multiplication facts and proficiency with division facts and fact extensions.	
Multiplication and division procedures				**Goal 4.** Use arrays, mental arithmetic, paper-and-pencil algorithms, and calculators to solve problems involving the multiplication of 2- and 3-digit whole numbers by 1-digit whole numbers; describe the strategies used.	**Goal 4.** Use mental arithmetic, paper-and-pencil algorithms, and calculators to solve problems involving the multiplication of multidigit whole numbers by 2-digit whole numbers and the division of multidigit whole numbers by 1-digit whole numbers; describe the strategies used and explain how they work.	**Goal 3.** Use mental arithmetic, paper-and-pencil algorithms, and calculators to solve problems involving the multiplication of whole numbers and decimals and the division of multidigit whole numbers and decimals by whole numbers; express remainders as whole numbers or fractions as appropriate; describe the strategies used and explain how they work.	**Goal 2.** Use mental arithmetic, paper-and-pencil algorithms, and calculators to solve problems involving the multiplication and division of whole numbers, decimals, and signed numbers; describe the strategies used and explain how they work.

Everyday Mathematics®

Content Strand: OPERATIONS AND COMPUTATION cont.

Program Goal: Compute Accurately cont.

Content	Kindergarten	First Grade	Second Grade	Third Grade	Fourth Grade	Fifth Grade	Sixth Grade
Procedures for addition and subtraction of fractions					**Goal 5.** Use manipulatives, mental arithmetic, and calculators to solve problems involving the addition and subtraction of fractions with like and unlike denominators; describe the strategies used.	**Goal 4.** Use mental arithmetic, paper-and-pencil algorithms, and calculators to solve problems involving the addition and subtraction of fractions and mixed numbers; describe the strategies used and explain how they work.	**Goal 3.** Use mental arithmetic, paper-and-pencil algorithms, and calculators to solve problems involving the addition and subtraction of fractions and mixed numbers; describe the strategies used and explain how they work.
Procedures for multiplication and division of fractions						**Goal 5.** Use area models, mental arithmetic, paper-and-pencil algorithms, and calculators to solve problems involving the multiplication of fractions and mixed numbers; use diagrams, a common-denominator method, and calculators to solve problems involving the division of fractions; describe the strategies used.	**Goal 4.** Use mental arithmetic, paper-and-pencil algorithms, and calculators to solve problems involving the multiplication and division of fractions and mixed numbers; describe the strategies used and explain how they work.

Everyday Mathematics®

Content Strand: OPERATIONS AND COMPUTATION *cont.*

Program Goal: Make Reasonable Estimates

Content	Kindergarten	First Grade	Second Grade	Third Grade	Fourth Grade	Fifth Grade	Sixth Grade
Computational estimation		**Goal 3.** Estimate reasonableness of answers to basic fact problems (e.g. Will 7 + 8 be more or less than 10?).	**Goal 3.** Make reasonable estimates for whole number addition and subtraction problems; explain how the estimates were obtained.	**Goal 5.** Make reasonable estimates for whole number addition and subtraction problems; explain how the estimates were obtained.	**Goal 6.** Make reasonable estimates for whole number and decimal addition and subtraction problems and whole number multiplication and division problems; explain how the estimates were obtained.	**Goal 6.** Make reasonable estimates for whole number and decimal addition, subtraction, multiplication, and division problems and fraction and mixed number addition and subtraction problems; explain how the estimates were obtained.	**Goal 5.** Make reasonable estimates for whole number, decimal, fraction, and mixed number addition, subtraction, multiplication, and division problems; explain how the estimates were obtained.

Program Goal: Understand Meanings of Operations

Content	Kindergarten	First Grade	Second Grade	Third Grade	Fourth Grade	Fifth Grade	Sixth Grade
Models for the operations	**Goal 2.** Identify join and take-away situations.	**Goal 4.** Identify change-to-more, change-to-less, comparison, and parts-and-total situations.	**Goal 4.** Identify and describe change, comparison, and parts-and-total situations; use repeated addition, arrays, and skip counting to model multiplication; use equal sharing and equal grouping to model division.	**Goal 6.** Recognize and describe change, comparison, and parts-and-total situations; use repeated addition, arrays, and skip counting to model multiplication; use equal sharing and equal grouping to model division.	**Goal 7.** Use repeated addition, skip counting, arrays, area, and scaling to model multiplication and division.	**Goal 7.** Use repeated addition, arrays, area, and scaling to model multiplication and division; use ratios expressed as words, fractions, percents, and with colons; solve problems involving ratios of parts of a set to the whole set.	**Goal 6.** Use ratios and scaling to model size changes and to solve size-change problems; represent ratios as fractions, percents, and decimals, and using a colon; model and solve problems involving part-to-whole and part-to-part ratios; model rate and ratio number stories with proportions; use and explain cross multiplication and other strategies to solve proportions.

Everyday Mathematics®

Content Strand: DATA AND CHANCE

Program Goal: Select and Create Appropriate Graphical Representations of Collected or Given Data

Content	Kindergarten	First Grade	Second Grade	Third Grade	Fourth Grade	Fifth Grade	Sixth Grade
Data collection and representation	**Goal 1.** Collect and organize data to create class-constructed tally charts, tables, and bar graphs.	**Goal 1.** Collect and organize data to create tally charts, tables, bar graphs, and line plots.	**Goal 1.** Collect and organize data or use given data to create tally charts, tables, bar graphs, and line plots.	**Goal 1.** Collect and organize data or use given data to create charts, tables, bar graphs, and line plots.	**Goal 1.** Collect and organize data or use given data to create charts, tables, bar graphs, line plots, and line graphs.	**Goal 1.** Collect and organize data or use given data to create bar, line, and circle graphs with reasonable titles, labels, keys, and intervals.	**Goal 1.** Collect and organize data or use given data to create bar, line, circle, and stem-and-leaf graphs with reasonable titles, labels, keys, and intervals.

Program Goal: Analyze and Interpret Data

	Kindergarten	First Grade	Second Grade	Third Grade	Fourth Grade	Fifth Grade	Sixth Grade
Data analysis	**Goal 2.** Use graphs to answer simple questions.	**Goal 2.** Use graphs to answer simple questions and draw conclusions; find the maximum and minimum of a data set.	**Goal 2.** Use graphs to ask and answer simple questions and draw conclusions; find the maximum, minimum, mode, and median of a data set.	**Goal 2.** Use graphs to ask and answer simple questions and draw conclusions; find the maximum, minimum, range, mode, and median of a data set.	**Goal 2.** Use the maximum, minimum, range, median, mode, and graphs to ask and answer questions, draw conclusions, and make predictions.	**Goal 2.** Use the maximum, minimum, range, median, mode, and mean and graphs to ask and answer questions, draw conclusions, and make predictions.	**Goal 2.** Use the minimum, range, median, mode, and mean and graphs to ask and answer questions, draw conclusions, and make predictions; compare and contrast the median and mean of a data set.

Program Goal: Understand and Apply Basic Concepts of Probability

	Kindergarten	First Grade	Second Grade	Third Grade	Fourth Grade	Fifth Grade	Sixth Grade
Qualitative probability	**Goal 3.** Describe events using *certain, possible, impossible,* and other basic probability terms.	**Goal 3.** Describe events using *certain, likely, unlikely, impossible* and other basic probability terms.	**Goal 3.** Describe events using *certain, likely, unlikely, impossible* and other basic probability terms; explain the choice of language.	**Goal 3.** Describe events using *certain, very likely, likely, unlikely, very unlikely, impossible,* and other basic probability terms; explain the choice of language.	**Goal 3.** Describe events using *certain, very likely, likely, unlikely, very unlikely, impossible* and other basic probability terms; *use more likely, equally likely, same chance, 50–50, less likely,* and other basic probability terms to compare events; explain the choice of language.	**Goal 3.** Describe events using *certain, very likely, likely, unlikely, very unlikely, impossible* and other basic probability terms; *use more likely, equally likely, same chance, 50–50, less likely,* and other basic probability terms to compare events; explain the choice of language.	

Everyday Mathematics®

Content Strand: DATA AND CHANCE *cont.*

Program Goal: Understand and Apply Basic Concepts of Probability *cont.*

Content	Kindergarten	First Grade	Second Grade	Third Grade	Fourth Grade	Fifth Grade	Sixth Grade
Quantitative probability				**Goal 4.** Predict the outcomes of simple experiments and test the predictions using manipulatives; express the probability of an event by using "___ out of ___" language.	**Goal 4.** Predict the outcomes of experiments and test the predictions using manipulatives; summarize the results and use them to predict future events; express the probability of an event as a fraction.	**Goal 4.** Predict the outcomes of experiments, test the predictions using manipulatives, and summarize the results; compare predictions based on theoretical probability with experimental results; use summaries and comparisons to predict future events; express the probability of an event as a fraction, decimal, or percent.	**Goal 3.** Use the Multiplication Counting Principle, tree diagrams, and other counting strategies to identify all possible outcomes for a situation; predict results of experiments, test the predictions using manipulatives, and summarize the findings; compare predictions based on theoretical probability with experimental results; calculate probabilities and express them as fractions, decimals, and percents; explain how sample size affects results; use the results to predict future events.

Everyday Mathematics®

Content Strand: MEASUREMENT AND REFERENCE FRAMES

Program Goal: Understand the Systems and Processes of Measurement; Use Appropriate Techniques, Tools, Units, and Formulas in Making Measurements

Content	Kindergarten	First Grade	Second Grade	Third Grade	Fourth Grade	Fifth Grade	Sixth Grade
Length, weight, and angles	**Goal 1.** Use nonstandard tools and techniques to estimate and compare weight and length; identify standard measuring tools.	**Goal 1.** Use nonstandard tools and techniques to estimate and compare weight and length; measure length with standard measuring tools.	**Goal 1.** Estimate length with and without tools; measure length to the nearest inch and centimeter; use standard and nonstandard tools to measure and estimate weight.	**Goal 1.** Estimate length with and without tools; measure length to the nearest $\frac{1}{2}$ inch and $\frac{1}{2}$ centimeter; draw and describe angles as records of rotations.	**Goal 1.** Estimate length with and without tools; measure length to the nearest $\frac{1}{4}$ inch and $\frac{1}{2}$ centimeter; estimate the size of angles without tools.	**Goal 1.** Estimate length with and without tools; measure length with tools to the nearest $\frac{1}{8}$ inch and millimeter; estimate the measure of angles with and without tools; use tools to draw angles with given measures.	**Goal 1.** Estimate length with and without tools; measure length with tools to the nearest $\frac{1}{16}$ inch and millimeter; estimate the measure of angles with and without tools; use tools to draw angles with given measures.
Area, perimeter, volume, and capacity			**Goal 2.** Count unit squares to find the area of rectangles.	**Goal 2.** Describe and use strategies to measure the perimeter of polygons; count unit squares to find the areas of rectangles.	**Goal 2.** Describe and use strategies to measure the perimeter and area of polygons, to estimate the area of irregular shapes, and to find the volume of rectangular prisms.	**Goal 2.** Describe and use strategies to find the perimeter of polygons and the area of circles; choose and use appropriate formulas to calculate the areas of rectangles, parallelograms, and triangles, and the volume of a prism; define *pi* as the ratio of a circle's circumference to its diameter.	**Goal 2.** Choose and use appropriate formulas to calculate the circumference of circles and to solve area, perimeter, and volume problems.
Units and systems of measurement			**Goal 3.** Describe relationships between days in a week and hours in a day.	**Goal 3.** Describe relationships among inches, feet, and yards; describe relationships between minutes in an hour, hours in a day, days in a week.	**Goal 3.** Describe relationships among U.S. customary units of length and among metric units of length.	**Goal 3.** Describe relationships among U.S. customary units of length; among metric units of length; and among U.S. customary units of capacity.	

Everyday Mathematics®

Content Strand: MEASUREMENT AND REFERENCE FRAMES *cont.*

Program Goal: Understand the Systems and Processes of Measurement; Use Appropriate Techniques, Tools, Units, and Formulas in Making Measurements *cont.*

Content	Kindergarten	First Grade	Second Grade	Third Grade	Fourth Grade	Fifth Grade	Sixth Grade
Money	**Goal 2.** Identify pennies, nickels, dimes, quarters, and dollar bills.	**Goal 2.** Know and compare the value of pennies, nickels, dimes, quarters, and dollar bills; make exchanges between coins.	**Goal 4.** Make exchanges between coins and bills.				

Program Goal: Use and Understand Reference Frames

Content	Kindergarten	First Grade	Second Grade	Third Grade	Fourth Grade	Fifth Grade	Sixth Grade
Temperature	**Goal 3.** Describe temperature using appropriate vocabulary, such as *hot, warm,* and *cold;* identify a thermometer as a tool for measuring temperature.	**Goal 3.** Identify a thermometer as a tool for measuring temperature; read temperatures on Fahrenheit and Celsius thermometers to the nearest 10°.	**Goal 5.** Read temperature on both the Fahrenheit and Celsius scales.				
Time	**Goal 4.** Describe and use measures of time periods relative to a day and week; identify tools that measure time.	**Goal 4.** Use a calendar to identify days, weeks, months, and dates; tell and show time to the nearest half and quarter hour on an analog clock.	**Goal 6.** Tell and show time to the nearest five minutes on an analog clock; tell and write time in digital notation.	**Goal 4.** Tell and show time to the nearest minute on an analog clock; tell and write time in digital notation.			
Coordinate systems					**Goal 4.** Use ordered pairs of numbers to name, locate, and plot points in the first quadrant of a coordinate grid.	**Goal 4.** Use ordered pairs of numbers to name, locate, and plot points in all four quadrants of a coordinate grid.	**Goal 3.** Use ordered pairs of numbers to name, locate, and plot points in all four quadrants of a coordinate grid.

Everyday Mathematics®

Program Goal: Investigate Characteristics and Properties of Two- and Three-Dimensional Geometric Shapes

Content	Kindergarten	First Grade	Second Grade	Third Grade	Fourth Grade	Fifth Grade	Sixth Grade
Lines and angles			**Goal 1.** Draw line segments and identify parallel line segments.	**Goal 1.** Identify and draw points, intersecting and parallel line segments and lines, rays, and right angles.	**Goal 1.** Identify, draw, and describe points, intersecting and parallel line segments and lines, rays, and right, acute, and obtuse angles.	**Goal 1.** Identify, describe, compare, name, and draw right, acute, obtuse, straight, and reflex angles; determine angle measures in vertical and supplementary angles and by applying properties of sums of angle measures in triangles and quadrangles.	**Goal 1.** Identify, describe, classify, name, and draw angles; determine angle measures by applying properties of orientations of angles and of sums of angle measures in triangles and quadrangles.
Plane and solid figures	**Goal 1.** Identify and describe plane and solid figures including circles, squares, rectangles, triangles, spheres, and cubes.	**Goal 1.** Identify and describe plane and solid figures including circles, squares, rectangles, triangles, spheres, cylinders, rectangular prisms, pyramids, cones, and cubes.	**Goal 2.** Identify, describe, and model plane and solid figures including circles, triangles, squares, rectangles, hexagons, trapezoids, rhombuses, spheres, cylinders, rectangular prisms, pyramids, cones, and cubes.	**Goal 2.** Identify, describe, model, and compare plane and solid figures including circles, polygons, spheres, cylinders, rectangular prisms, pyramids, cones, and cubes using appropriate geometric terms including the terms *face, edge, vertex,* and *base.*	**Goal 2.** Describe, compare, and classify plane and solid figures, including polygons, circles, spheres, cylinders, rectangular prisms, cones, cubes, and pyramids, using appropriate geometric terms including *vertex, base, face, edge,* and *congruent.*	**Goal 2.** Describe, compare, and classify plane and solid figures using appropriate geometric terms; identify congruent figures and describe their properties.	**Goal 2.** Identify and describe similar and congruent figures and describe their properties; construct a figure that is congruent to another figure using a compass and straightedge.

Program Goal: Apply Transformations and Symmetry in Geometric Situations

Content	Kindergarten	First Grade	Second Grade	Third Grade	Fourth Grade	Fifth Grade	Sixth Grade
Transformations and symmetry	**Goal 2.** Identify shapes having line symmetry.	**Goal 2.** Identify shapes having line symmetry; complete line-symmetric shapes or designs.	**Goal 3.** Create and complete two-dimensional symmetric shapes or designs.	**Goal 3.** Create and complete two-dimensional symmetric shapes or designs; locate multiple lines of symmetry in a two-dimensional shape.	**Goal 3.** Identify, describe, and sketch examples of reflections; identify and describe examples of translations and rotations.	**Goal 3.** Identify, describe, and sketch examples of reflections, translations, and rotations.	**Goal 3.** Identify, describe, and sketch (including plotting on the coordinate plane) instances of reflections, translations, and rotations.

Everyday Mathematics®

Content Strand: PATTERNS, FUNCTIONS, AND ALGEBRA

Program Goal: Understand Patterns and Functions

Content	Kindergarten	First Grade	Second Grade	Third Grade	Fourth Grade	Fifth Grade	Sixth Grade
Patterns and functions	**Goal 1.** Extend, describe, and create visual, rhythmic, and movement patterns; use rules, which will lead to functions, to sort, make patterns, and play "What's My Rule?" and other games.	**Goal 1.** Extend, describe, and create numeric, visual, and concrete patterns; solve problems involving function machines, "What's My Rule?" tables, and Frames-and-Arrows diagrams.	**Goal 1.** Extend, describe, and create numeric, visual, and concrete patterns; describe rules for patterns and use them to solve problems; use words and symbols to describe and write rules for functions involving addition and subtraction and use those rules to solve problems.	**Goal 1.** Extend, describe, and create numeric patterns; describe rules for patterns and use them to solve problems; use words and symbols to describe and write rules for functions involving addition, subtraction, and multiplication and use those rules to solve problems.	**Goal 1.** Extend, describe, and create numeric patterns; describe rules for patterns and use them to solve problems; use words and symbols to describe and write rules for functions that involve the four basic arithmetic operations and use those rules to solve problems.	**Goal 1.** Extend, describe, and create numeric patterns; describe rules for patterns and use them to solve problems; write rules for functions involving the four basic arithmetic operations; represent functions using words, symbols, tables, and graphs and use those representations to solve problems.	**Goal 1.** Extend, describe, and create numeric patterns; describe rules for patterns and use them to solve problems; represent patterns and rules using algebraic notation; represent functions using words, algebraic notation, tables, and graphs; translate from one representation to another and use representations to solve problems involving functions.

Program Goal: Use Algebraic Notation to Represent and Analyze Situations and Structures

Content	Kindergarten	First Grade	Second Grade	Third Grade	Fourth Grade	Fifth Grade	Sixth Grade
Algebraic notation and solving number sentences	**Goal 2.** Read and write expressions and number sentences using the symbols +, −, and =.	**Goal 2.** Read, write, and explain expressions and number sentences using the symbols +, −, and = and the symbols > and < with cues; solve equations involving addition and subtraction.	**Goal 2.** Read, write, and explain expressions and number sentences using the symbols +, −, =, >, and <; solve number sentences involving addition and subtraction; write expressions and number sentences to model number stories.	**Goal 2.** Read, write, and explain number sentences using the symbols +, −, ×, ÷, =, >, and <; solve number sentences; write expressions and number sentences to model number stories.	**Goal 2.** Use conventional notation to write expressions and number sentences using the four basic arithmetic operations; determine whether number sentences are true or false; solve open sentences and explain the solutions; write expressions and number sentences to model number stories.	**Goal 2.** Determine whether number sentences are true or false; solve open number sentences and explain the solutions; use a letter variable to write an open sentence to model a number story; use a pan-balance model to solve linear equations in one unknown.	**Goal 2.** Determine whether equalities and inequalities are true or false; solve open number sentences and explain the solutions; use a pan-balance model to solve linear equations in one or two unknowns; use trial-and-error and equivalent equations strategies to solve linear equations in one unknown.

Everyday Mathematics®

Program Goal: Use Algebraic Notation to Represent and Analyze Situations and Structures *cont.*

Content	Kindergarten	First Grade	Second Grade	Third Grade	Fourth Grade	Fifth Grade	Sixth Grade
Order of operations				**Goal 3.** Recognize that numeric expressions can have different values depending on the order in which operations are carried out; understand that grouping symbols can be used to affect the order in which operations are carried out.	**Goal 3.** Evaluate numeric expressions containing grouping symbols; insert grouping symbols to make number sentences true.	**Goal 3.** Evaluate numeric expressions containing grouping symbols and nested grouping symbols; insert grouping symbols and nested grouping symbols to make number sentences true; describe and use the precedence of multiplication and division over addition and subtraction.	**Goal 3.** Describe and apply the conventional order of operations.
Properties of the arithmetic operations		**Goal 3.** Apply the Commutative Property of Addition and the Additive Identity to basic addition fact problems.	**Goal 3.** Describe the Commutative and Associative Properties of Addition and apply them to mental arithmetic problems.	**Goal 4.** Describe and apply the Commutative and Associative Properties of Addition, the Commutative Property of Multiplication, and the Multiplicative Identity.	**Goal 4.** Apply the Distributive Property of Multiplication over Addition to the partial-products multiplication algorithm.	**Goal 4.** Describe and apply properties of arithmetic.	**Goal 4.** Describe and apply properties of arithmetic and multiplicative and additive inverses.

Assessment Overviews

This section summarizes the assessment opportunities in each unit. Ongoing assessments, such as the Informing Instruction and Recognizing Student Achievement notes, are listed by lesson. Portfolio opportunities, paired or linked Math Boxes, and Writing/Reasoning prompts are also highlighted. You will find information on periodic assessments as well. Modifications for each unit's Progress Check Written Assessment, tips for implementing Open Response tasks (including rubrics for each task), and sample student responses for each rubric level are provided.

Contents

Assessment Overview

In this unit, children are introduced to a variety of routines that provide them with opportunities to explore, compare, and order numbers. Use the information in this section to develop your assessment plan for Unit 1.

Ongoing Assessment

Opportunities for using and collecting ongoing assessment information are highlighted in Informing Instruction and Recognizing Student Achievement notes. Student products, along with observations and suggested writing prompts, provide a range of useful assessment information.

Informing Instruction

The Informing Instruction notes highlight children's thinking and point out common misconceptions. Informing Instruction in Unit 1: Lessons 1-2, 1-5, 1-7, and 1-13.

Recognizing Student Achievement

The Recognizing Student Achievement notes highlight specific tasks from which teachers can collect assessment data to monitor and document children's progress toward meeting Grade-Level Goals.

Lesson	Content Assessed	Where to Find It
1♦1	**Count by 1s.** [Number and Numeration Goal 1]	*TLG*, p. 17
1♦2	**Count by 1s and 5s.** [Number and Numeration Goal 1]	*TLG*, p. 21
1♦3	**Compare numbers.** [Number and Numeration Goal 7]	*TLG*, p. 27
1♦4	**Write the numbers 1 and 2.** [Number and Numeration Goal 3]	*TLG*, p. 31
1♦5	**Name numbers that come before and after a given number.** [Number and Numeration Goal 7]	*TLG*, p. 34
1♦6	**Tell the number that is *one more* or *one less*.** [Number and Numeration Goal 7]	*TLG*, p. 39
1♦7	**Write the numbers 3 and 4.** [Number and Numeration Goal 3]	*TLG*, p. 45
1♦8	**Make tally marks for a number.** [Number and Numeration Goal 6]	*TLG*, p. 49
1♦9	**Write the numbers 5 and 6.** [Number and Numeration Goal 3]	*TLG*, p. 55
1♦10	**Count hops on a number line.** [Operations and Computation Goal 2]	*TLG*, p. 57
1♦11	**Compare numbers.** [Number and Numeration Goal 7]	*TLG*, p. 62
1♦12	**Count by 2s.** [Number and Numeration Goal 1]	*TLG*, p. 65
1♦13	**Solve simple number stories.** [Operations and Computation Goal 4]	*TLG*, p. 73

Math Boxes

Math Boxes, one of several types of tasks highlighted in the Recognizing Student Achievement notes, have an additional useful feature. Math Boxes in most lessons are paired or linked with Math Boxes in one or two other lessons that have similar problems. Paired or linked Math Boxes are introduced in Unit 2.

Writing/Reasoning Prompts

Throughout Grade 1, a variety of writing prompts encourage children to explain their strategies and thinking, to reflect on their learning, and to make connections to other mathematics or life experiences. Writing/Reasoning Prompts are introduced in Unit 3.

Portfolio Opportunities

Portfolios are a versatile tool for assessment. They help children reflect on their mathematical growth and help teachers understand and document that growth. Each unit identifies several student products that can be selected and stored in a portfolio. Here are some of the Unit 1 suggestions:

Lesson	Portfolio Opportunities	Where to Find It
1♦2	Children create counting books based on a theme of their choice.	*TLG*, p. 24
1♦3	Children examine dot patterns shown on dice and write the corresponding numbers.	*TLG*, p. 28
1♦3	Children use pattern block templates to build geometric patterns.	*TLG*, p. 28
1♦12	Children explore temperature and weather by making booklets about temperature zones.	*TLG*, p. 69
1♦13	Children practice writing the numbers 1 through 6.	*TLG*, p. 74

Periodic Assessment

Every Progress Check lesson includes opportunities to observe children's progress and to collect student products in a variety of ways—Self Assessment, Oral and Slate Assessment, Written Assessment, and an Open Response task. For more details, see the first page of Progress Check 1, Lesson 1-14 on page 76, of the *Teacher's Lesson Guide*.

Progress Check Modifications

Written Assessments are one way children demonstrate what they know. The table below shows modifications for the Written Assessment in this unit. Use these to maximize opportunities for children to demonstrate what they know. Modifications can be given individually or written on the board for the class.

Problem(s)	Modifications for Written Assessment
1, 2, 5	For Problems 1, 2, and 5, use a number line or number grid to help you solve the problems.
3	For Problem 3, explain how the two tallies are alike and how they are different.
6	For Problem 6, show both numbers with counters. Line up the counters for the two numbers next to each other to see which number is larger.

Assessment Handbook, p. 139

The Written Assessment for the Unit 1 Progress Check is on page 139.

Open Response, *Counting Buttons*

35-45 Min.

Description

For this task, children count a collection of objects in two different ways—by 1s and by skip-counting.

Focus

◆ **Skip count with or without number grids and number lines.**
   [Number and Numeration Goal 1]

◆ **Count collections of objects.**
   [Number and Numeration Goal 2]

Implementation Tips

◆ The open-response task for this unit can be recorded in two ways. For Option 1, you record children's mathematical thinking and solutions as you observe their work and ask them questions. For Option 2, children record their own mathematical thinking and solutions on the Assessment Master. For both options, it is important to discuss children's solutions and model how to record mathematical thinking so that children become more independent.

◆ Provide counters or buttons so children can model the problem.

◆ If you use buttons, give children a few minutes to explore the buttons before using them to model the problem.

Modifications for Meeting Diverse Needs

◆ Enlarge the illustration of the buttons and have children place one counter on each button in the illustration before counting the buttons.

◆ Have children count faster in two ways. Have them explain why counting by 10s could be faster than counting by 2s.

Improving Open Response Skills

After children complete the task, have them model a variety of solution strategies and share or display their explanations in words and pictures.

Note: The wording and formatting of the text on the student samples that follow may vary slightly from the actual task your children will complete. These minor discrepancies will not affect the implementation of the task.

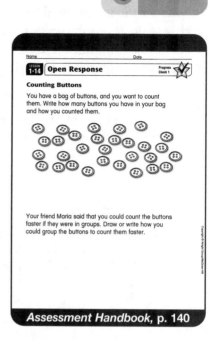

Assessment Handbook, p. 140

Within the image:

Name _____ Date _____

1·14 Open Response
Progress Check 1

Counting Buttons

You have a bag of buttons, and you want to count them. Write how many buttons you have in your bag and how you counted them.

Your friend Maria said that you could count the buttons faster if they were in groups. Draw or write how you could group the buttons to count them faster.

Rubric

This rubric is designed to help you assess levels of mathematical performance on this task. It emphasizes mathematical understanding with only a mention of clarity of explanation. Consider the expectations of standardized tests in your area when applying a rubric. Modify this sample rubric as appropriate.

4	Finds the correct total. Skip counts correctly. Records a picture that accurately shows the groups. Clearly explains how the count matches the picture.
3	Finds the correct total. Skip counts correctly. Records a picture, but the groups might not be illustrated. Explains how the count matches the picture, but the language might be imprecise or difficult to follow.
2	Attempts to use skip counting to solve the problem. Might record a picture, but it might not clearly illustrate a grouping strategy. The explanation does not match the picture.
1	Provides no evidence of a skip-counting strategy. Does not include a picture illustrating a counting strategy.
0	Does not attempt to understand or solve the problem.

Sample Student Responses

This Level 4 paper illustrates the following features: The count by ones to thirty is correct. For the faster count, equal groups of two are illustrated, and the count to thirty is correct. The explanation is clear and matches the illustration.

This Level 4 paper illustrates the following features: The count by ones to thirty is correct. For the faster count, equal groups of ten are illustrated, and the count to thirty is correct. The explanation is clear and matches the illustration.

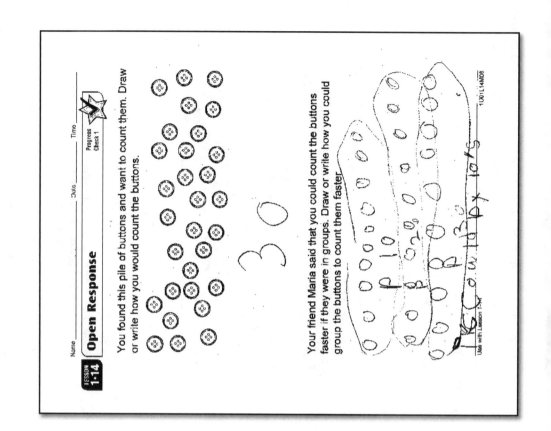

This Level 3 paper illustrates the following features: The count by ones to thirty is correct. For the faster count, counting by threes is illustrated, but the groupings are not easily deciphered. There is an explanation that matches the illustration.

This Level 3 paper illustrates the following features: The count by ones to thirty is correct. For the faster count, counting faster by tens is illustrated but the groupings are not easily deciphered. There is an explanation that matches the illustration.

Name ______ Date ______ Time ______

LESSON 1·14 **Open Response** Progress Check 1

You found this pile of buttons and want to count them. Draw or write how you would count the buttons.

30

Your friend Maria said that you could count the buttons faster if they were in groups. Draw or write how you could group the buttons to count them faster.

I Put them in Piuls OF the

Use with Lesson 1-14 1U01L14M08

Name ______ Date ______ Time ______

LESSON 1·14 **Open Response** Progress Check 1

You found this pile of buttons and want to count them. Draw or write how you would count the buttons.

30

Your friend Maria said that you could count the buttons faster if they were in groups. Draw or write how you could group the buttons to count them faster.

I cent By 10s

Use with Lesson 1-14 1U01L14M08

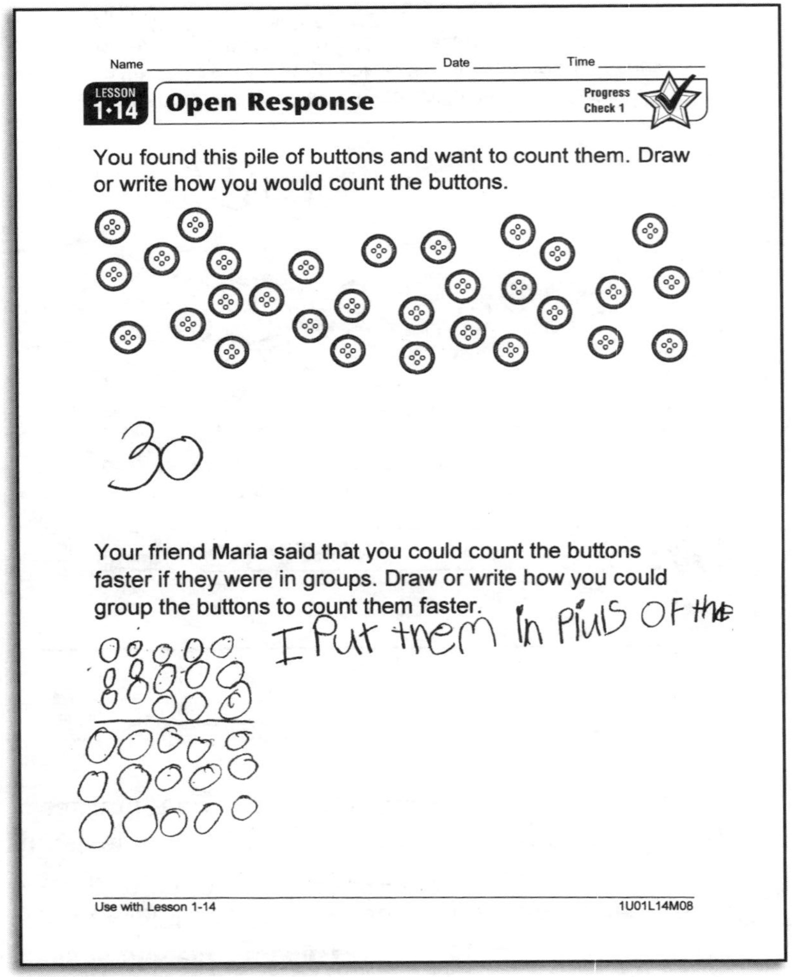

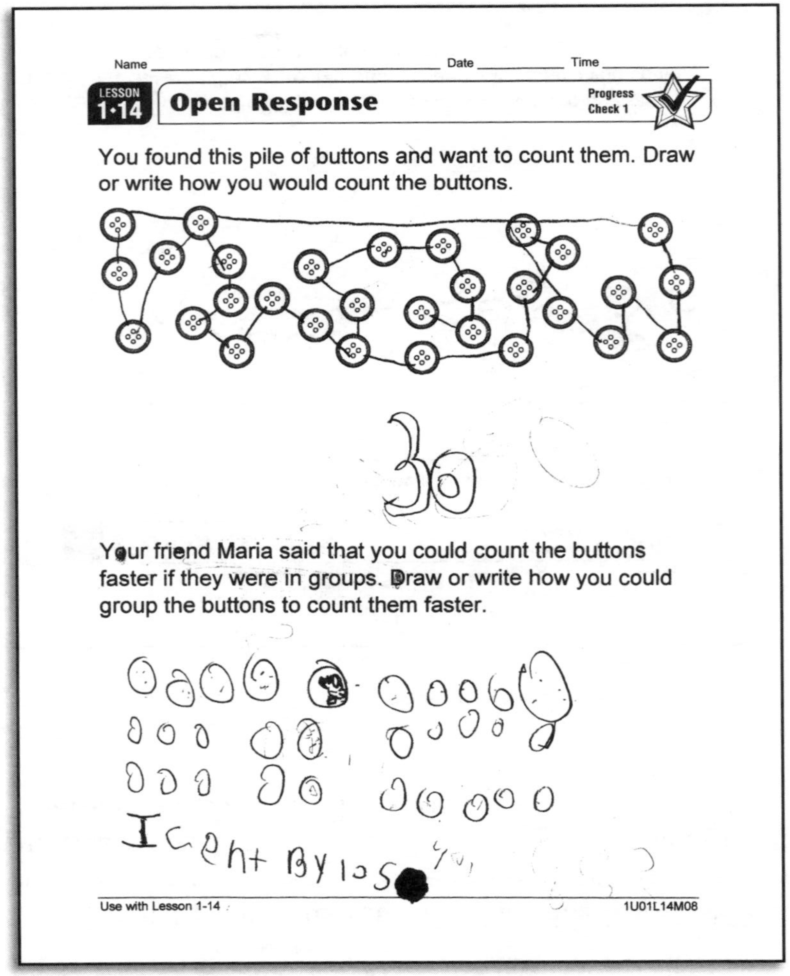

This Level 2 paper illustrates the following features: The count by ones to thirty is correct. For the faster count, the explanation describes counting by twos, but the illustration does not match the explanation.

This Level 1 paper illustrates the following features: The count by ones to thirty is correct. For the faster count, the count is by ones again.

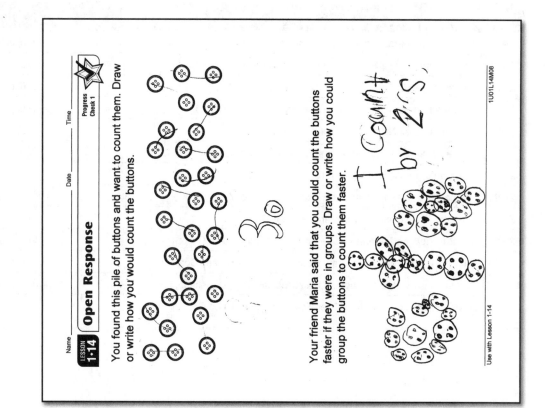

Name _____ Date _____ Time _____

LESSON 1·14 **Open Response** Progress Check 1

You found this pile of buttons and want to count them. Draw or write how you would count the buttons.

30

Your friend Maria said that you could count the buttons faster if they were in groups. Draw or write how you could group the buttons to count them faster.

I count by 2's.

Use with Lesson 1-14   1U01L14M08

Name _____ Date _____ Time _____

LESSON 1·14 **Open Response** Progress Check 1

You found this pile of buttons and want to count them. Draw or write how you would count the buttons.

30

Your friend Maria said that you could count the buttons faster if they were in groups. Draw or write how you could group the buttons to count them faster.

I Counted by 1

Use with Lesson 1-14   1U01L14M08

Assessment Overview

In this unit, children work with time and money concepts. Children are also introduced to number stories and number models. Use the information in this section to develop your assessment plan for Unit 2.

Ongoing Assessment

Opportunities for using and collecting ongoing assessment information are highlighted in Informing Instruction and Recognizing Student Achievement notes. Student products, along with observations and suggested writing prompts, provide a range of useful assessment information.

Informing Instruction

The Informing Instruction notes highlight children's thinking and point out common misconceptions. Informing Instruction in Unit 2: Lessons 2-1, 2-2, 2-3, 2-4, 2-6, and 2-13.

Recognizing Student Achievement

The Recognizing Student Achievement notes highlight specific tasks from which teachers can collect assessment data to monitor and document children's progress toward meeting Grade-Level Goals.

Lesson	Content Assessed	Where to Find It
2◆1	**Compare numbers.** [Number and Numeration Goal 7]	*TLG*, p. 97
2◆2	**Write the numbers 7 and 8.** [Number and Numeration Goal 3]	*TLG*, p. 102
2◆3	**Find sums of 10.** [Operations and Computation Goal 1]	*TLG*, p. 106
2◆4	**Write the numbers 9 and 0.** [Number and Numeration Goal 3]	*TLG*, p. 112
2◆5	**Order numbers.** [Number and Numeration Goal 7]	*TLG*, p. 117
2◆6	**Find equivalent names for numbers.** [Number and Numeration Goal 6]	*TLG*, p. 122
2◆7	**Count on a number grid.** [Operations and Computation Goal 2]	*TLG*, p. 127
2◆8	**Compare quantities.** [Number and Numeration Goal 7]	*TLG*, p. 131
2◆9	**Count by 5s.** [Number and Numeration Goal 1]	*TLG*, p. 136
2◆10	**Count nickels and pennies.** [Operations and Computation Goal 2]	*TLG*, p. 142
2◆11	**Tell time to the hour.** [Measurement and Reference Frames Goal 4]	*TLG*, p. 148
2◆12	**Find sums of 1-digit numbers.** [Operations and Computation Goal 2]	*TLG*, p. 153
2◆13	**Count nickels and pennies.** [Operations and Computation Goal 2]	*TLG*, p. 159

Math Boxes

Math Boxes, one of several types of tasks highlighted in the Recognizing Student Achievement notes, have an additional useful feature. Math Boxes in most lessons are paired or linked with Math Boxes in one or two other lessons that have similar problems. Paired or linked Math Boxes in Unit 2: 2-3 and 2-5; 2-4 and 2-6; 2-7 and 2-9; 2-8, 2-10, and 2-12; and 2-11 and 2-13.

Writing/Reasoning Prompts

Throughout Grade 1, a variety of writing prompts encourage children to explain their strategies and thinking, to reflect on their learning, and to make connections to other mathematics or life experiences. Writing/Reasoning Prompts begin in Unit 3.

Portfolio Opportunities

Portfolios are a versatile tool for assessment. They help children reflect on their mathematical growth and help teachers understand and document that growth. Each unit identifies several student products that can be selected and stored in a portfolio. Here are some of the Unit 2 suggestions:

Lesson	Portfolio Opportunities	Where to Find It
2•1	Children write and compare numbers.	*TLG*, p. 97
2•3	Children record sums of ten.	*TLG*, p. 106
2•5	Children further explore time by illustrating their daily activities according to the time of day.	*TLG*, p. 118
2•6	Children practice writing the numbers 0–9.	*TLG*, p. 122
2•7	Children use straightedges to draw pattern-block shapes, compare the lengths of their sides, and identify the longest side of each shape.	*TLG*, p. 128
2•11	Children further explore estimating totals by grabbing and counting handfuls of coins.	*TLG*, p. 149
2•12	Children investigate addition by recording addends and sums during games of *High Roller*.	*TLG*, p. 153

Periodic Assessment

Every Progress Check lesson includes opportunities to observe children's progress and to collect student products in a variety of ways—Self Assessment, Oral and Slate Assessment, Written Assessment, and an Open Response task. For more details, see the first page of Progress Check 2, Lesson 2-14 on page 162, of the *Teacher's Lesson Guide*.

Progress Check Modifications

Written Assessments are one way children demonstrate what they know. The table below shows modifications for the Written Assessment in this unit. Use these to maximize opportunities for children to demonstrate what they know. Modifications can be given individually or written on the board for the class.

Problem(s)	Modifications for Written Assessment
1	For Problem 1, model the tallies with craft sticks. Use the craft sticks to help you answer the question.
2	For Problem 2, write the value of each coin above the coin. Use counters to help you find the total.
4	For Problem 4, use counters to model the problems.
5	For Problem 5, tell what number is circled and crossed out. What is the next number that would be circled and crossed out? How do you know?

Assessment Handbook, p. 142

The Written Assessment for the Unit 2 Progress Check is on pages 142–143.

Open Response, *Counting Coins*

Description

For this task, children calculate coin combinations and compare money amounts.

Focus

◆ **Know and compare values of pennies and nickels.**
[Measurement and Reference Frames Goal 2]

◆ **Calculate and compare the values of coin combinations.**
[Operations and Computation Goal 2]

Implementation Tips

◆ The open-response task for this unit can be recorded in two ways. For Option 1, you record children's mathematical thinking and solutions as you observe their work and ask them questions. For Option 2, children record their own mathematical thinking and solutions on the Assessment Master. For both options, it is important to discuss children's solutions and model how to record mathematical thinking so that children become more independent.

◆ Provide tool-kit nickels and pennies.

◆ Review the meaning of *greatest*.

◆ Have children organize their coins with nickels first to make them easier to count.

Modifications for Meeting Diverse Needs

◆ Have children draw five circles before filling in the coin abbreviations and record the value inside of the circles they draw (instead of the letter that represents the coin).

◆ Have children record all the ways they could draw five coins from the jar and explain how they know they found all of the possible combinations.

Improving Open Response Skills

After children complete the task, on the Class Data Pad make a list of the different ways children explained why they chose all nickels for Problem 3—for example, because nickels are worth more than pennies; because nickels are five cents and pennies are one cent. Have children compare the language they used. Look for mathematical terms in the list such as *greater than, worth, cents, nickels* and so on.

Note: The wording and formatting of the text on the student samples that follow may vary slightly from the actual task your children will complete. These minor discrepancies will not affect the implementation of the task.

Name _____ Date _____

LESSON 2·14 | Open Response | Progress Check 2

Counting Coins

Bill and Janet have a jar of nickels and pennies.

1. Bill takes 5 coins out of the jar. He has both nickels and pennies. Draw 5 coins that Bill could take out and tell the total value of the coins.

Coins	Value

2. Janet takes 5 coins out of the jar. She has both nickels and pennies. She has more money than Bill has. Draw 5 coins that Janet could take out and tell the total value of the coins.

Coins	Value

3. Draw 5 coins from the jar that would have the **greatest** total value. Explain how you found your answer.

Coins	Value

Assessment Handbook, p. 144

Rubric

This rubric is designed to help you assess levels of mathematical performance on this task. It emphasizes mathematical understanding with only a mention of clarity of explanation. Consider the expectations of standardized tests in your area when applying a rubric. Modify this sample rubric as appropriate.

4   Draws a combination of five pennies and nickels for Problems 1 and 2. Calculates values correctly. Makes a combination with nickels and pennies for Problem 2 that is greater in value than the value of Problem 1. Uses five nickels for Problem 3. Explains why nickels are used exclusively for Problem 3—because nickels are worth more than pennies.

3   Draws five coins for each problem. Calculates values correctly. Makes a combination for Problem 2 that is greater in value than the value of Problem 1. Uses five nickels for Problem 3. Explains why nickels are used exclusively for Problem 3, but the explanation might be incomplete.

2   Draws five coins for each problem. Calculates values correctly. Makes a combination for Problem 2 that might be greater in value than the value of Problem 1. Might use five nickels for Problem 3. Does not explain his or her choice for Problem 3, or the explanation is unclear.

1   Draws coins but there is no evidence of a knowledge of coin values. Might calculate totals incorrectly. Does not make combinations with increasing totals. Does not explain his or her choice for Problem 3, or the explanation does not make sense in the context of the problem.

0   Does not attempt to understand or solve the problem.

Sample Student Responses

This Level 4 paper illustrates the following features: Problems 1, 2, and 3 are completed correctly. The total for Bill's coin combination is worth less than Janet's. A combination of all nickels is chosen for Problem 3, and the explanation indicates that this is because they are worth more than pennies.

This Level 3 paper illustrates the following features: Problems 1, 2, and 3 are completed correctly. The total for Bill's coin combination is worth less than Janet's. A combination of all nickels is chosen for Problem 3, but the explanation is incomplete.

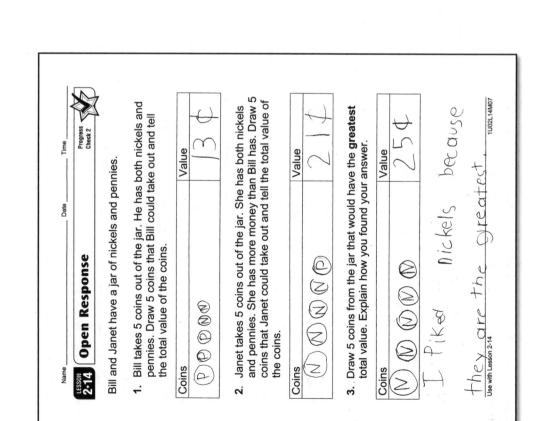

This Level 2 paper illustrates the following features: Problem 1 is completed correctly. The total for Bill's coin combination is worth less than Janet's. There are no pennies in Janet's combination. A combination of all nickels is chosen for Problem 3, but the explanation is missing.

This Level 3 paper illustrates the following features: Problems 1 and 3 are completed correctly. The total for Bill's coin combination is worth less than Janet's. There are no pennies in Janet's combination. A combination of all nickels is chosen for Problem 3 and the explanation indicates that this is because they are worth more than pennies.

Name _____ Date _____ Time _____

LESSON 2·14 Open Response

Bill and Janet have a jar of nickels and pennies.

1. Bill takes 5 coins out of the jar. He has both nickels and pennies. Draw 5 coins that Bill could take out and tell the total value of the coins.

Coins	Value
N N P P P	17¢

2. Janet takes 5 coins out of the jar. She has both nickels and pennies. She has more money than Bill has. Draw 5 coins that Janet could take out and tell the total value of the coins.

Coins	Value
N N N N N	25¢

3. Draw 5 coins from the jar that would have the **greatest** total value. Explain how you found your answer.

Coins	Value
N N N N N	25 ¢

Use with Lesson 2-14   1U02L14M07

Name _____ Date _____ Time _____

Progress Check 2

LESSON 2·14 Open Response

Bill and Janet have a jar of nickels and pennies.

1. Bill takes 5 coins out of the jar. He has both nickels and pennies. Draw 5 coins that Bill could take out and tell the total value of the coins.

Coins	Value
N N N P	21¢

2. Janet takes 5 coins out of the jar. She has both nickels and pennies. She has more money than Bill has. Draw 5 coins that Janet could take out and tell the total value of the coins.

Coins	Value
N N N P	25¢

3. Draw 5 coins from the jar that would have the **greatest** total value. Explain how you found your answer.

Coins	Value
N N N N N	25¢

Becase panes are lastand Neko are greatest

Use with Lesson 2-14   1U02L14M07

This Level 2 paper illustrates the following features: Problem 1 is completed correctly. The total for Bill's coin combination is worth less than Janet's. A combination of all nickels is chosen for Problem 3, but the explanation is incomplete.

This Level 1 paper illustrates the following features: The total for the coins pictured in Problem 1 is incorrect. The total for Bill's coin combination is worth less than Janet's. There are no pennies in Janet's combination. No attempt is made to solve Problem 3.

Assessment Overview

In this unit, children work with patterns in a variety of contexts, further explore telling time, and continue to calculate totals for coin combinations. Use the information in this section to develop your assessment plan for Unit 3.

Ongoing Assessment

Opportunities for using and collecting ongoing assessment information are highlighted in Informing Instruction and Recognizing Student Achievement notes. Student products, along with observations and suggested writing prompts, provide a range of useful assessment information.

Informing Instruction

The Informing Instruction notes highlight children's thinking and point out common misconceptions. Informing Instruction in Unit 3: Lessons 3-4, 3-5, 3-7, 3-8, 3-9, 3-10, 3-11, and 3-12.

Recognizing Student Achievement

The Recognizing Student Achievement notes highlight specific tasks from which teachers can collect assessment data to monitor and document children's progress toward meeting Grade-Level Goals.

Lesson	Content Assessed	Where to Find It
3•1	**Create and extend patterns.** [Patterns, Functions, and Algebra Goal 1]	*TLG*, p. 184
3•2	**Distinguish between even and odd numbers.** [Number and Numeration Goal 5]	*TLG*, p. 191
3•3	**Compare numbers.** [Number and Numeration Goal 7]	*TLG*, p. 197
3•4	**Count spaces on a number grid.** [Operations and Computation Goal 2]	*TLG*, p. 200
3•5	**Skip count.** [Number and Numeration Goal 1]	*TLG*, p. 206
3•6	**Write number models for subtraction.** [Patterns, Functions, and Algebra Goal 2]	*TLG*, p. 211
3•7	**Use a tally chart to answer questions.** [Data and Chance Goal 2]	*TLG*, p. 217
3•8	**Count up and back from a given number.** [Number and Numeration Goal 1]	*TLG*, p. 220
3•9	**Solve Frames-and-Arrows problems.** [Patterns, Functions, and Algebra Goal 1]	*TLG*, p. 226
3•10	**Count by 5s and then by 1s.** [Number and Numeration Goal 1]	*TLG*, p. 230
3•11	**Make exchanges between coins.** [Measurement and Reference Frames Goal 2]	*TLG*, p. 238
3•12	**Solve parts-and-total number stories.** [Operations and Computation Goal 4]	*TLG*, p. 242
3•13	**Make sums of 10.** [Operations and Computation Goal 1]	*TLG*, p. 249
3•14	**Find dice sums.** [Operations and Computation Goal 2]	*TLG*, p. 254

Math Boxes

Math Boxes, one of several types of tasks highlighted in the Recognizing Student Achievement notes, have an additional useful feature. Math Boxes in most lessons are paired or linked with Math Boxes in one or two other lessons that have similar problems. Paired or linked Math Boxes in Unit 3: 3-1 and 3-3; 3-2 and 3-4; 3-5 and 3-7; 3-6 and 3-8; 3-9 and 3-11; 3-10 and 3-13; and 3-12 and 3-14.

Writing/Reasoning Prompts

In Unit 3, a variety of writing prompts encourage children to explain their strategies and thinking, to reflect on their learning, and to make connections to other mathematics or life experiences. Here are some of the Unit 3 suggestions:

Lesson	Writing/Reasoning Prompts	Where to Find It
3✦2	Explain how you know the value of a group of coins.	*TLG*, p. 192
3✦7	Explain how you know whether a number is even or odd.	*TLG*, p. 217
3✦8	Explain why it is important to use a calendar.	*TLG*, p. 222
3✦10	Explain how to find a missing number to make a sum of 10.	*TLG*, p. 233

Portfolio Opportunities

Portfolios are a versatile tool for assessment. They help children reflect on their mathematical growth and help teachers understand and document that growth. Each unit identifies several student products that can be selected and stored in a portfolio. Here are some of the Unit 3 suggestions:

Lesson	Portfolio Opportunities	Where to Find It
3✦1	Children draw and extend a pattern.	*TLG*, p. 184
3✦6	Children model a subtraction problem.	*TLG*, p. 211
3✦11	Children explain how to find the missing number in a skip-counting pattern.	*TLG*, p. 239
3✦14	Children explain why they use a number line to solve a problem.	*TLG*, p. 254

Periodic Assessment

Every Progress Check lesson includes opportunities to observe children's progress and to collect student products in a variety of ways—Self Assessment, Oral and Slate Assessment, Written Assessment, and an Open Response task. For more details, see the first page of Progress Check 3, Lesson 3-15 on page 256, of the *Teacher's Lesson Guide*.

Progress Check Modifications

Written Assessments are one way children demonstrate what they know. The table below shows modifications for the Written Assessment in this unit. Use these to maximize opportunities for children to demonstrate what they know. Modifications can be given individually or written on the board for the class.

Problem(s)	Modifications for Written Assessment
1	For Problem 1, use 10 pennies and *Math Masters,* page 24 to help you find the missing numbers.
2, 3, 7	For Problems 2, 3, and 7, skip count on a calculator to help you find your answers.
4	For Problems 4 and 5, show the same amount using fewer coins. Explain what you did to find your answer.

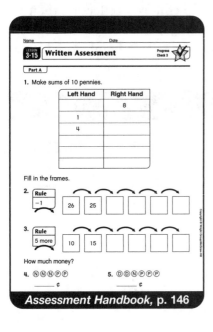

Assessment Handbook, p. 146

The Written Assessment for the Unit 3 Progress Check is on pages 146–147.

Open Response, *The Bike Shop*

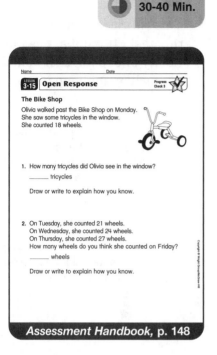

30-40 Min.

Description

For this task, children identify patterns and skip count by 3s.

Focus

◆ **Use numeric patterns to solve a problem.**
[Patterns, Functions, and Algebra Goal 1]

◆ **Count collections of objects.**
[Numbers and Numeration Goal 2]

Implementation Tips

◆ The open-response task for this unit can be recorded in two ways. For Option 1, you record children's mathematical thinking and solutions as you observe their work and ask them questions. For Option 2, children record their own mathematical thinking and solutions on the Assessment Master. For both options, it is important to discuss children's solutions and model how to record mathematical thinking so that children become more independent.

◆ Discuss what a tricycle is. Show a picture if possible.

◆ Have counters, number lines, and number grids accessible for children to do their counting.

Modifications for Meeting Diverse Needs

◆ Distribute counters and small pieces of paper so children can model tricycles by placing 3 counters (wheels) on each small piece of paper. Have children use a calculator to help them skip count by 3s.

◆ Ask children to predict how many wheels Olivia might see on a particular day. For example, if there were 21 wheels on Tuesday and Tuesday is the seventh day, how many wheels were there on the day before? How many wheels will there be 3 days later?

Improving Open Response Skills

After children complete the task, list and discuss the most important components of a successful paper. For example, both problems have an answer, a picture or words explain how they solved the problems, or groups of three are described and drawn somewhere within their answers.

Note: The wording and formatting of the text on the student samples that follow may vary slightly from the actual task your children will complete. These minor discrepancies will not affect the implementation of the task.

Rubric

This rubric is designed to help you assess levels of mathematical performance on this task. It emphasizes mathematical understanding with only a mention of clarity of explanation. Consider the expectations of standardized tests in your area when applying a rubric. Modify this sample rubric as appropriate.

4	Answers both parts correctly. Clearly explains his or her solution strategy. Recognizes the pattern of adding three for each day for Problem 2 and explains how to use the pattern to solve the problem.
3	Answers both parts correctly. Explains his or her solution strategy, but the explanation might be unclear or incomplete. It might not mention the pattern, but there is evidence that he or she recognizes the pattern of adding three for each day.
2	Understands that this is a counting problem, but might make errors or be unable to apply a strategy to solve the problem.
1	Attempts to solve the problem, but demonstrates little understanding of the problem.
0	Does not attempt to understand or solve the problem.

Sample Student Responses

This Level 4 paper illustrates the following features: The answers to Problems 1 and 2 are correct. The explanation for Problem 1 demonstrates an understanding of the pattern of groups of three. The explanation for Problem 2 clearly shows evidence that the pattern of adding three was used to find the total.

This Level 4 paper illustrates the following features: The answers to Problems 1 and 2 are correct. The explanation for Problem 1 demonstrates an understanding of skip counting on the number line by threes. The explanation for Problem 2 clearly shows evidence that the pattern of adding three was used to find the total.

Name _____ Date _____ Time _____

LESSON 3·15 **Open Response** Progress Check 3

Olivia walked past the Bike Shop on Monday.
She saw some tricycles in the window.
She counted 18 wheels.

1. How many tricycles did Olivia see in the window?

Draw or write to explain how you know.

*I conted by three's
I used the number line*

2. On Tuesday, she counted 21 wheels.
On Wednesday, she counted 24 wheels.
On Thursday, she counted 27 wheels.
How many wheels do you think she counted on Friday?

Draw or write to explain how you know.

*I started with 21
I conted up 6 more
I got 24 I conted up
6 more I got 27 I conted up
6 more I got 30*

Name _____ Date _____ Time _____

LESSON 3·15 **Open Response** Progress Check 3

Olivia walked past the Bike Shop on Monday.
She saw some tricycles in the window.
She counted 18 wheels.

1. How many tricycles did Olivia see in the window?

Draw or write to explain how you know.

2. On Tuesday, she counted 21 wheels.
On Wednesday, she counted 24 wheels.
On Thursday, she counted 27 wheels.
How many wheels do you think she counted on Friday?

Draw or write to explain how you know.

*the gestain is clonting by 3rs, so
I counted 3 up from 21 and get
30*

This Level 2 paper illustrates the following features: The answer to Problem 1 is correct. The explanation for Problem 1 demonstrates an understanding of the pattern of groups of three. The answer and explanation for Problem 2 do not include evidence of understanding the problem.

LESSON 3·15 Open Response

Progress Check 3

Olivia walked past the Bike Shop on Monday. She saw some tricycles in the window. She counted 18 wheels.

1. How many tricycles did Olivia see in the window? 6

Draw or write to explain how you know.

I cotid by thre's with catrs

2. On Tuesday, she counted 21 wheels.
   On Wednesday, she counted 24 wheels.
   On Thursday, she counted 27 wheels.
   How many wheels do you think she counted on Friday? 22

Draw or write to explain how you know.

be cus She did ent See sifaunt towt

This Level 3 paper illustrates the following features: The answers to Problems 1 and 2 are correct. The explanation for Problem 1 demonstrates an understanding of the pattern of groups of three. The explanation for Problem 2 shows some evidence of a strategy of counting on the number line for finding the total.

LESSON 3·15 Open Response

Progress Check 3

Olivia walked past the Bike Shop on Monday. She saw some tricycles in the window. She counted 18 wheels.

1. How many tricycles did Olivia see in the window?

Draw or write to explain how you know.

6

2. On Tuesday, she counted 21 wheels.
   On Wednesday, she counted 24 wheels.
   On Thursday, she counted 27 wheels.
   How many wheels do you think she counted on Friday?

Draw or write to explain how you know.

30

2 22 23 24 25 26 27 28 29

This Level 2 paper illustrates the following features: The answer and explanation for Problem 1 do not demonstrate any understanding of the problem. The explanation for Problem 2 indicates an understanding that the solution can be reached by skip counting.

This Level 1 paper illustrates the following features: Problem 1 has the correct answer, but there is no evidence of how the answer was reached. The answer and explanation for Problem 2 do not demonstrate an understanding of the problem.

Name _____ Date _____ Time _____

LESSON 3·15 Open Response Progress Check 3

Olivia walked past the Bike Shop on Monday.
She saw some tricycles in the window.
She counted 18 wheels.

1. How many tricycles did Olivia see in the window? 6

Draw or write to explain how you know.

fingers numberLine

[hand drawing] 8-9-10-11-12

2. On Tuesday, she counted 21 wheels.
On Wednesday, she counted 24 wheels.
On Thursday, she counted 27 wheels.
How many wheels do you think she counted on Friday? 72

Draw or write to explain how you know.

8-9-10-11-12-13-14-15-16
number Line

Name _____ Date _____ Time _____

LESSON 3·15 Open Response Progress Check 3

Olivia walked past the Bike Shop on Monday.
She saw some tricycles in the window.
She counted 18 wheels.

1. How many tricycles did Olivia see in the window?

Draw or write to explain how you know.

36 tricycles because 8+8
is 16 and counted 21 wheels 18 more

2. On Tuesday, she counted 21 wheels.
On Wednesday, she counted 24 wheels.
On Thursday, she counted 27 wheels.
How many wheels do you think she counted on Friday?

Draw or write to explain how you know.

30 wheels because
I counted By threes

Unit 4 Assessment Overview

In this unit, children explore linear measure with standard and nonstandard units, fact power, and patterns in number grids. Use the information in this section to develop your assessment plan for Unit 4.

Ongoing Assessment

Opportunities for using and collecting ongoing assessment information are highlighted in Informing Instruction and Recognizing Student Achievement notes. Student products, along with observations and suggested writing prompts, provide a range of useful assessment information.

Informing Instruction

The Informing Instruction notes highlight children's thinking and point out common misconceptions. Informing Instruction in Unit 4: Lessons 4-2, 4-3, 4-4, 4-5, 4-10, and 4-11.

Recognizing Student Achievement

The Recognizing Student Achievement notes highlight specific tasks from which teachers can collect assessment data to monitor and document children's progress toward meeting Grade-Level Goals.

Lesson	Content Assessed	Where to Find It
4◆1	Skip count by 2s. [Number and Numeration Goal 1]	*TLG*, p. 275
4◆2	Find complements of numbers. [Operations and Computation Goal 2]	*TLG*, p. 284
4◆3	Solve Frames-and-Arrows problems. [Patterns, Functions, and Algebra Goal 1]	*TLG*, p. 289
4◆4	Measure in feet. [Measurement and Reference Frames Goal 1]	*TLG*, p. 292
4◆5	Find domino sums and compare quantities. [Number and Numeration Goal 7]	*TLG*, p. 300
4◆6	Solve parts-and-total number stories. [Operations and Computation Goal 4]	*TLG*, p. 303
4◆7	Solve easy dice sums. [Operations and Computation Goal 2]	*TLG*, p. 311
4◆8	Tell time. [Measurement and Reference Frames Goal 4]	*TLG*, p. 316
4◆9	Measure to the nearest inch. [Measurement and Reference Frames Goal 1]	*TLG*, p. 322
4◆10	Answer probability questions. [Data and Chance Goal 3]	*TLG*, p. 328
4◆11	Tell time to the quarter-hour. [Measurement and Reference Frames Goal 4]	*TLG*, p. 333
4◆12	Write easy addition facts. [Operations and Computation Goal 1]	*TLG*, p. 336

Math Boxes

Math Boxes, one of several types of tasks highlighted in the Recognizing Student Achievement notes, have an additional useful feature. Math Boxes in most lessons are paired or linked with Math Boxes in one or two other lessons that have similar problems. Paired or linked Math Boxes in Unit 4: 4-1 and 4-3; 4-2 and 4-4; 4-5 and 4-7; 4-6 and 4-8; 4-9 and 4-11; and 4-10 and 4-12.

Writing/Reasoning Prompts

In Unit 4, a variety of writing prompts encourage children to explain their strategies and thinking, to reflect on their learning, and to make connections to other mathematics or life experiences. Here are some of the Unit 4 suggestions:

Lesson	Writing/Reasoning Prompts	Where to Find It
4◆3	Explain how drawing a picture can help you to solve a number story.	*TLG*, p. 289
4◆4	Explain why using a thermometer is important when making everyday decisions.	*TLG*, p. 295
4◆5	Explain how you know which pet is most popular from reading a line plot.	*TLG*, p. 300
4◆8	Explain how you draw a line segment.	*TLG*, p. 317
4◆12	Explain how you know which color chip you will likely grab from the bag.	*TLG*, p. 338

Portfolio Opportunities

Portfolios are a versatile tool for assessment. They help children reflect on their mathematical growth and help teachers understand and document that growth. Each unit identifies several student products that can be selected and stored in a portfolio. Here are some of the Unit 4 suggestions:

Lesson	Portfolio Opportunities	Where to Find It
4◆5	Children find domino sums and compare quantities.	*TLG*, p. 300
4◆9	Children draw and label before-school activities using sequence language.	*TLG*, p. 322
4◆9	Children make a storybook timeline.	*TLG*, p. 323
4◆11	Children explain why using a ruler is important.	*TLG*, p. 333

Periodic Assessment

Every Progress Check lesson includes opportunities to observe children's progress and to collect student products in a variety of ways—Self Assessment, Oral and Slate Assessment, Written Assessment, and an Open Response task. For more details, see the first page of Progress Check 4, Lesson 4-13 on page 340, of the *Teacher's Lesson Guide*.

Progress Check Modifications

Written Assessments are one way children demonstrate what they know. The table below shows modifications for the Written Assessment in this unit. Use these to maximize opportunities for children to demonstrate what they know. Modifications can be given individually or written on the board for the class.

Problem(s)	Modifications for Written Assessment
2	For Problem 2, describe patterns you can use to help you fill in the number grid.
3	For Problem 3, circle one cycle of the pattern. Then fill in the missing shape.
5	For Problem 5, skip count backward on a calculator to help you find the answers.
10	For Problem 10, use counters to help you solve the problems.

Assessment Handbook, p. 150

The Written Assessment for the Unit 4 Progress Check is on pages 150–151.

Open Response, *Measuring the Page*

30–40 Min.

Description

For this task, children determine the best way to measure the width of a page and use this strategy to measure the width of the task page with pennies.

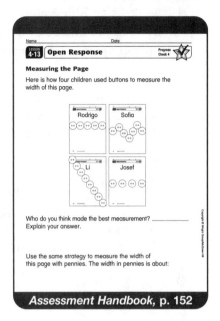

Assessment Handbook, p. 152

Focus

◆ **Use nonstandard tools and techniques to estimate length.**

[Measurement and Reference Frames Goal 1]

Implementation Tips

◆ The open-response task for this unit can be recorded in two ways. For Option 1, you record children's mathematical thinking and solutions as you observe their work and ask them questions. For Option 2, children record their own mathematical thinking and solutions on the Assessment Master. For both options, it is important to discuss children's solutions and model how to record mathematical thinking so that children become more independent.

◆ Briefly review the meaning of measuring the width of something (versus the length).

Modifications for Meeting Diverse Needs

◆ Have children trace pennies across the page to illustrate how they measured.

◆ Have children compare the different measurements the four children in the task got when they measured with buttons to their classroom experience of measuring with children's shoes.

Improving Open Response Skills

After children complete the task, have them discuss the various errors in Sofia's, Li's, and Josef's measurements. List key vocabulary words on the board—for example, *diagonal, spaces, across, gaps,* and *straight.* After the discussion, have children take their own papers and try to improve or enhance their explanations.

Note: The wording and formatting of the text on the student samples that follow may vary slightly from the actual task your children will complete. These minor discrepancies will not affect the implementation of the task.

Rubric

This rubric is designed to help you assess levels of mathematical performance on this task. It emphasizes mathematical understanding with only a mention of clarity of explanation. Consider the expectations of standardized tests in your area when applying a rubric. Modify this sample rubric as appropriate.

4   Chooses Rodrigo. The explanation refers to the mistakes other children made—that there should be no gaps between units and that the units should be lined up straight across the width of the page. Measures the page to be about 11 or 12 pennies.

3   Chooses Rodrigo. The explanation refers to at least one of the other children's mistakes—that there should be no gaps between units or that the units should be lined up straight across the page. Measures the page to be about 11 or 12 pennies.

2   Chooses Rodrigo. Explains choosing Rodrigo, but there is little evidence of understanding the errors the other children made. Measures the page to be somewhere between 10 and 13 pennies.

1   Might not choose Rodrigo. Does not explain the choice or the explanation makes no sense in the context of the problem. There is an attempt to measure the page, but the measurement might not be between 10 and 13 pennies.

0   Does not attempt to understand or solve the problem.

Sample Student Responses

This Level 4 paper illustrates the following features: Rodrigo's was chosen as the best measurement. The explanation describes all three mistakes—that Josef had spaces; Li was not straight; and Sofia was squiggly. The width of the page is determined to be about 11 pennies.

This Level 4 paper illustrates the following features: Rodrigo's was chosen as the best measurement. The explanation describes all three mistakes—that Sofia did zigzags; Li didn't measure correctly; and Josef had spaces. The width of the page is determined to be about 12 pennies, and the traced pennies illustrate the strategy that is used.

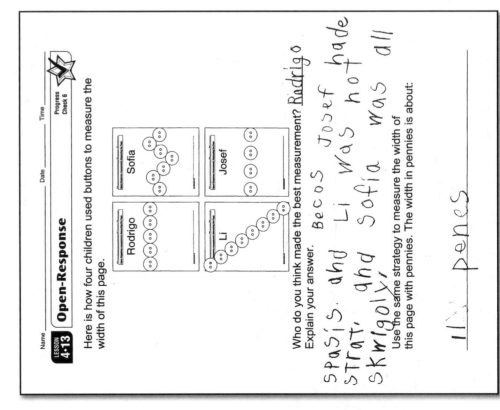

This Level 3 paper illustrates the following features: Rodrigo's was chosen as the best measurement. The explanation describes one mistake—to have a good measure, it cannot zigzag (shown with a picture). The width of the page was determined to be about 11 pennies.

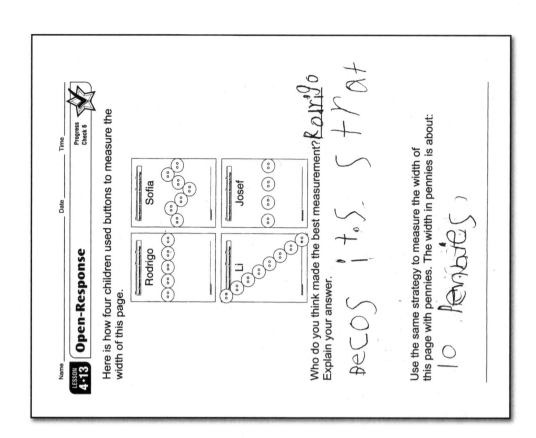

LESSON
4·13

Open-Response

Progress
Check 6

Here is how four children used buttons to measure the width of this page.

Rodrigo   Sofia

Li   Josef

Who do you think made the best measurement?
Explain your answer. becuase it bares
it goeal macthes
For it coanthot

Rodrigo

Use the same strategy to measure the width of
this page with pennies. The width in pennies is about: ||

11 pennies

This Level 2 paper illustrates the following features: Rodrigo's was chosen as the best measurement. The explanation demonstrates some evidence of understanding how to measure width straight across. The width of the page was determined to be about 10 pennies.

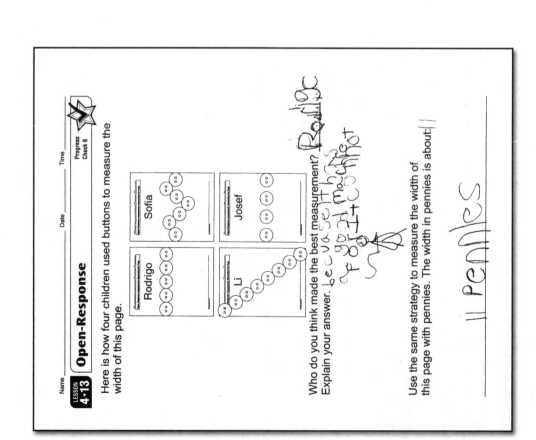

LESSON
4·13

Open-Response

Progress
Check 6

Here is how four children used buttons to measure the width of this page.

Rodrigo   Sofia

Li   Josef

Who do you think made the best measurement?
Explain your answer. Rorigo

becos its strat

Use the same strategy to measure the width of
this page with pennies. The width in pennies is about:

10 Pennies

This Level 1 paper illustrates the following features: Josef's was chosen as the best measurement because he spaced the pennies. The explanation does not present any evidence of understanding how to measure width. The width of the page was determined to be about $12\frac{1}{2}$ pennies.

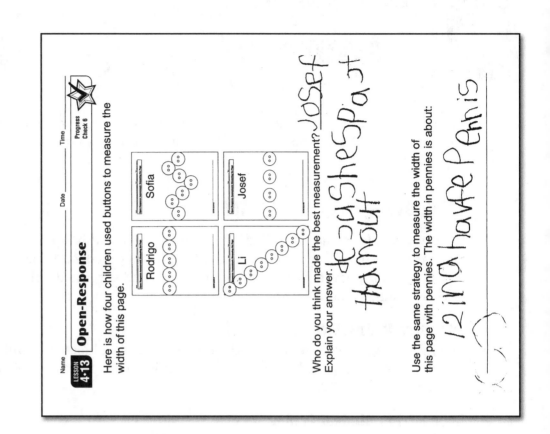

This Level 2 paper illustrates the following features: Rodrigo's was chosen as the best measurement. The explanation demonstrates some evidence of understanding how to measure width with units in a line. The width of page was determined to be about 11 pennies. The units are missing on the measurement.

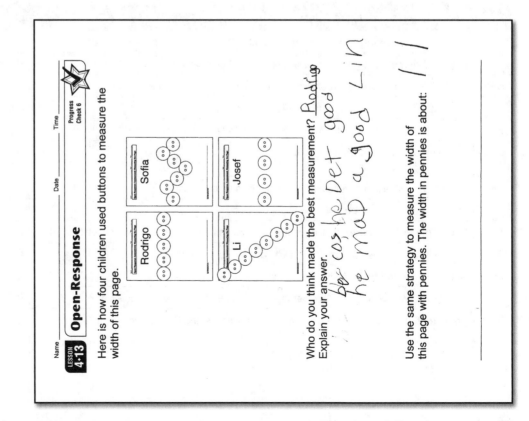

Assessment Overview

In this unit, children continue their work with place value, number stories, and fact power. Use the information in this section to develop your assessment plan for Unit 5.

Ongoing Assessment

Opportunities for using and collecting ongoing assessment information are highlighted in Informing Instruction and Recognizing Student Achievement notes. Student products, along with observations and suggested writing prompts, provide a range of useful assessment information.

Informing Instruction
The Informing Instruction notes highlight children's thinking and point out common misconceptions. Informing Instruction in Unit 5: Lessons 5-1, 5-3, 5-4, 5-5, 5-6, 5-9, and 5-12.

Recognizing Student Achievement
The Recognizing Student Achievement notes highlight specific tasks from which teachers can collect assessment data to monitor and document children's progress toward meeting Grade-Level Goals.

Lesson	Content Assessed	Where to Find It
5♦1	**Name numbers represented by base-10 blocks.** [Number and Numeration Goal 3]	*TLG*, p. 360
5♦2	**Find complements of numbers.** [Operations and Computation Goal 2]	*TLG*, p. 366
5♦3	**Solve Frames-and-Arrows problems.** [Patterns, Functions, and Algebra Goal 1]	*TLG*, p. 372
5♦4	**Find equivalent names for numbers.** [Number and Numeration Goal 6]	*TLG*, p. 378
5♦5	**Compare lengths of objects.** [Measurement and Reference Frames Goal 1]	*TLG*, p. 382
5♦6	**Compare numbers through hundreds using < and >.** [Patterns, Functions, and Algebra Goal 2]	*TLG*, p. 386
5♦7	**Compare numbers of pennies.** [Number and Numeration Goal 7]	*TLG*, p. 390
5♦8	**Identify digits in numbers.** [Number and Numeration Goal 3]	*TLG*, p. 394
5♦9	**Show time to the quarter-hour on a clock.** [Measurement and Reference Frames Goal 4]	*TLG*, p. 401
5♦10	**Solve simple number stories.** [Operations and Computation Goal 4]	*TLG*, p. 403
5♦11	**Write turn-around facts.** [Patterns, Functions, and Algebra Goal 3]	*TLG*, p. 410
5♦12	**Use thermometers to record temperature.** [Measurement and Reference Frames Goal 3]	*TLG*, p. 417
5♦13	**Compare the values of coin combinations.** [Operations and Computation Goal 2]	*TLG*, p. 422

Math Boxes

Math Boxes, one of several types of tasks highlighted in the Recognizing Student Achievement notes, have an additional useful feature. Math Boxes in most lessons are paired or linked with Math Boxes in one or two other lessons that have similar problems. Paired or linked Math Boxes in Unit 5: 5-1 and 5-3; 5-2 and 5-4; 5-5 and 5-7; 5-6 and 5-8; 5-9, 5-11, and 5-13; and 5-10 and 5-12.

Writing/Reasoning Prompts

In Unit 5, a variety of writing prompts encourage children to explain their strategies and thinking, to reflect on their learning, and to make connections to other mathematics or life experiences. Here are some of the Unit 5 suggestions:

Lesson	Writing/Reasoning Prompts	Where to Find It
5♦2	Explain how you count base-10 blocks.	*TLG*, p. 367
5♦8	Explain what a pattern is.	*TLG*, p. 396
5♦9	Explain how to use < and > to compare numbers.	*TLG*, p. 401
5♦12	Explain how you find the temperature.	*TLG*, p. 417

Portfolio Opportunities

Portfolios are a versatile tool for assessment. They help children reflect on their mathematical growth and help teachers understand and document that growth. Each unit identifies several student products that can be selected and stored in a portfolio. Here are some of the Unit 5 suggestions:

Lesson	Portfolio Opportunities	Where to Find It
5♦1	Children solve Frames-and-Arrows problems.	*TLG*, p. 361
5♦5	Children tell how many tens are in a number.	*TLG*, p. 382
5♦7	Children solve comparison problems.	*TLG*, p. 390
5♦8	Children tell a number story using a theme from the science or social studies curriculum.	*TLG*, p. 397
5♦9	Children explain how to use < and > to compare numbers.	*TLG*, p. 401

Periodic Assessment

Every Progress Check lesson includes opportunities to observe children's progress and to collect student products in a variety of ways—Self Assessment, Oral and Slate Assessment, Written Assessment, and an Open Response task. For more details, see the first page of Progress Check 5, Lesson 5-14 on page 419, of the *Teacher's Lesson Guide*.

Progress Check Modifications

Written Assessments are one way children demonstrate what they know. The table below shows modifications for the Written Assessment in this unit. Use these to maximize opportunities for children to demonstrate what they know. Modifications can be given individually or written on the board for the class.

Problem(s)	Modifications for Written Assessment
2, 3	For Problems 2 and 3, build the numbers with base-10 blocks. Remember that the "mouth" opens to "swallow" the larger number.
5, 6	For Problems 5 and 6, use a number grid to help you solve the problems.
7, 8	For Problems 7 and 8, describe two ways that the dominoes are alike and two ways that the dominoes are different.

Assessment Handbook, p. 154

The Written Assessment for the Unit 5 Progress Check is on pages 154–155.

Open Response, *Making Numbers*

Description

For this task, children use place value to make the greatest and least 2-digit numbers, to add two 2-digit numbers using base-10 blocks, and to write a number model for the addition problem.

Focus

◆ **Model whole numbers using base-10 blocks.**
[Number and Numeration Goal 3]

◆ **Compare whole numbers using base-10 blocks.** [Number and Numeration Goal 7]

◆ **Add whole numbers using base-10 blocks.**
[Operations and Computation Goal 2]

◆ **Write number sentences using the symbols = and +.**
[Patterns, Functions, and Algebra Goal 2]

Assessment Handbook, p. 156

Implementation Tips

◆ The open-response task for this unit can be recorded in two ways. For Option 1, you record children's mathematical thinking and solutions as you observe their work and ask them questions. For Option 2, children record their own mathematical thinking and solutions on the Assessment Master. For both options, it is important to discuss children's solutions and model how to record mathematical thinking so that children become more independent.

◆ Provide base-10 blocks for children to model the numbers. Review the symbols for recording base-10 blocks.

◆ Provide number and symbol cards for children to use to create their number models.

Modifications for Meeting Diverse Needs

◆ Have children use the same two digits to form both numbers.

◆ Have children record their total using the fewest base-10 blocks and describe in words how they added their two numbers.

Improving Open Response Skills

After children complete the task, create a student paper with mistakes. Have children find and correct the mistakes. When they have finished, discuss the errors they found. Possible errors include: more than three cards are circled; the numbers formed do not use the three cards; the numbers made might have the tens and ones digits reversed; make the base-10 block representations correct, but make one without trading; write a number model with an incorrect sum and the = symbol on the left instead of the right.

Note: The wording and formatting of the text on the student samples that follow may vary slightly from the actual task your children will complete. These minor discrepancies will not affect the implementation of the task.

Rubric

This rubric is designed to help you assess levels of mathematical performance on this task. It emphasizes mathematical understanding with only a mention of clarity of explanation. Consider the expectations of standardized tests in your area when applying a rubric. Modify this sample rubric as appropriate.

4 Circles three digits and uses them to construct two 2-digit numbers. Constructs the smallest and largest 2-digit numbers possible. Represents the addends separately or the sum using base-10 blocks. Writes the number sentence for finding the sum.

3 Circles three digits used to construct two 2-digit numbers. Constructs the larger number with the larger of the two digits in the tens place and the smaller number with the smaller of the two digits in the ones place. Represents the addends separately or the sum using base-10 blocks, but there might be minor counting errors. Writes the number sentence for finding the sum.

2 Circles some digits used to construct two 2-digit numbers. Constructs the 2-digit numbers with minor errors. There is evidence of understanding how to represent numbers using base-10 blocks, but there might be errors. Writes a number sentence for finding the sum in which the symbols are used correctly, but there might be a computation error.

1 Circles some digits and uses them to construct two 2-digit numbers. Constructs two 2-digit numbers. Attempts to represent the numbers or the sum using base-10 blocks, but there might be errors. Writes a number sentence with computation errors and might incorrectly use symbols.

0 Does not attempt to understand or solve the problem.

Sample Student Responses

This Level 4 paper illustrates the following features: Three digits are circled and used to make the largest and smallest possible numbers. The two addends are represented with base-10 blocks. The number sentence and its sum are written correctly.

This Level 4 paper illustrates the following features: Three digits are circled and used to make the largest and smallest possible numbers. The sum is represented with base-10 blocks. (No exchanges have been made.) The number sentence and its sum are written correctly.

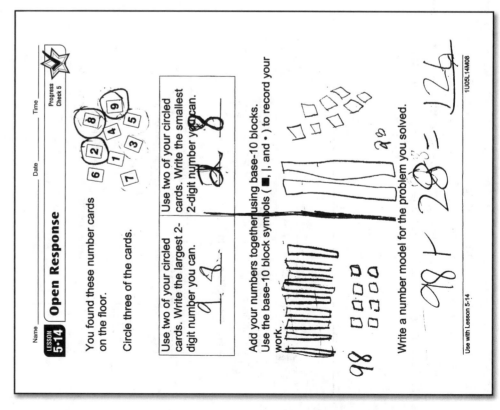

Name _____ Date _____ Time _____

Progress Check 5

LESSON 5·14 **Open Response**

You found these number cards on the floor.

6 2 8 9
7 1 4
3 5

Circle three of the cards.

Use two of your circled cards. Write the largest 2-digit number you can.	Use two of your circled cards. Write the smallest 2-digit number you can.
96	46

Add your numbers together using base-10 blocks. Use the base-10 block symbols (■, |, and •) to record your work.

Write a number model for the problem you solved.

96 + 46 = 142

Use with Lesson 5-14   1U05L14M08

Name _____ Date _____ Time _____

Progress Check 5

LESSON 5·14 **Open Response**

You found these number cards on the floor.

6 2 8 9
7 1 4
3 5

Circle three of the cards.

Use two of your circled cards. Write the largest 2-digit number you can.	Use two of your circled cards. Write the smallest 2-digit number you can.
98	28

Add your numbers together using base-10 blocks. Use the base-10 block symbols (■, |, and •) to record your work.

Write a number model for the problem you solved.

98 + 28 = 126

Use with Lesson 5-14   1U05L14M08

This Level 3 paper illustrates the following features: Three digits are circled and used to make a larger and a smaller number. 69 is not the smallest number possible with these three digits. The sum is represented with base-10 blocks. (No exchanges have been made.) The number sentence and its sum are written correctly except for the sum of 167, which has a zero inserted incorrectly.

Name _____ Date _____ Time _____

LESSON 5·14 **Open Response**

Progress Check 5

You found these number cards on the floor.

Circle three of the cards.

6 2 8 9 1 4 3 5 7 3

Use two of your circled cards. Write the largest 2-digit number you can.	Use two of your circled cards. Write the smallest 2-digit number you can.
98	69

Add your numbers together using base-10 blocks. Use the base-10 block symbols (■, |, and •) to record your work.

Write a number model for the problem you solved.

98+69=1067

Use with Lesson 5-14

1U05L14M08

This Level 3 paper illustrates the following features: Three digits are circled and used to make a larger and a smaller number. 81 is not the largest number possible and 19 is not the smallest number possible with these three digits. The sum is represented with base-10 blocks. The number sentence and its sum are written correctly.

Name _____ Date _____ Time _____

LESSON 5·14 **Open Response**

Progress Check 5

You found these number cards on the floor.

Circle three of the cards.

6 2 8 9 1 4 3 5 7

Use two of your circled cards. Write the largest 2-digit number you can.	Use two of your circled cards. Write the smallest 2-digit number you can.
8	1 0

Add your numbers together using base-10 blocks. Use the base-10 block symbols (■, |, and •) to record your work.

Write a number model for the problem you solved.

81+19=100

Use with Lesson 5-14

1U05L14M08

This Level 1 paper illustrates the following features: Three digits are circled and used to make the largest and smallest possible numbers. One addend is represented with base-10 blocks, but the other number represented does not relate to the smallest or largest one. The number sentence is missing.

This Level 2 paper illustrates the following features: Four digits are circled and three are used to make the largest and smallest numbers possible with those 3 digits. The addends are represented with base-10 blocks, but each block count is off by one. The number sentence is written correctly, but its sum is off by one. The error in the sum does not match the error in the base-10 block illustrations.

LESSON 5·14 — Open Response — Progress Check 5

You found these number cards on the floor.

Circle three of the cards.

Use two of your circled cards. Write the largest 2-digit number you can.

Use two of your circled cards. Write the smallest 2-digit number you can.

Add your numbers together using base-10 blocks. Use the base-10 block symbols (■, |, and •) to record your work.

Write a number model for the problem you solved.

Use with Lesson 5-14 — 1U05L14M08

LESSON 5·14 — Open Response — Progress Check 5

You found these number cards on the floor.

Circle three of the cards.

Use two of your circled cards. Write the largest 2-digit number you can.

Use two of your circled cards. Write the smallest 2-digit number you can.

Add your numbers together using base-10 blocks. Use the base-10 block symbols (■, |, and •) to record your work.

Write a number model for the problem you solved.

Use with Lesson 5-14 — 1U05L14M08

Mid-Year Assessment Goals

The Mid-Year Assessment (pages 187–190) provides an additional opportunity that you may use as part of your balanced assessment plan. It covers some of the important concepts and skills presented in *First Grade Everyday Mathematics*. It should be used to complement the ongoing and periodic assessments that appear within lessons and at the end of units. The following tables provide the goals for all the problems in Part A and Part B of the Mid-Year Assessment.

Part A Recognizing Student Achievement

Problems 1–8 provide summative information and may be used for grading purposes.

Problem(s)	Description	Grade-Level Goal
1, 7	Count collections of objects accurately and reliably.	Number and Numeration Goal 2
1	Identify even and odd numbers.	Number and Numeration Goal 5
2	Write whole numbers up to 1,000.	Number and Numeration Goal 3
2	Order whole numbers.	Number and Numeration Goal 7
3	Count by 2s and 10s.	Number and Numeration Goal 1
4	Extend visual patterns.	Patterns, Functions, and Algebra Goal 1
5	Show time to the nearest hour and half-hour on an analog clock.	Measurement and Reference Frames Goal 4
6	Measure length using standard measuring tools.	Measurement and Reference Frames Goal 1
7	Use tally marks to give equivalent names for whole numbers.	Number and Numeration Goal 6
7, 8	Use tally marks to solve problems involving addition and subtraction of 1-digit whole numbers with 1- or 2-digit whole numbers; calculate the values of combinations of coins.	Operations and Computation Goal 2
7	Identify comparison situations.	Operations and Computation Goal 4
7	Organize data to create tally charts.	Data and Chance Goal 1
7	Use tally charts to answer simple questions.	Data and Chance Goal 2
8	Know the values of pennies, nickels, and dimes.	Measurement and Reference Frames Goal 2

Part B Informing Instruction

Problems 9–12 provide formative information that can be useful in planning future instruction.

Problem(s)	Description	Grade-Level Goal
9	Demonstrate proficiency with + 0, + 1, doubles, and sum-equals-ten addition facts.	Operations and Computation Goal 1
10	Count back by 5s.	Number and Numeration Goal 1
10	Solve problems involving the addition and subtraction of 1-digit whole numbers with 1- or 2-digit whole numbers.	Operations and Computation Goal 2
10	Solve problems involving Frames-and-Arrows diagrams.	Patterns, Functions, and Algebra Goal 1
11	Solve problems involving the addition and subtraction of 1-digit whole numbers with 1- or 2-digit whole numbers.	Operations and Computation Goal 2
11	Identify change-to-less, change-to-more, and parts-and-totals situations.	Operations and Computation Goal 4
11	Write and explain number sentences using the symbols +, −, and =; solve equations involving addition and subtraction.	Patterns, Functions, and Algebra Goal 2
12	Calculate the values of combinations of coins.	Operations and Computation Goal 2
12	Know the values of pennies, nickels, and dimes; make exchanges between coins.	Measurement and Reference Frames Goal 2

Assessment Overview

In this unit, children continue their work to build their fact power with basic addition and subtraction facts. Use the information in this section to develop your assessment plan for Unit 6.

Ongoing Assessment

Opportunities for using and collecting ongoing assessment information are highlighted in Informing Instruction and Recognizing Student Achievement notes. Student products, along with observations and suggested writing prompts, provide a range of useful assessment information.

Informing Instruction

The Informing Instruction notes highlight children's thinking and point out common misconceptions. Informing Instruction in Unit 6: Lessons 6-3, 6-6, 6-8, 6-9, and 6-10.

Recognizing Student Achievement

The Recognizing Student Achievement notes highlight specific tasks from which teachers can collect assessment data to monitor and document children's progress toward meeting Grade-Level Goals.

Lesson	Content Assessed	Where to Find It
6◆1	Find a number between two numbers. [Number and Numeration Goal 7]	*TLG*, p. 537
6◆2	Write addition problems with a sum of 7. [Operations and Computation Goal 2]	*TLG*, p. 543
6◆3	Solve parts and total problems. [Operations and Computation Goal 4]	*TLG*, p. 549
6◆4	Do "stop-and-start" counting. [Number and Numeration Goal 1]	*TLG*, p. 554
6◆5	Use the Addition/Subtraction Facts Table to solve addition problems. [Operations and Computation Goal 2]	*TLG*, p. 561
6◆6	Analyze and interpret data. [Data and Chance Goal 2]	*TLG*, p. 567
6◆7	Solve easy addition facts. [Operations and Computation Goal 1]	*TLG*, p. 572
6◆8	Find the rule in "What's My Rule?" problems. [Patterns, Functions, and Algebra Goal 1]	*TLG*, p. 575
6◆9	Answer probability questions. [Data and Chance Goal 3]	*TLG*, p. 584
6◆10	Solve number stories. [Operations and Computation Goal 4]	*TLG*, p. 588
6◆11	Show and tell time. [Measurement and Reference Frames Goal 4]	*TLG*, p. 594
6◆12	Solve and record addition problems. [Operations and Computation Goal 2]	*TLG*, p. 601

Math Boxes

Math Boxes, one of several types of tasks highlighted in the Recognizing Student Achievement notes, have an additional useful feature. Math Boxes in most lessons are paired or linked with Math Boxes in one or two other lessons that have similar problems. Paired or linked Math Boxes in Unit 6: 6-1 and 6-3; 6-2 and 6-4; 6-5 and 6-7; 6-6 and 6-8; 6-9 and 6-11; and 6-10 and 6-12.

Writing/Reasoning Prompts

In Unit 6, a variety of writing prompts encourage children to explain their strategies and thinking, to reflect on their learning, and to make connections to other mathematics or life experiences. Here are some of the Unit 6 suggestions:

Lesson	Writing/Reasoning Prompts	Where to Find It
6•1	Explain how turn-around facts increase your fact power.	TLG, p. 540
6•4	Explain how you know what to write in the name-collection box.	TLG, p. 557
6•5	Explain what a fact family is.	TLG, p. 561
6•10	Explain how you count a handful of coins.	TLG, p. 592

Portfolio Opportunities

Portfolios are a versatile tool for assessment. They help children reflect on their mathematical growth and help teachers understand and document that growth. Each unit identifies several student products that can be selected and stored in a portfolio. Here are some of the Unit 6 suggestions:

Lesson	Portfolio Opportunities	Where to Find It
6•3	Children record the domino-card pairs they win in the game *Concentration* using number sentences.	TLG, p. 552
6•7	Children determine how many of one kind of a smaller pattern block are needed to cover a larger pattern block.	TLG, p. 570
6•8	Children compare numbers on a graph.	TLG, p. 578
6•11	Children explain how they know which color they are more likely to spin.	TLG, p. 596

Periodic Assessment

Every Progress Check lesson includes opportunities to observe children's progress and to collect student products in a variety of ways—Self Assessment, Oral and Slate Assessment, Written Assessment, and an Open Response task. For more details, see the first page of Progress Check 6, Lesson 6-12 on page 604, of the *Teacher's Lesson Guide*.

Progress Check Modifications

Written Assessments are one way children demonstrate what they know. The table below shows modifications for the Written Assessment in this unit. Use these to maximize opportunities for children to demonstrate what they know. Modifications can be given individually or written on the board for the class.

Problem(s)	Modifications for Written Assessment
3, 4	For Problems 3 and 4, record at least one name for the number that uses BOTH addition and subtraction.
5	For Problem 5, use coins to model the totals on both sides of the problem.
7, 8	For Problems 7 and 8, cut a strip of paper that is about 6 cm long. Use this strip of paper to make your estimates.
9	For Problem 9, use a number grid to help you solve the problems.

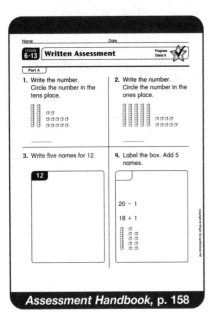

Assessment Handbook, p. 158

The Written Assessment for the Unit 6 Progress Check is on pages 158–159.

Open Response, *Necklace Patterns*

30-40 Min.

Description

For this task, children create and continue a pattern and represent an amount with a coin combination.

Focus

◆ **Solve problems involving addition.**
[Operations and Computation Goal 2]

◆ **Make coin combinations for a given amount.**
[Measurement and Reference Frames Goal 2]

◆ **Create and continue a visual pattern.**
[Patterns, Functions, and Algebra Goal 1]

Implementation Tips

◆ **Have children record the total value of the beads they used so you have enough information to tell if their coin combinations are correct.**

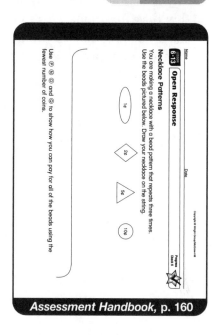

Assessment Handbook, p. 160

◆ By this time in the year, children have gained experience communicating their mathematical thinking and should be moving towards independence. Have children record their solutions and mathematical thinking on the Assessment Master.
It is still important to share solutions as a whole class.

◆ Provide children with coins to model the problem.

◆ Provide a template so children can trace the shapes for their necklace patterns.

Modifications for Meeting Diverse Needs

◆ Have children color-code the shapes to help them with the pattern. Have children label each bead in the necklace with its value.

◆ Have children do two different equivalent coin combinations for the total value and explain a strategy for how they can use coin exchanges to make multiple coin combinations for the total value.

Improving Open Response Skills

Before children begin the task, have them read the task. Discuss and make a list of what a paper must include in order to be complete. For example, it requires a necklace with a pattern that repeats three times and a coin combination that is equal to the value of the beads used in the necklace pattern.

Note: The wording and formatting of the text on the student samples that follow may vary slightly from the actual task your children will complete. These minor discrepancies will not affect the implementation of the task.

Rubric

The rubric is designed to help you assess levels of mathematical performance on this task. It emphasizes mathematical understanding with only a mention of clarity of explanation. Consider the expectations of standardized tests in your area when applying a rubric. Modify this sample rubric as appropriate.

4 Creates a pattern that repeats at least three times. Correctly computes the total value of the bead necklace that is drawn. Records a coin combination representing the total value of the necklace using the fewest possible coins.

3 Creates a pattern that repeats at least three times. Correctly computes the total value of the bead necklace that is drawn. Records a coin combination representing the total value of the necklace.

2 Creates a repeating pattern. Computes the total value of the bead necklace that is drawn with only minor errors. Records a coin combination related to the actual total or to a recorded total that might have minor calculation errors.

1 Creates no apparent pattern. There is no total or an incorrect total for the beads. The coin combination is missing or does not relate to the total number of beads or to a recorded total.

0 Does not attempt to understand or solve the problem.

Sample Student Responses

This Level 4 paper illustrates the following features: The four-bead pattern is repeated three times. The total value of the pattern is correctly computed. The coin combination shows the total value with the fewest coins.

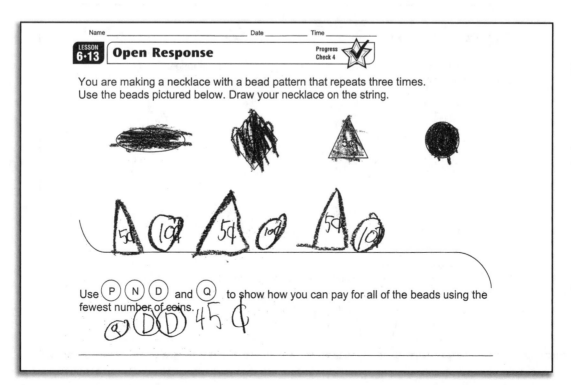

This Level 4 paper illustrates the following features: The two-bead pattern is repeated three times. The total value of the pattern is correctly computed. The coin combination shows the total value with the fewest coins.

This Level 3 paper illustrates the following features: The two-bead pattern is repeated more than three times. The total value of the pattern is correctly computed. The coin combination shows the total value, but not with the fewest number of coins.

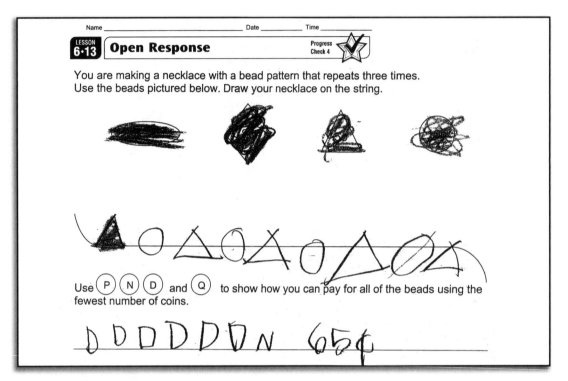

This Level 2 paper illustrates the following features: The three-bead pattern is repeated three times. The total value of the pattern is correctly computed. The coin combination does not show the total value.

This Level 2 paper illustrates the following features: The three-bead pattern has a reversal so that it does not repeat three times. The total value of the pattern is correctly computed. The coin combination shows the total value.

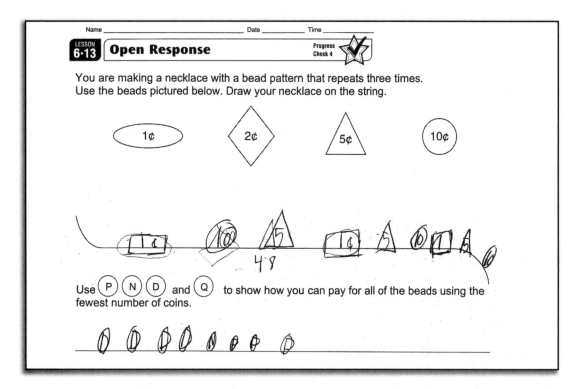

This Level 1 paper illustrates the following features: There is no evidence of a repeating pattern. There is no total given for the cost, and the coin combination has no connection to the value of the beads in the necklace.

Unit 7 Assessment Overview

In this unit, children explore the attributes of, and compare and contrast 2- and 3-dimensional shapes. Use the information in this section to develop your assessment plan for Unit 7.

Ongoing Assessment

Opportunities for using and collecting ongoing assessment information are highlighted in Informing Instruction and Recognizing Student Achievement notes. Student products, along with observations and suggested writing prompts, provide a range of useful assessment information.

Informing Instruction

The Informing Instruction notes highlight children's thinking and point out common misconceptions. Informing Instruction in Unit 7: Lessons 7-1, 7-4, 7-6, and 7-7.

Recognizing Student Achievement

The Recognizing Student Achievement notes highlight specific tasks from which teachers can collect assessment data to monitor and document children's progress toward meeting Grade-Level Goals.

Lesson	Content Assessed	Where to Find It
7◆1	**Solve change-to-less problems.** [Operations and Computation Goal 4]	*TLG,* p. 625
7◆2	**Write fact families.** [Patterns, Functions, and Algebra Goal 3]	*TLG,* p. 628
7◆3	**Identify 2-dimensional shapes.** [Geometry Goal 1]	*TLG,* p. 635
7◆4	**Count the value of quarters.** [Measurement and Reference Frames Goal 2]	*TLG,* p. 639
7◆5	**Name numbers represented by base-10 blocks.** [Number and Numeration Goal 3]	*TLG,* p. 645
7◆6	**Identify attributes of attribute blocks.** [Geometry Goal 1]	*TLG,* p. 652
7◆7	**Identify cylinders.** [Geometry Goal 1]	*TLG,* p. 657

Math Boxes

Math Boxes, one of several types of tasks highlighted in the Recognizing Student Achievement notes, have an additional useful feature. Math Boxes in most lessons are paired or linked with Math Boxes in one or two other lessons that have similar problems. Paired or linked Math Boxes in Unit 7: 7-1 and 7-3; 7-2, 7-4, and 7-6; and 7-5 and 7-7.

Writing/Reasoning Prompts

In Unit 7, a variety of writing prompts encourage children to explain their strategies and thinking, to reflect on their learning, and to make connections to other mathematics or life experiences. Here are some of the Unit 7 suggestions:

Lesson	Writing/Reasoning Prompts	Where to Find It
7♦3	Explain what a rectangle is.	*TLG*, p. 636
7♦5	Explain what a polygon is.	*TLG*, p. 647
7♦6	Explain patterns on the number grid.	*TLG*, p. 652

Portfolio Opportunities

Portfolios are a versatile tool for assessment. They help children reflect on their mathematical growth and help teachers understand and document that growth. Each unit identifies several student products that can be selected and stored in a portfolio. Here are some of the Unit 7 suggestions:

Lesson	Portfolio Opportunities	Where to Find It
7♦3	Children explain what a rectangle is.	*TLG*, p. 636
7♦3	Children make a design using pattern-block shapes and then make a graph showing the frequency of the shapes they used.	*TLG*, p. 637
7♦5	Children explain what a polygon is.	*TLG*, p. 647
7♦6	Children describe patterns on the number grid.	*TLG*, p. 652
7♦6	Children draw and color at least three shapes in an attribute train.	*TLG*, p. 652

Periodic Assessment

Every Progress Check lesson includes opportunities to observe children's progress and to collect student products in a variety of ways—Self Assessment, Oral and Slate Assessment, Written Assessment, and an Open Response task. For more details, see the first page of Progress Check 7, Lesson 7-8 on page 658 of the *Teacher's Lesson Guide*.

Progress Check Modifications

Written Assessments are one way children demonstrate what they know. The table below shows modifications for the Written Assessment in this unit. Use these to maximize opportunities for children to demonstrate what they know. Modifications can be given individually or written on the board for the class.

Problem(s)	Modifications for Written Assessment
1	For Problem 1, build each number on a place-value mat with base-10 blocks before recording the answer.
5	For Problem 5, underline each "color" word with the matching crayon before coloring the shapes.
7	For Problem 7, add two more rows of your own *in* and *out* numbers.
9	For Problem 9, use tool-kit coins to show 68¢, and record the coins you use.

Assessment Handbook, p. 162

The Written Assessment for the Unit 7 Progress Check is on pages 162–163.

Open Response, *Shapes That Belong in a Group*

30-40 Min.

Description

For this task, children sort shapes from the pattern-block template into two groups according to attributes.

Focus

◆ **Identify and describe plane and solid figures.** [Geometry Goal 1]

◆ **Solve problems involving rules.** [Patterns, Functions, and Algebra Goal 1]

Implementation Tips

By this time in the year, children have gained experience communicating their mathematical thinking and should be moving towards independence. Have children record their solutions and mathematical thinking on the Assessment Master. It is still important to share solutions as a whole class.

Name   *Date*

7-8 | **Open Response** | Progress Check 7

Shapes That Belong in a Group

Think: Which shapes from your Pattern-Block Template belong together in a group?

Use your template to draw 3 shapes that go together in the box "Shapes That Belong in the Group." In the other box, draw 3 shapes that do not belong in the group.

Shapes That Belong in the Group	Shapes That Do Not Belong in the Group

Explain or show how you know if a shape belongs in the group.

Assessment Handbook, p. 164

◆ To remind children what the task is asking them to do, record two rectangles on the board. In the left-hand rectangle, write These Belong. In the right-hand rectangle, write These Do Not Belong. Give an example. List a few of the children's names in the Belong side. List the teacher's name and other adults (mom, dad, and so on) in the Do-Not-Belong side. Discuss who fits on the Belong side and why. *(Children)*

Modifications for Meeting Diverse Needs

◆ Have children use attribute blocks. They can trace three blocks that belong and three that do not. The attribute blocks give them concrete materials to work with and provide more choices for the rules for putting the shapes in the Belong side.

◆ Have children describe several attributes the shapes that Belong have in common.

Improving Open Response Skills

Before children begin the task, have them review the problem and generate a list of vocabulary words that they might use in the explanation; for example, *corners, points, sides, polygons, straight, curved.*

Note: The wording and formatting of the text on the student samples that follow may vary slightly from the actual task your children will complete. These minor discrepancies will not affect the implementation of the task.

Rubric

This rubric is designed to help you assess levels of mathematical performance on this task. It emphasizes mathematical understanding with only a mention of clarity of explanation. Consider the expectations of standardized tests in your area when applying a rubric. Modify this sample rubric as appropriate.

4   Constructs a group in which several shapes belong together. Identifies three shapes that fit in the group and three shapes that do not fit in the group. Clearly describes at least one attribute that is true for the group of shapes that belong together and one that is not true for the other group. The explanation makes sense and does not include extra or confusing information.

3   Constructs a group in which several shapes belong together. Identifies three shapes that fit in the group and three shapes that do not fit in the group. Describes at least one attribute that is true for the group of shapes that belong together and one that is not true for the other group. The explanation might be unclear or might include some extra or confusing information.

2   Attempts to construct a group in which several shapes belong together, but there might be errors. Attempts to describe an attribute, and the description makes sense in the context of the problem, but it might not be clearly related to the examples.

1   Attempts to place shapes into two groups, but there might not be apparent categories. The description might not explain the qualifying attribute, or it might not make sense in the context of the problem.

0   Does not attempt to solve the problem.

Sample Student Responses

This Level 4 paper clearly illustrates that the shapes that fit in the Belong group have 2 attributes in common: They have corners and sides. The shapes in the Do-Not-Belong group are all circles, which do not have corners or sides.

This Level 4 paper clearly illustrates that the shapes that fit in the Belong group have several attributes in common: They are polygons with 4 corners and sides. Circles are placed correctly in the Do-Not-Belong group.

Name _____ Date _____ Time _____

Open Response

Progress Check 7

Think: which shapes from your pattern-block template belong together in a group.

Use your template to draw 3 shapes that go together in the box "Shapes That Belong in the Group." In the other box, draw 3 shapes that do not belong in the group.

Shapes that Belong in the Group	Shapes that Do Not Belong in the Group

Explain or show how you know if a shape belongs in the group.

there all Polygons   there not Polygons
they all have 4 corner and sides.   they Don't have sides and cones

---

Name _____ Date _____ Time _____

LESSON 7·8 **Open Response**

Progress Check 7

Think: which shapes from your pattern-block template belong together in a group.

Use your template to draw 3 shapes that go together in the box "Shapes That Belong in the Group." In the other box, draw 3 shapes that do not belong in the group.

Shapes that Belong in the Group	Shapes that Do Not Belong in the Group

Explain or show how you know if a shape belongs in the group.

thes have Conos and Sos

This Level 3 paper illustrates that the shapes in the Belong group can "fit" in a hexagon. There seems to be a distinction between shapes that spatially just fit inside and shapes that can be used to replicate the hexagon. The shapes in the Do-Not-Belong group cannot be used to replicate a hexagon.

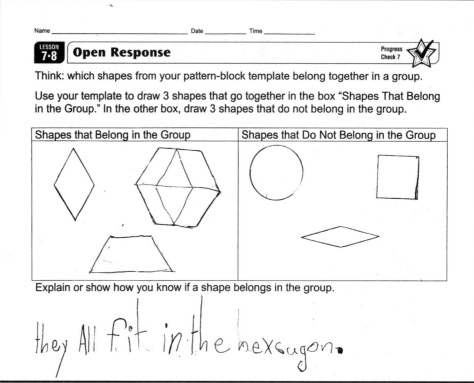

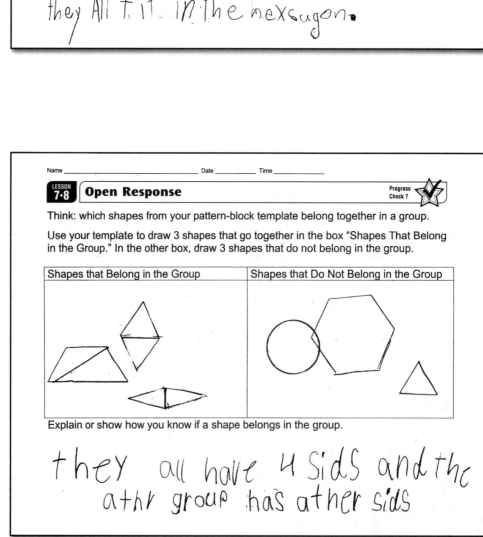

This Level 3 paper correctly illustrates that the shapes fitting in the Belong group have 1 attribute in common: They all have 4 sides. The shapes in the Do-Not-Belong group do not have 4 sides.

This Level 1 paper illustrates that there is a triangle in each group, and the description does not make sense.

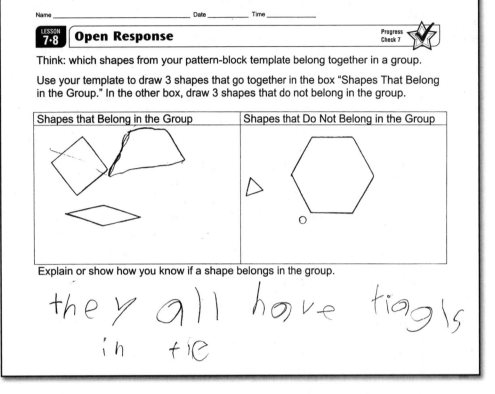

Name _____ Date _____ Time _____

Open Response

Progress Check 7

Think: which shapes from your pattern-block template belong together in a group.

Use your template to draw 3 shapes that go together in the box "Shapes That Belong in the Group." In the other box, draw 3 shapes that do not belong in the group.

Shapes that Belong in the Group	Shapes that Do Not Belong in the Group

Explain or show how you know if a shape belongs in the group.

they all have tiagls in fie

This Level 2 paper illustrates that the shapes fitting in the Belong group have no points. They are all circles. Some of the shapes in the Do-Not-Belong group have points, but there is also a circle in this group.

Name _____ Date _____ Time _____

LESSON 7·8
Open Response

Progress Check 7

Think: which shapes from your pattern-block template belong together in a group.

Use your template to draw 3 shapes that go together in the box "Shapes That Belong in the Group." In the other box, draw 3 shapes that do not belong in the group.

Shapes that Belong in the Group	Shapes that Do Not Belong in the Group

Explain or show how you know if a shape belongs in the group.

The srkls They a rehave notosl
The hax gon kat makā he shkl

Assessment Overview

In this unit, children build on their previous experience with money and place value, and they begin to explore fraction concepts more formally. Use the information in this section to develop your assessment plan for Unit 8.

Ongoing Assessment

Opportunities for using and collecting ongoing assessment information are highlighted in Informing Instruction and Recognizing Student Achievement notes. Student products, along with observations and suggested writing prompts, provide a range of useful assessment information.

Informing Instruction

The Informing Instruction notes highlight children's thinking and point out common misconceptions. Informing Instruction in Unit 8: Lessons 8-2, 8-3, 8-5, 8-7, and 8-9.

Recognizing Student Achievement

The Recognizing Student Achievement notes highlight specific tasks from which teachers can collect assessment data to monitor and document children's progress toward meeting Grade-Level Goals.

Lesson	Content Assessed	Where to Find It
8•1	Count money. [Operations and Computation Goal 2]	*TLG*, p. 678
8•2	Compare numbers using <, >, and = . [Patterns, Functions, and Algebra Goal 2]	*TLG*, p. 683
8•3	Model numbers with base-10 blocks. [Number and Numeration Goal 3]	*TLG*, p. 689
8•4	Solve subtraction facts. [Operations and Computation Goal 1]	*TLG*, p. 696
8•5	Find 10 more and 10 less than numbers and circle the tens digit. [Number and Numeration Goal 3]	*TLG*, p. 699
8•6	Divide a region into halves. [Number and Numeration Goal 4]	*TLG*, p. 705
8•7	Draw the missing half of a symmetrical figure. [Geometry Goal 2]	*TLG*, p. 712
8•8	Determine the likelihood of spinning a certain number. [Data and Chance Goal 3]	*TLG*, p. 717
8•9	Name 2-dimensional shapes. [Geometry Goal 1]	*TLG*, p. 720

Math Boxes

Math Boxes, one of several types of tasks highlighted in the Recognizing Student Achievement notes, have an additional useful feature. Math Boxes in most lessons are paired or linked with Math Boxes in one or two other lessons that have similar problems. Paired or linked Math Boxes in Unit 8: 8-1 and 8-3; 8-2 and 8-4; 8-5, 8-7, and 8-9; and 8-6 and 8-8.

Writing/Reasoning Prompts

In Unit 8, a variety of writing prompts encourage children to explain their strategies and thinking, to reflect on their learning, and to make connections to other mathematics or life experiences. Here are some of the Unit 8 suggestions:

Lesson	Writing/Reasoning Prompts	Where to Find It
8◆1	Explain why it is important to know addition facts.	*TLG*, p. 680
8◆2	Explain what a prism is.	*TLG*, p. 686
8◆6	Explain how you make change.	*TLG*, p. 707
8◆7	Explain how you know how many hundreds are in a number.	*TLG*, p. 712

Portfolio Opportunities

Portfolios are a versatile tool for assessment. They help children reflect on their mathematical growth and help teachers understand and document that growth. Each unit identifies several student products that can be selected and stored in a portfolio. Here are some of the Unit 8 suggestions:

Lesson	Portfolio Opportunities	Where to Find It
8◆2	Children show combinations of coins that total one dollar.	*TLG*, p. 687
8◆6	Children explain how to make change.	*TLG*, p. 707
8◆7	Children make a fraction book.	*TLG*, p. 713
8◆8	Children make a "fraction creature."	*TLG*, p. 718
8◆9	Children test circles, squares, and triangles for symmetry.	*TLG*, p. 723

Periodic Assessment

Every Progress Check lesson includes opportunities to observe children's progress and to collect student products in a variety of ways—Self Assessment, Oral and Slate Assessment, Written Assessment, and an Open Response task. For more details, see the first page of Progress Check 8, Lesson 8-10 on page 724 of the *Teacher's Lesson Guide*.

Progress Check Modifications

Written Assessments are one way children demonstrate what they know. The table below shows modifications for the Written Assessment in this unit. Use these to maximize opportunities for children to demonstrate what they know. Modifications can be given individually or written on the board for the class.

Problem(s)	Modifications for Written Assessment
1	For Problem 1, trace and cut out the shapes and fold them in half. Then shade $\frac{1}{2}$ of each shape.
3	For Problem 3, write one name that uses both addition and subtraction.
4	For Problem 4, build the number on a place-value mat with base-10 blocks before recording the number.
7	For Problem 7, use pattern blocks to figure out the fraction name for each part.

Assessment Handbook, p. 166

The Written Assessment for the Unit 8 Progress Check is on pages 166–167.

Open Response, *School Box*

45-55 Min.

Description

For this task, children draw fractions of a collection.

Focus

◆ **Count collections of objects.**
[Number and Numeration Goal 2]

◆ **Use drawings to model equal parts of a collection and describe the model.**
[Number and Numeration Goal 4]

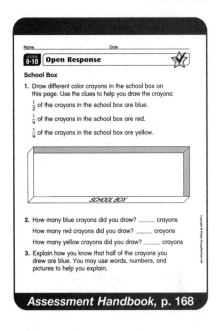

Assessment Handbook, p. 168

Implementation Tips

By this time in the year, children have gained experience communicating their mathematical thinking and should be moving towards independence. Have children record their solutions and mathematical thinking on the Assessment Master. It is still important to share solutions as a whole class.

◆ Have children make a plan before they start drawing and coloring.

◆ Remind children of the lesson where they shared pennies equally.

Modifications for Meeting Diverse Needs

◆ Give children a starting number of crayons in the form of a manipulative such as craft sticks, for example, a set of 12 or 16. Have them divide the set in half and then into quarters and record their work for the problem.

◆ Have children solve the problem in two different ways. Ask them to explain a pattern they see in the solutions. (*Sample answer: I noticed that the number of red and yellow crayons together would always be the same as the number of blue crayons.*)

Improving Open Response Skills

After children complete the task, display Level 4 of the rubric on the board or overhead, and review it with the children. Have them translate Level 4 of the rubric into their own words. Record the children's language on chart paper and display the description. Have children refer to the posted Level 4 description to improve their work before turning in their papers.

Note: The wording and formatting of the text on the student samples that follow may vary slightly from the actual task your children will complete. These minor discrepancies will not affect the implementation of the task.

Rubric

This rubric is designed to help you assess levels of mathematical performance on this task. It emphasizes mathematical understanding with only a mention of clarity of explanation. Consider the expectations of standardized tests in your area when applying a rubric. Modify this sample rubric as appropriate.

4 — Draws a collection of crayons of which one-half are blue, one-quarter are red, and one-quarter are yellow. Records numbers in Problem 2 that match the drawing in Problem 1. Explains why half the crayons are blue. The explanation matches the illustration in Problem 1.

3 — Draws a collection of crayons, of which one-half are blue, one-quarter are red, and one-quarter are yellow. Records numbers in Problem 2 that match the drawing in Problem 1. Uses numbers or language that demonstrate an understanding of fractions, for example, *equal group* or *half of;* however, the explanation might be incomplete or unclear.

2 — Draws a collection of crayons that illustrates some understanding of half. Records numbers in Problem 2 that match the drawing in Problem 1. Attempts an explanation in Problem 3, but it might be incorrect or make little sense in the context of the problem.

1 — Draws a collection of crayons, but does not show an understanding of the problem. Records numbers in Problem 2 that might relate to the illustration in Problem 1. Might attempt an explanation in Problem 3, but it might make no sense in the context of the problem.

0 — Does not attempt to solve the problem.

Sample Student Responses

This Level 4 paper illustrates the following features: There are 6 blue crayons, 3 red crayons, and 3 yellow crayons. The explanation is written correctly in a number sentence. The explanation indicates an understanding that half of the crayons are blue and that there must be a total of 12 crayons if there are 6 blue crayons.

This Level 4 paper illustrates the following features: There are 6 blue crayons, 3 red crayons, and 3 yellow crayons. The written explanation clearly describes a strategy of modeling the problem with pennies to find the number of crayons.

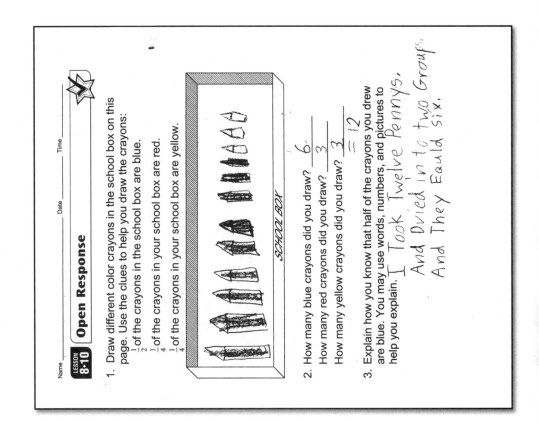

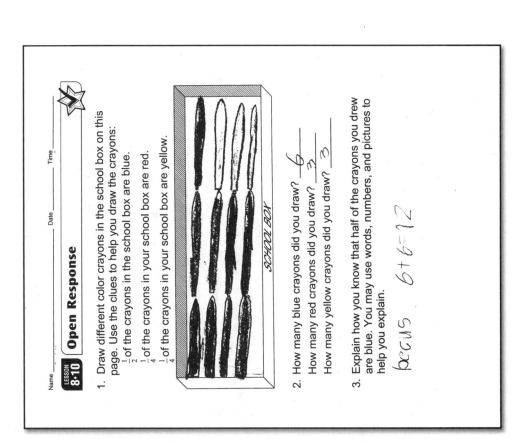

This Level 3 paper illustrates the following features: There are 4 blue crayons, 2 red crayons, and 2 yellow crayons. The written explanation implies taking some number and finding that half of it is 4. There are 4 blue crayons drawn together in the center. No more information is provided.

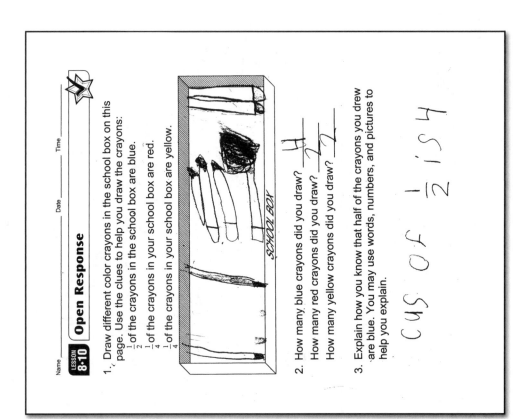

This Level 3 paper illustrates the following features: There are 4 blue crayons, 2 red crayons, and 2 yellow crayons. The written explanation describes modeling the problem with 8 crayons, taking half away, and having 2 red and 2 yellow crayons left. The drawing does not match the explanation, but the work is all correct.

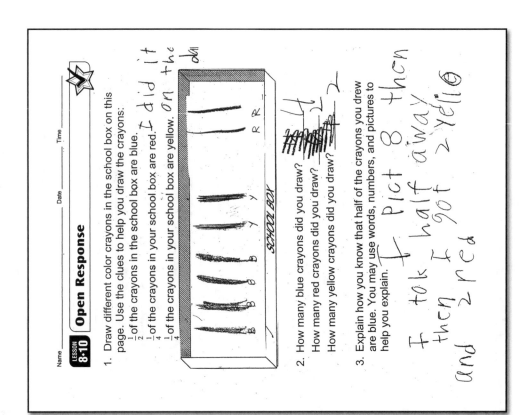

This Level 2 paper illustrates the following features: The answers drawn and listed are correct. The explanation suggests some understanding of a relationship between equal groups and fractions, but it does not appear to relate to the context of the problem.

This Level 1 paper illustrates the following features: Each color of crayon represents $\frac{1}{3}$ of the total. The answers given do not relate to the numbers represented in the illustration, but like the illustration, the 3 colors are evenly distributed. No explanation is given.

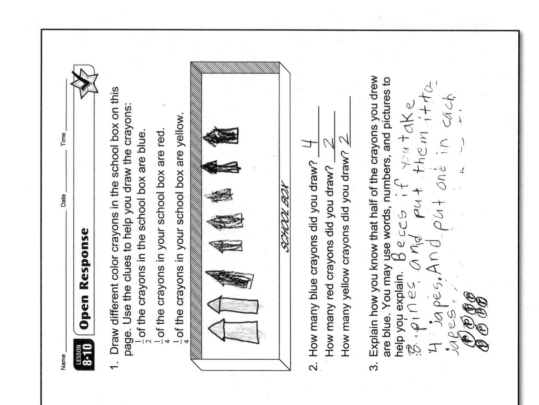

In this unit, children explore adding and subtracting with multiples of ten, and continue to develop fraction concepts. Use the information in this section to develop your assessment plan for Unit 9.

Ongoing Assessment

Opportunities for using and collecting ongoing assessment information are highlighted in Informing Instruction and Recognizing Student Achievement notes. Student products, along with observations and suggested writing prompts, provide a range of useful assessment information.

Informing Instruction

The Informing Instruction notes highlight children's thinking and point out common misconceptions. Informing Instruction in Unit 9: Lessons 9-4, 9-5, 9-6, and 9-8.

Recognizing Student Achievement

The Recognizing Student Achievement notes highlight specific tasks from which teachers can collect assessment data to monitor and document children's progress toward meeting Grade-Level Goals.

Lesson	Content Assessed	Where to Find It
9•1	**Order numbers to 110.** [Number and Numeration Goal 7]	*TLG*, p. 744
9•2	**Use a number grid to add and subtract.** [Operations and Computation Goal 2]	*TLG*, p. 748
9•3	**Name 2-dimensional shapes.** [Geometry Goal 1]	*TLG*, p. 756
9•4	**Find fractions of a collection.** [Number and Numeration Goal 4]	*TLG*, p. 761
9•5	**Create numbers using specified digits.** [Number and Numeration Goal 3]	*TLG*, p. 764
9•6	**Divide shapes into equal parts.** [Number and Numeration Goal 4]	*TLG*, p. 771
9•7	**Solve number-grid puzzles.** [Patterns, Functions, and Algebra Goal 1]	*TLG*, p. 777
9•8	**Estimate sums.** [Operations and Computation Goal 3]	*TLG*, p. 779

Math Boxes

Math Boxes, one of several types of tasks highlighted in the Recognizing Student Achievement notes, have an additional useful feature. Math Boxes in most lessons are paired or linked with Math Boxes in one or two other lessons that have similar problems. Paired or linked Math Boxes in Unit 9: 9-1 and 9-3; 9-2 and 9-4; 9-5 and 9-7; and 9-6 and 9-8.

Writing/Reasoning Prompts

In Unit 9, a variety of writing prompts encourage children to explain their strategies and thinking, to reflect on their learning, and to make connections to other mathematics or life experiences. Here are some of the Unit 9 suggestions:

Lesson	Writing/Reasoning Prompts	Where to Find It
9◆2	Explain the pattern found in a set of sums.	*TLG*, p. 751
9◆3	Explain how you know who has more money.	*TLG*, p. 756
9◆5	Explain what a fraction of a shape is.	*TLG*, p. 766
9◆8	Explain what a fraction of a collection is.	*TLG*, p. 781

Portfolio Opportunities

Portfolios are a versatile tool for assessment. They help children reflect on their mathematical growth and help teachers understand and document that growth. Each unit identifies several student products that can be selected and stored in a portfolio. Here are some of the Unit 9 suggestions:

Lesson	Portfolio Opportunities	Where to Find It
9◆3	Children list the shapes they used to create a design.	*TLG*, p. 756
9◆5	Children use pattern blocks to make their own symmetrical designs on sheets of paper.	*TLG*, p. 766
9◆6	Children explore unit fractions by drawing shapes with equal parts.	*TLG*, p. 773
9◆8	Children explore equivalent fractions by placing fractional pieces on whole fraction strips.	*TLG*, p. 782

Periodic Assessment

Every Progress Check lesson includes opportunities to observe children's progress and to collect student products in a variety of ways—Self Assessment, Oral and Slate Assessment, Written Assessment, and an Open Response task. For more details, see the first page of Progress Check 9, Lesson 9-9 on page 783 of the *Teacher's Lesson Guide*.

Progress Check Modifications

Written Assessments are one way children demonstrate what they know. The table below shows modifications for the Written Assessment in this unit. Use these to maximize opportunities for children to demonstrate what they know. Modifications can be given individually or written on the board for the class.

Problem(s)	Modifications for Written Assessment
1	For Problem 1, use counters to solve each problem.
2	For Problem 2, use quarter-sheets of paper to represent the people and 12 counters to represent the cookies.
3	For Problem 3, use your tool-kit coins to model the problem.
6	For Problem 6, explain how you figured out what number to write for the second number.

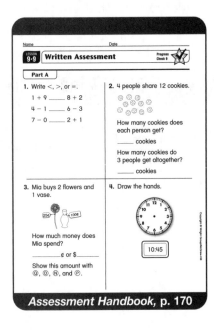

Assessment Handbook, p. 170

The Written Assessment for the Unit 9 Progress Check is on pages 170–171.

Open Response, *Number-Grid Patterns*

30-40 Min.

Description

For this task, children complete a number-grid puzzle, and then identify and describe an error in the puzzle.

Focus

◆ **Identify place value of digits in whole numbers.** [Number and Numeration Goal 3]

◆ **Extend numeric patterns and use them to solve problems.**
[Patterns, Functions, and Algebra Goal 1]

Implementation Tips

By this time in the year, children have gained experience communicating their mathematical thinking and should be moving towards independence. Have children record their solutions and mathematical thinking on the Assessment Master. It is still important to share solutions as a whole class.

◆ Have children add missing boxes to help them figure out where the mistake is.

Modifications for Meeting Diverse Needs

◆ Provide children with a section of a blank number grid that has the given numbers filled in. Have children model the numbers with base-10 longs and cubes, adding longs and taking away cubes as necessary. They fill in the resulting numbers in the grid as they go.

◆ Change the range of numbers in the problem by adding a third digit, for example, 337, 347, and so on, or even a fourth digit, for example, 1,037 or 1,047.

Improving Open Response Skills

After children complete the task, display explanations describing how patterns can be used to find the missing numbers and the mistake. For each explanation, have children determine what information could be added to make the explanation more complete. Consider using the Level 4 and Level 3 Sample Student Responses on pages 123 and 124 of this book.

Note: The wording and formatting of the text on the student samples that follow may vary slightly from the actual task your children will complete. These minor discrepancies will not affect the implementation of the task.

Assessment Handbook, p. 172

Rubric

This rubric is designed to help you assess levels of mathematical performance on this task. It emphasizes mathematical understanding with only a mention of clarity of explanation. Consider the expectations of standardized tests in your area when applying a rubric. Modify this sample rubric as appropriate.

4 — Fills in all numbers correctly. Identifies and corrects the mistake. Clearly explains the strategy used to identify and correct the mistake. Includes some reference to patterns in the number grid in the explanation.

3 — Fills in all numbers correctly. Identifies and corrects the mistake. Explains a strategy used to identify and correct the mistake. The explanation includes some reference to patterns in the number grid, but the explanation might be incomplete.

2 — Fills in numbers demonstrating an understanding of the number grid. Identifies the mistake and tries to fix it. Attempts to explain the strategy used. The explanation makes sense but omits some steps and might not make reference to patterns on the grid.

1 — Attempts to fill in missing numbers, but there might be errors. Might identify the mistake but not the correct number. Might attempt to explain the strategy used, but the explanation might show no evidence of understanding the problem.

0 — Does not attempt to solve the problem.

Sample Student Responses

This Level 4 paper illustrates the following features: All the correct numbers are entered in the grid. Several additional boxes are drawn to help solve the puzzle. The explanation clearly describes using the +10, −10, +1, −1 pattern in the grid and matches the work illustrated.

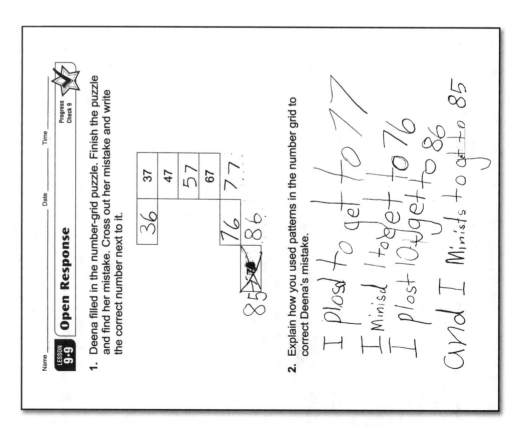

This Level 4 paper illustrates the following features: All the correct numbers are entered in the grid. The explanation describes thinking about what number would have to be in the box next to the error (86 because it is under 76) and then counting back one to correct the error.

This Level 3 paper illustrates the following features: All the correct numbers are entered in the grid. The explanation makes reference to filling in the box above the error (75) to correct the error, but the explanation needs some clarification.

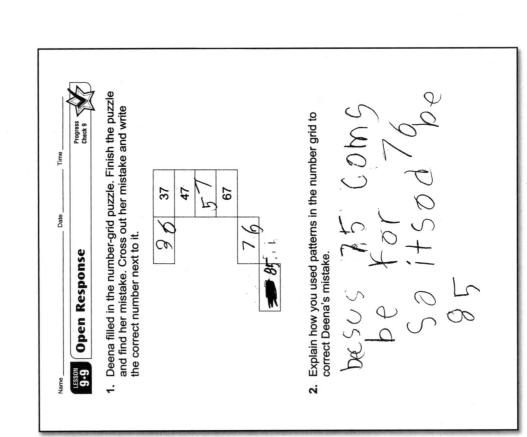

LESSON 9·9

Open Response

Progress Check 9

1. Deena filled in the number-grid puzzle. Finish the puzzle and find her mistake. Cross out her mistake and write the correct number next to it.

9 6	37
	47
5 7	
	67

76
85 ~~78~~

2. Explain how you used patterns in the number grid to correct Deena's mistake.

becsus 75 coms
be for 76 e
so itsod be
85

This Level 3 paper illustrates the following features: All the correct numbers are entered in the grid. The explanation describes the pattern in the ones place of the column farthest to the right (all 7s), and then describes going back 1. The explanation needs some clarification.

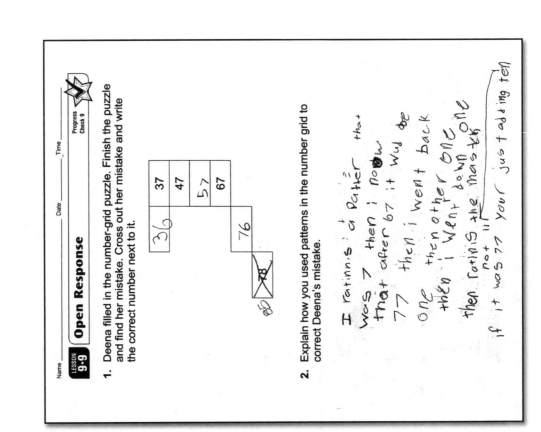

LESSON 9·9

Open Response

Progress Check 9

1. Deena filled in the number-grid puzzle. Finish the puzzle and find her mistake. Cross out her mistake and write the correct number next to it.

36	37
	47
5 7	
	67

76
~~78~~
85

2. Explain how you used patterns in the number grid to correct Deena's mistake.

I ratins a patter that
was 7 then i no
that after 67 it wus be
77 then i went back
one then other one
then i went down one
then ratins the mas tek
not i
if it was 77 you just ading ten

This Level 2 paper illustrates the following features: All the correct numbers are entered in the grid. The explanation refers to counting on the number grid, but there is no specific reference to particular numbers or to number-grid patterns.

This Level 1 paper illustrates the following features: Some of the correct numbers are entered in the grid. Numbers that are not directly below another number in the grid are incorrect. The last three entries are sequential, which demonstrates no evidence of using number-grid patterns.

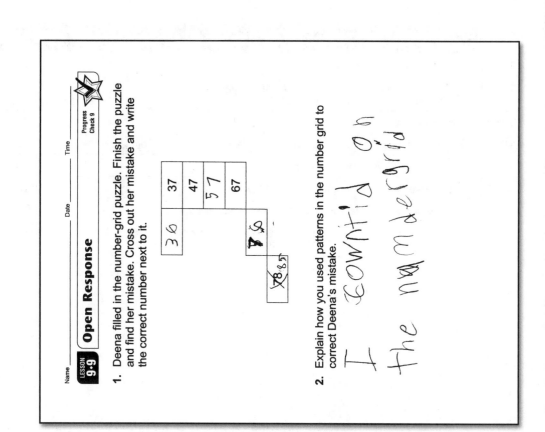

Unit 10 Assessment Overview

In this unit, children review many of the key concepts developed during the year including linear measurement, data, time, and arithmetic. Use the information in this section to develop your assessment plan for Unit 10.

Ongoing Assessment

Opportunities for using and collecting ongoing assessment information are highlighted in Informing Instruction and Recognizing Student Achievement notes. Student products, along with observations and suggested writing prompts, provide a range of useful assessment information.

Informing Instruction
The Informing Instruction notes highlight children's thinking and point out common misconceptions. Informing Instruction in Unit 10: Lessons 10-2, 10-4, 10-6, and 10-7.

Recognizing Student Achievement
The Recognizing Student Achievement notes highlight specific tasks from which teachers can collect assessment data to monitor and document children's progress toward meeting Grade-Level Goals.

Lesson	Content Assessed	Where to Find It
10◆1	**Find data landmarks.** [Data and Chance Goal 2]	*TLG*, p. 803
10◆2	**Identify the number of minutes in movements of the minute hand.** [Measurement and Reference Frames Goal 4]	*TLG*, p. 806
10◆3	**Compare numbers.** [Number and Numeration Goal 7]	*TLG*, p. 812
10◆4	**Find the difference between two money amounts.** [Operations and Computation Goal 2]	*TLG*, p. 819
10◆5	**Estimate sums.** [Operations and Computation Goal 3]	*TLG*, p. 823
10◆6	**Compare temperatures.** [Measurement and Reference Frames Goal 3]	*TLG*, p. 828
10◆7	**Solve number-grid puzzles.** [Patterns, Functions, and Algebra Goal 1]	*TLG*, p. 835

Math Boxes

Math Boxes, one of several types of tasks highlighted in the Recognizing Student Achievement notes, have an additional useful feature. Math Boxes in most lessons are paired or linked with Math Boxes in one or two other lessons that have similar problems. Paired or linked Math Boxes in Unit 10: 10-1 and 10-3; 10-2, 10-4, and 10-6; and 10-5 and 10-7.

Writing/Reasoning Prompts

In Unit 10, a variety of writing prompts encourage children to explain their strategies and thinking, to reflect on their learning, and to make connections to other mathematics or life experiences. Here are some of the Unit 10 suggestions:

Lesson	Writing/Reasoning Prompts	Where to Find It
10◆2	Explain how to solve a number-grid puzzle.	*TLG*, p. 809
10◆3	Explain how you add 10 to a number.	*TLG*, p. 814
10◆7	Explain how to read a clock.	*TLG*, p. 836

Portfolio Opportunities

Portfolios are a versatile tool for assessment. They help children reflect on their mathematical growth and help teachers understand and document that growth. Each unit identifies several student products that can be selected and stored in a portfolio. Here are some of the Unit 10 suggestions:

Lesson	Portfolio Opportunities	Where to Find It
10◆2	Children explain how to solve a number-grid puzzle.	*TLG*, p. 809
10◆3	Children explain how to add 10 to a number.	*TLG*, p. 814
10◆4	Children write and solve number stories based on magazine and newspaper ads.	*TLG*, p. 820
10◆7	Children create number patterns on scroll sheets.	*TLG*, p. 836
10◆7	Children explain how to read a clock.	*TLG*, p. 836

Periodic Assessment

Every Progress Check lesson includes opportunities to observe children's progress and to collect student products in a variety of ways—Self Assessment, Oral and Slate Assessment, Written Assessment, and an Open Response task. For more details, see the first page of Progress Check 10, Lesson 10-8 on page 839 of the *Teacher's Lesson Guide*.

Progress Check Modifications

Written Assessments are one way children demonstrate what they know. The table below shows modifications for the Written Assessment in this unit. Use these to maximize opportunities for children to demonstrate what they know. Modifications can be given individually or written on the board for the class.

Problem(s)	Modifications for Written Assessment
1	For Problem 1, draw some of the missing boxes to solve the puzzles.
2	For Problem 2, use tool-kit coins to solve the problems.
5, 6	For Problems 5 and 6, build the numbers on a place-value mat with base-10 blocks.
9	For Problem 9, explain how you found your answer.

The Written Assessment for the Unit 10 Progress Check is on pages 174–175.

Name _____ Date _____

LESSON 10·8 Written Assessment

Progress Check 10

Part A

1. Complete the number-grid puzzles.

186	187	
		198
	207	

		103
	112	
121		

2. I buy an apple for 15¢. I buy gum for $0.72.
   I pay 25¢. I pay $1.00.
   How much change do I get? How much change do I get?
   _____ ¢ $_____ . _____

3. Write <, >, or =.

   154 ☐ 372   727 ☐ 272

   94 ☐ 149   233 ☐ 322

   406 ☐ 406   510 ☐ 501

4. Fill in the missing number.

   6 + _____ = 10   _____ − 6 = 6

   _____ + 1 = 7   3 − 0 = _____

   4 + 4 = _____   10 − _____ = 9

Assessment Handbook, p. 174

Open Response, *Counting Books*

Assessment Handbook, p. 176

Description

For this task, children calculate the numbers of books two children have based on relationships between their numbers of books.

Focus

◆ **Use manipulatives, number grids, tally marks, or mental arithmetic to solve problems involving addition and subtraction.**
[Operations and Computation Goal 2]

◆ **Solve equations involving addition and subtraction.**
[Patterns, Functions, and Algebra Goal 2]

Implementation Tips

By this time in the year, children have gained experience communicating their mathematical thinking and should be moving towards independence. Have children record their solutions and mathematical thinking on the Assessment Master. It is still important to share solutions as a whole class.

◆ Provide counters for children to model the problem.

◆ Remind children that they can illustrate an write an explanation of how they solved the problem.

Modifications for Meeting Diverse Needs

◆ Before beginning the problem, have children list all of the addition facts that total nine. Have children discuss how this can help them solve the problem.

◆ Have children write another similar problem.

Improving Open Response Skills

After children complete the task, have them discuss their solution strategies in small groups. Have children work together to list each step for solving the problem. For each step they list, have them discuss why they did that step. Have the groups share their findings with the class. Draw two columns on the board or overhead; label one column What and the other column Why. List each of their steps in the What column and the reason for each step in the Why column. Remind children that when they explain their answers, the explanation can include both of these parts.

Note: The wording and formatting of the text on the student samples that follow may vary slightly from the actual task your children will complete. These minor discrepancies will not affect the implementation of the task.

Rubric

This rubric is designed to help you assess levels of mathematical performance on this task. It emphasizes mathematical understanding with only a mention of clarity of explanation. Consider the expectations of standardized tests in your area when applying a rubric. Modify this sample rubric as appropriate.

4 Determines that Roel has 6 books and Carol has 3 books. Indicates that 9 is the total and that one person has 3 more books than the other one does. Explains a strategy that matches the work, but the explanation might omit some steps.

3 Determines that one person has 6 books and the other has 3 books. Indicates that 9 is the total or that one person has 3 more books than the other one does. Attempts to explain or show a strategy, but the explanation might be incomplete or might not match the work shown.

2 There is evidence of some understanding of the problem. Attempts to explain or illustrate a strategy. The explanation might be confusing or incorrect, but there is some information that is consistent with solving the problem.

1 Attempts to solve the problem. Might show some work, but there might be no evidence of a solution strategy or of understanding the problem.

0 Does not attempt to solve the problem.

Sample Student Responses

This Level 4 paper illustrates the following features: The illustration shows 9 tallies used to represent the total number of books. The tallies are crossed off as the books are distributed between Roel and Carol. The explanation describes giving the last block of 3 tallies to Roel since he had 3 more books than Carol.

This Level 4 paper illustrates the following features: The work is shown as a number model, and the answer is stated in words. The explanation describes choosing 6 and 3 because their sum is 9 and because 6 is 3 more than 3.

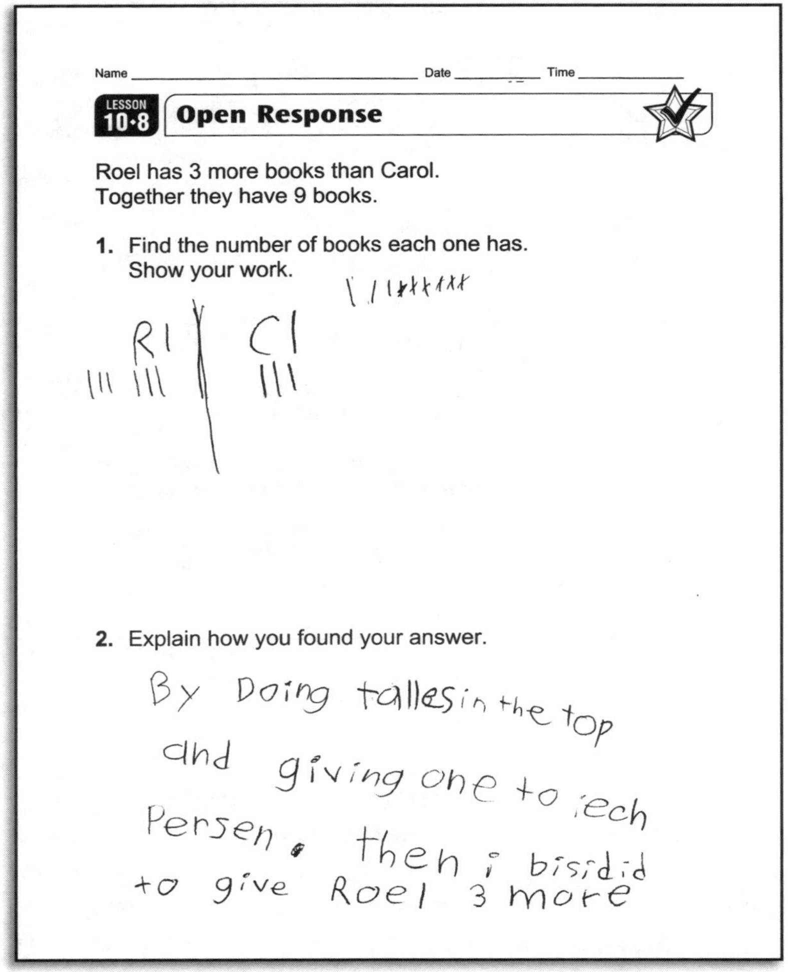

Name _____ Date _____ Time _____

LESSON 10·8 Open Response

Roel has 3 more books than Carol.
Together they have 9 books.

1. Find the number of books each one has.
Show your work.

6 + 3 = 9

Roel has 6 and
Carol has 3.

2. Explain how you found your answer.

6 + 3 = 9
Because

6 is 3 more then 3.

Name _____ Date _____ Time _____

LESSON 10·8 Open Response

Roel has 3 more books than Carol.
Together they have 9 books.

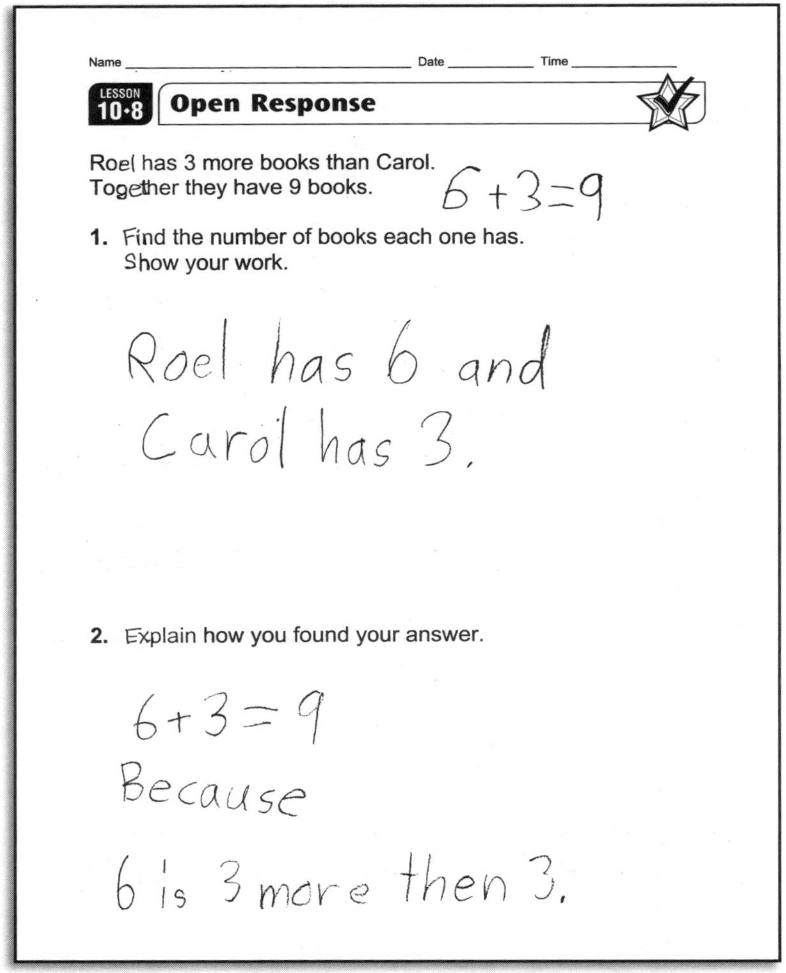

1. Find the number of books each one has.
Show your work.

R |||| C |||
R ||||

2. Explain how you found your answer.

By Doing tallies in the top
and giving one to each
persen then i bis did
to give Roel 3 more

This Level 3 paper illustrates the following features: The answer is displayed in a t-chart. Above Roel, there is a statement that he has 3 more. There is an indication that the focus is on figuring out that 6 is 3 more than 3. There is no work on the page that refers to 9 as the total.

LESSON 10·8 Open Response

Roel has 3 more books than Carol.
Together they have 9 books.

1. Find the number of books each one has. Show your work.

3 more
Roel | Carol
6 | 3
3+3=6

2. Explain how you found your answer.

threethree=six

3+3=6

This Level 3 paper illustrates the following features: There is a list of addition facts with addends that total 9. The addition fact that has a difference of 3 between the 2 addends is selected as the answer (6 and 3). The explanation says, "I cotinde [counted]," but there is no additional information.

LESSON 10·8 Open Response

Roel has 3 more books than Carol.
Together they have 9 books.

1. Find the number of books each one has. Show your work.

4+t Carol.4+5=9.
Roel.6+3=9.
Carol.7+2=9.
Roel.8+1=9.

Roel haves 6 3
Carol haves 3

2. Explain how you found your answer.

I cotinde.

---

132   Assessment Handbook

This Level 2 paper illustrates the following features: 9 rectangles are drawn and 3 of them are crossed off. There is an attempt at writing a number sentence for 9 − 3 = 6, but the notation has errors. There is no additional information offered in the explanation.

This Level 1 paper illustrates the following features: There is an attempt to organize the information, and there is an incorrect number model. There is no work on the page that demonstrates an understanding of the problem.

Name _____ Date _____ Time _____

LESSON 10·8 Open Response

Roel has 3 more books than Carol.
Together they have 9 books.

1. Find the number of books each one has.
   Show your work.

   Roel Carol

2. Explain how you found your answer.

Name _____ Date _____ Time _____

LESSON 10·8 Open Response

Roel has 3 more books than Carol.
Together they have 9 books.

1. Find the number of books each one has.
   Show your work.

   Ros Carol

2. Explain how you found your answer.

   I Fun My
   asn

End-of-Year Assessment Goals

The End-of-Year Assessment (pages 191–196) provides an additional opportunity that you may use as part of your balanced assessment plan. It covers many of the important concepts and skills presented in *First Grade Everyday Mathematics*. It should be used to complement the ongoing and periodic assessments that appear within lessons and at the end of units. The following tables provide goals for all the problems in Part A and Part B of the End-of-Year Assessment.

Part A Recognizing Student Achievement

Problems 1–14 provide summative information and may be used for grading purposes.

Problem(s)	Description	Grade-Level Goal
1	Use drawings to model halves, thirds, and fourths as equal parts of a region.	Number and Numeration Goal 4
2	Compare whole numbers.	Number and Numeration Goal 7
2	Read, write, and explain expressions using the symbols <, >, = with cues.	Patterns, Functions, and Algebra Goal 2
3	Identify plane and solid figures including circles, squares, spheres, pyramids, cones, and cubes.	Geometry Goal 1
4	Demonstrate proficiency with +/− 0, +/− 1, doubles, and sum-equals-ten addition facts.	Operations and Computation Goal 1
4	Use mental arithmetic to solve problems involving the addition and subtraction of 1-digit whole numbers with 1- or 2-digit whole numbers.	Operations and Computation Goal 2
4	Apply the Commutative Property of Addition and the Additive Identity to basic addition fact problems.	Patterns, Functions, and Algebra Goal 3
5	Collect and organize data to create a bar graph.	Data and Chance Goal 1
5	Use graphs to answer simple questions and draw conclusions; find the maximum and minimum of a data set.	Data and Chance Goal 2
6	Identify shapes having line symmetry.	Geometry Goal 2
7	Describe events using basic probability terms.	Data and Chance Goal 3
8	Read temperatures on Fahrenheit thermometers to the nearest 10°.	Measurement and Reference Frames Goal 3
9	Measure length using standard measuring tools.	Measurement and Reference Frames Goal 1
10	Use manipulatives, drawings, tally marks, and numerical expressions involving addition and subtraction of 1- or 2-digit numbers to give equivalent names for whole numbers to 100.	Number and Numeration Goal 6
11	Show time to the nearest quarter-hour on an analog clock.	Measurement and Reference Frames Goal 4

Problem(s)	Description *continued*	Grade-Level Goal
12	Calculate the values of combinations of coins.	Operations and Computation Goal 2
12	Know the values of pennies, nickels, dimes, and quarters; make exchanges between coins.	Measurement and Reference Frames Goal 2
13	Solve problems involving function machines and "What's My Rule?" tables.	Patterns, Functions, and Algebra Goal 1
14	Count collections of objects accurately and reliably.	Number and Numeration Goal 2
14	Write whole numbers up to 1,000; identify places in such numbers.	Number and Numeration Goal 3

Part B Informing Instruction

Problems 15–20 provide formative information.

Problem(s)	Description	Grade-Level Goal
15	Calculate and compare the values of combinations of coins.	Operations and Computation Goal 2
15	Know the values of pennies, nickels, dimes, quarters, and dollar bills.	Measurement and Reference Frames Goal 2
15	Solve problems involving the addition or subtraction of whole numbers.	Operations and Computation Goal 2
16	Use drawings to model halves as equal parts of a collection.	Number and Numeration Goal 4
17	Use number grids to solve problems involving the addition and subtraction of whole numbers.	Operations and Computation Goal 2
18	Use manipulatives, number grids, tally marks, and mental arithmetic to solve problems involving the addition and subtraction of 1-digit whole numbers with 1- or 2-digit whole numbers.	Operations and Computation Goal 2
18	Extend numeric patterns.	Patterns, Functions, and Algebra Goal 1
19	Use manipulatives, number grids, tally marks, and mental arithmetic to solve problems involving the addition and subtraction of 2-digit whole numbers with 2-digit whole numbers.	Operations and Computation Goal 2
19	Identify parts-and-total situations.	Operations and Computation Goal 4
19	Write and explain number sentences using the symbols +, −, and =.	Patterns, functions, and Algebra Goal 2
20	Tell time to the nearest 5 minutes on an analog clock.	Measurement and Reference Frames Goal 4

Assessment Masters

Contents

LESSON 1·14   **Self Assessment**   Progress Check 1

Put a check in the box that tells how you do each skill.

Skills	I can do this by myself. I can explain how to do this.	I can do this by myself.	I can do this with help.
1. Count by 1s.			
2. Count by 2s.			
3. Count by 5s.			
4. Make tally marks.			
5. Find numbers before and after.			
6. Count on a number line.			

LESSON 1·14 | **Written Assessment**

Part A

1. Count by 1s.

8, 9, 10, _____, _____, _____, _____, _____

2. Write the numbers that come before and after.

_____ 4 _____   _____ 9 _____

3. Make tally marks for each number below.

7 = _____   12 = _____

4. Write the numbers from 1 through 6.
Circle the number that you write best.

_____

- -

_____

Part B

5. Count by 2s.

2, 4, _____, _____, _____, _____, _____

Count by 5s.

5, 10, _____, 20, _____, _____, _____, _____

6. Circle the winner of this round of *Top-It*.

| 12 | 13 |

LESSON 1·14 Open Response

Counting Buttons

You have a bag of buttons, and you want to count them. Write how many buttons you have in your bag and how you counted them.

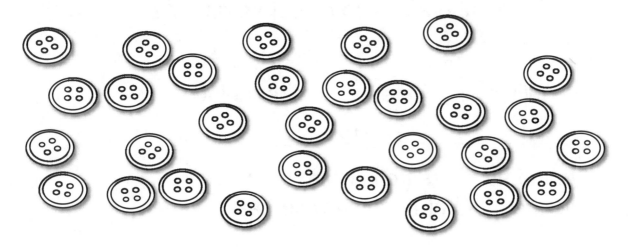

Your friend Maria said that you could count the buttons faster if they were in groups. Draw or write how you could group the buttons to count them faster.

LESSON 2·14 Self Assessment

Progress Check 2

Put a check in the box that tells how you do each skill.

Skills	I can do this by myself. I can explain how to do this.	I can do this by myself.	I can do this with help.
1. Write 7, 8, 9, and 0.			
2. Solve number stories.			
3. Count pennies.			
4. Count nickels.			
5. Tell time to the hour.			
6. Read a tally chart.			

LESSON 2·14 **Written Assessment**

Part A

1. How many children lost 1 tooth?

_____ children

Teeth Lost	Tallies
0	卌
1	卌 //
2	///

2. How much money does Sarah have?

_____ ¢

How much money does Bill have?

_____ ¢

Circle the amount that is more.

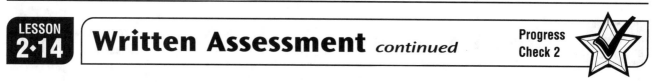

3. Draw the hour hand and the minute hand.

4 o'clock

Part B

4. Add or subtract.

$8 + 1 = $ _____

$5 - 1 = $ _____

$4 + 0 = $ _____

$10 - 1 = $ _____

5.

1 2 3 4 5 6 7 8 9 10 11 12 13

Circle counts by 2s.

Cross out counts by 5s.

Open Response

Counting Coins

Bill and Janet have a jar of nickels and pennies.

1. Bill takes 5 coins out of the jar. He has both nickels and pennies. Draw 5 coins that Bill could take out and tell the total value of the coins.

Coins	Value

2. Janet takes 5 coins out of the jar. She has both nickels and pennies. She has more money than Bill has. Draw 5 coins that Janet could take out and tell the total value of the coins.

Coins	Value

3. Draw 5 coins from the jar that would have the **greatest** total value. Explain how you found your answer.

Coins	Value

LESSON 3·15 | **Self Assessment**

Put a check in the box that tells how you do each skill.

Skills	I can do this by myself. I can explain how to do this.	I can do this by myself.	I can do this with help.
1. Do Frames-and-Arrows problems.			
2. Find sums of 10.			
3. Continue patterns.			
4. Count money.			
5. Tell time to the half-hour.			
6. Skip count.			

LESSON 3·15 | Written Assessment

Progress
Check 3

Part A

1. Make sums of 10 pennies.

Left Hand	Right Hand
	8
1	
4	

Fill in the frames.

2.

Rule
−1

26 | 25 | ☐ | ☐ | ☐ | ☐

3.

Rule
5 more

10 | 15 | ☐ | ☐ | ☐ | ☐

How much money?

4. Ⓝ Ⓝ Ⓝ Ⓟ Ⓟ

_____ ¢

5. Ⓓ Ⓓ Ⓝ Ⓟ Ⓟ Ⓟ

_____ ¢

LESSON 3·15 | **Written Assessment** *continued*

6. Draw the next four shapes.

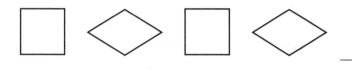

___ ___ ___ ___

Part B

7. Fill in the rule and the frames.

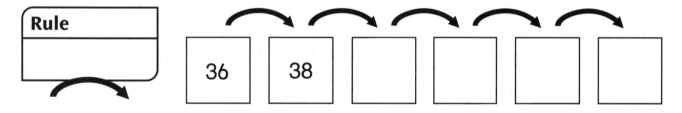

| Rule | | 36 | 38 | | | | |

8. What time is it?

half-past ___ o'clock

9. Draw the hands.

half-past 8 o'clock

Open Response

The Bike Shop

Olivia walked past the Bike Shop on Monday.
She saw some tricycles in the window.
She counted 18 wheels.

1. How many tricycles did Olivia see in the window?

   _____ tricycles

   Draw or write to explain how you know.

2. On Tuesday, she counted 21 wheels.
   On Wednesday, she counted 24 wheels.
   On Thursday, she counted 27 wheels.
   How many wheels do you think she counted on Friday?

   _____ wheels

   Draw or write to explain how you know.

LESSON 4·13 | **Self Assessment**

Put a check in the box that tells how you do each skill.

Skills	 I can do this by myself. I can explain how to do this.	I can do this by myself.	I can do this with help.
1. Solve addition facts.			
2. Use the number grid.			
3. Solve change-to-more and change-to-less problems.			
4. Make amounts of money with the fewest coins.			
5. Tell time to the quarter-hour.			
6. Tell which is longer and which is shorter.			

Written Assessment

Progress
Check 4

Part A

1. Fill in the missing numbers.

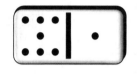

Total
8

Part	Part

2. Fill in the missing numbers in the number grid.

61					67			
		74						80

3. Draw the missing shape.

□ △ △ ○ □ △ ___ ○

4. How much money has Wes saved?

Ⓝ Ⓝ Ⓟ Ⓟ Ⓟ Ⓟ Ⓟ Ⓟ _____ ¢

Show the same amount using fewer coins.
Use Ⓟ, Ⓝ, and Ⓓ.

LESSON 4·13 | **Written Assessment** *continued*

5. Fill in the missing numbers.

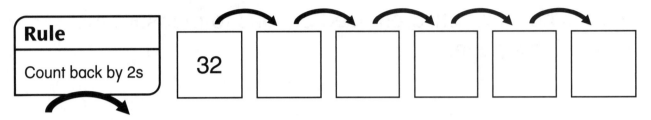

| **Rule** |
| Count back by 2s |

32

6. Write an addition fact to go with the dice.

_____ + _____ = _____

Part B

7. Circle the shorter line segment.

_____

_____

8. What time is it?

quarter-to ___ o'clock

9. Draw the hour hand and the minute hand.

quarter-after 1 o'clock

10. Add.

$7 + 0 =$ _____ $5 + 1 =$ _____ $6 + 4 =$ _____

Open Response

Progress
Check 4

Measuring the Page

Here is how four children used buttons to measure the width of this page.

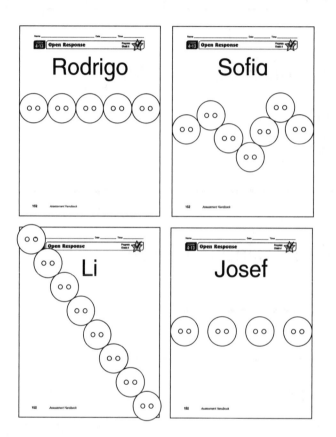

Who do you think made the best measurement? _____
Explain your answer.

Use the same strategy to measure the width of this page with pennies. The width in pennies is about:

LESSON 5·14 | Self Assessment

Put a check in the box that tells how you do each skill.

Skills	I can do this by myself. I can explain how to do this.	I can do this by myself.	I can do this with help.
1. Use a thermometer.			
2. Use base-10 blocks to make numbers.			
3. Answer questions using a tally chart.			
4. Count coins.			
5. Solve "What's My Rule?" problems.			
6. Solve easy facts.			

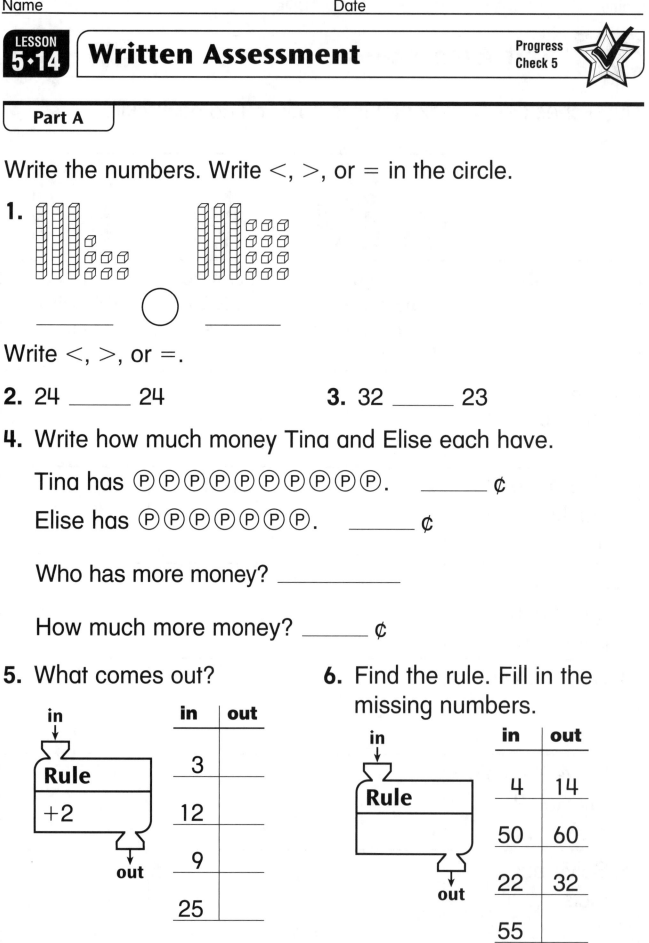

LESSON 5·14 Written Assessment

Progress Check 5

Part A

Write the numbers. Write <, >, or = in the circle.

1.

_____ ◯ _____

Write <, >, or =.

2. 24 _____ 24

3. 32 _____ 23

4. Write how much money Tina and Elise each have.

Tina has ⓅⓅⓅⓅⓅⓅⓅⓅⓅⓅ.   _____ ¢

Elise has ⓅⓅⓅⓅⓅⓅⓅ.   _____ ¢

Who has more money? _____

How much more money? _____ ¢

5. What comes out?

in ↓

Rule
+2

out ↓

in	out
3	
12	
9	
25	

6. Find the rule. Fill in the missing numbers.

in ↓

Rule

out ↓

in	out
4	14
50	60
22	32
55	
	100

LESSON 5·14 | **Written Assessment** *continued*

Write addition facts.

7.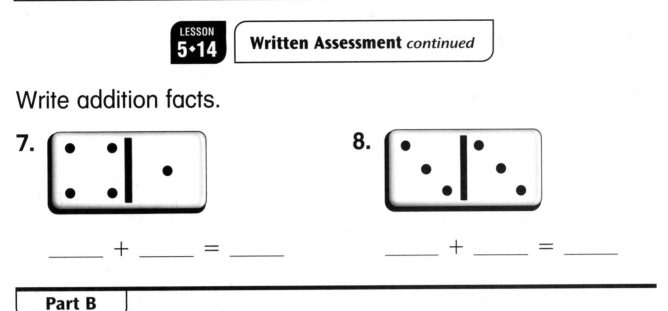

____ + ____ = ____

8.

____ + ____ = ____

Part B

9. Show each temperature. Color the warmer temperature yellow. Color the cooler temperature blue.

°F
70—
60—
50—
40—
30—

40°F

°F
70—
60—
50—
40—
30—

65°F

10. Draw the hands.

quarter-before 6 o'clock

Use the tally chart to answer the questions.

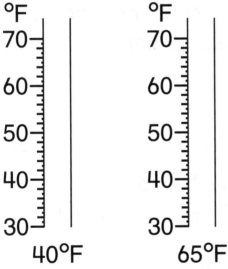

Animals' Legs	
Animals with No Legs	ЖНТ ЖНТ ЖНТ ЖНТ //
Animals with 2 Legs	ЖНТ ЖНТ ЖНТ ///
Animals with 4 Legs	ЖНТ ЖНТ ЖНТ

11. How many animals have no legs?

_____ animals

12. Do more animals have 2 legs or 4 legs?

_____ legs

Making Numbers

You found these number cards on the floor.

Circle three of the cards.

| 6 | 2 | 8 |

| 1 | 4 | 9 |

| 7 | 3 | 5 |

Use two of your circled cards. Write the largest possible 2-digit number.	Use two of your circled cards. Write the smallest possible 2-digit number.
_____	_____

Add your numbers together using base-10 blocks. Use base-10 block symbols (■, |, and •) to record your work.

Write a number model for the problem you solved.

LESSON 6·13 | **Self Assessment**

Put a check in the box that tells how you do each skill.

Skills	I can do this by myself. I can explain how to do this.	I can do this by myself.	I can do this with help.
1. Fill name-collection boxes.			
2. Use $<$, $>$, $=$.			
3. Name the ones place and tens place in numbers.			
4. Estimate the length of objects.			
5. Write turn-around facts.			
6. Solve change-to-more and change-to-less number stories.			

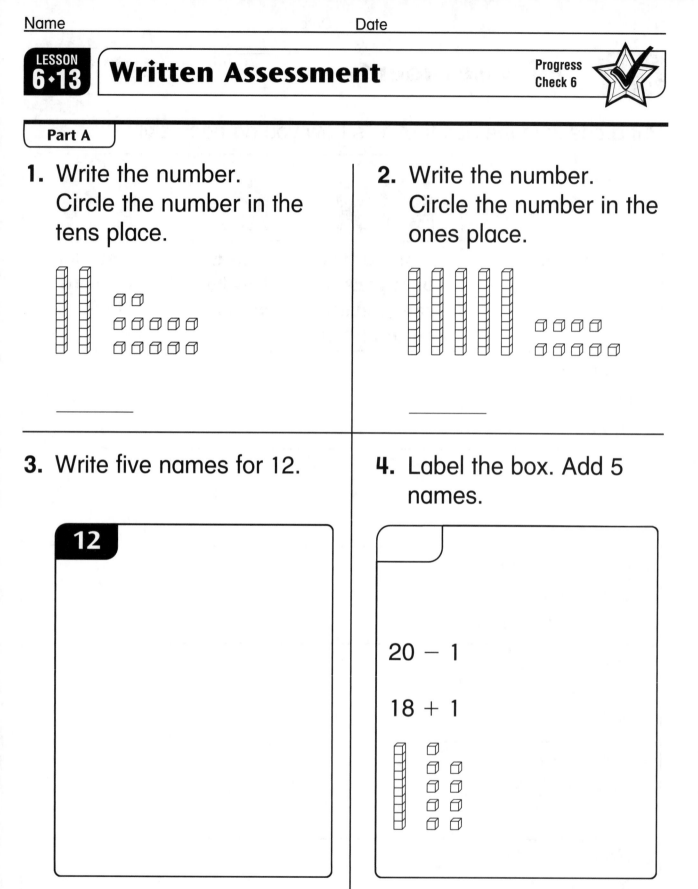

LESSON 6·13 | **Written Assessment** | Progress Check 6

Part A

1. Write the number.
   Circle the number in the tens place.

   _____

2. Write the number.
   Circle the number in the ones place.

   _____

3. Write five names for 12.

   12

4. Label the box. Add 5 names.

   20 − 1

   18 + 1

LESSON 6·13 | **Written Assessment** *continued*

5. Write <, >, =.

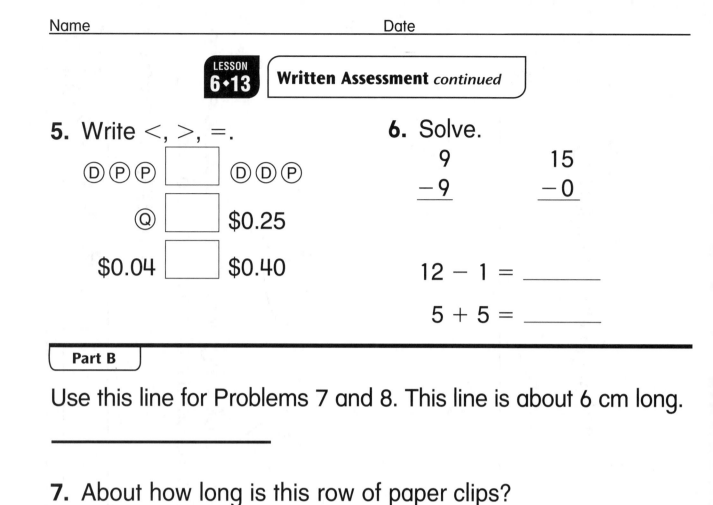

Ⓓ Ⓟ Ⓟ ☐ Ⓓ Ⓓ Ⓟ

Ⓠ ☐ $0.25

$0.04 ☐ $0.40

6. Solve.

$$\begin{array}{r} 9 \\ -9 \\ \hline \end{array} \qquad \begin{array}{r} 15 \\ -0 \\ \hline \end{array}$$

$12 - 1 =$ _____

$5 + 5 =$ _____

Part B

Use this line for Problems 7 and 8. This line is about 6 cm long.

7. About how long is this row of paper clips?

_____ cm

8. About how long is this row of coins?

_____ cm

9. Write the sums. Draw lines to match turn-around facts.

$16 + 1 =$ _____ $20 + 0 =$ _____

$4 + 6 =$ _____ $1 + 16 =$ _____

$0 + 20 =$ _____ $6 + 4 =$ _____

LESSON 6·13 | Open Response

Necklace Patterns

You are making a necklace with a bead pattern that repeats three times.
Use the beads pictured below. Draw your necklace on the string.

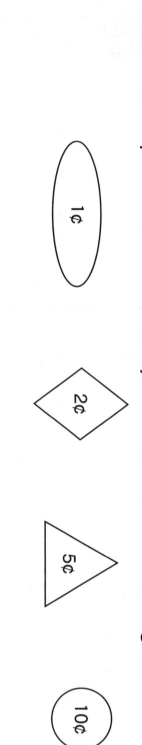

1¢   2¢   5¢   10¢

Use ⓟ ⓝ ⓓ and ⓠ to show how you can pay for all of the beads using the fewest number of coins.

LESSON 7·8 Self Assessment

Put a check in the box that tells how you do each skill.

	I can do this by myself. I can explain how to do this.	I can do this by myself.	I can do this with help.
1. Name shapes.			
2. Answer questions about data.			
3. Find the rule in function machines.			
4. Write fact families.			
5. Show amounts of money with coins.			
6. Draw hands on an analog clock.			

LESSON 7·8 | **Written Assessment** | Progress Check 7

Part A

1. Use ☐ | •

Show 124. | Show 49.

2. Write the fact family.

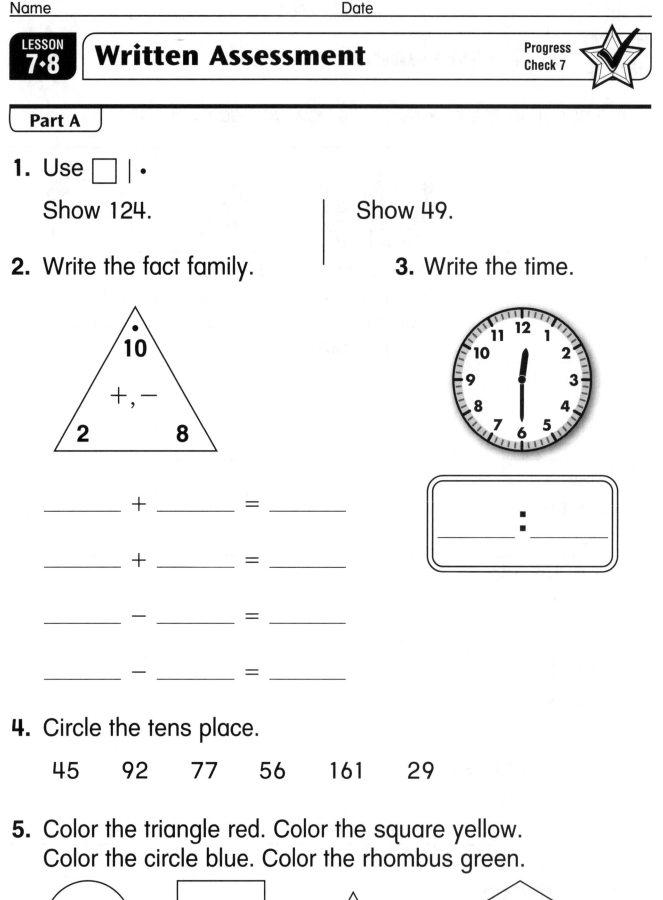

3. Write the time.

_____ + _____ = _____

_____ + _____ = _____

_____ − _____ = _____

_____ − _____ = _____

4. Circle the tens place.

45   92   77   56   161   29

5. Color the triangle red. Color the square yellow.
Color the circle blue. Color the rhombus green.

LESSON 7·8 | **Written Assessment** *continued*

6. How many letters do the greatest number of children have in their names? _____

How many letters do the fewest number of children have in their names? _____

Letters in Names

Number of Children

```
            X
            X   X
        X   X   X
        X   X   X
    X   X   X   X
    X   X   X   X
   ─────────────────
    2   3   4   5
```

Number of Letters

Part B

7. Complete the table. Fill in the missing rule.

in	out
4	8
7	11
13	17
20	24

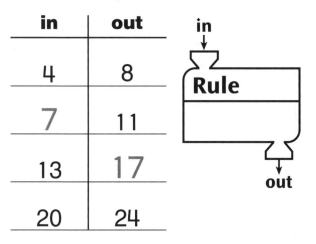

8. Draw the hands.

11:15

9. Show 68¢ in two ways. Use Ⓠ, Ⓓ, Ⓝ, and Ⓟ.

LESSON 7·8

Open Response

Shapes That Belong in a Group

Think: Which shapes from your Pattern-Block Template belong together in a group?

Use your template to draw 3 shapes that go together in the box "Shapes That Belong in the Group." In the other box, draw 3 shapes that do not belong in the group.

Shapes That Belong in the Group	Shapes That Do Not Belong in the Group

Explain or show how you know if a shape belongs in the group.

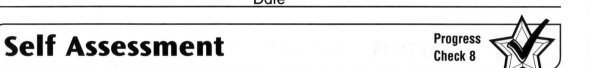

Self Assessment

Put a check in the box that tells how you do each skill.

Skills	I can do this by myself. I can explain how to do this.	I can do this by myself.	I can do this with help.
1. Complete symmetrical shapes.			
2. Find fractions.			
3. Fill name-collection boxes.			
4. Know math facts.			
5. Identify 3-dimensional shapes.			
6. Solve number stories.			

LESSON 8·10 — Written Assessment

Progress Check 8

Part A

1. Divide each shape in half. Shade one half of each shape.

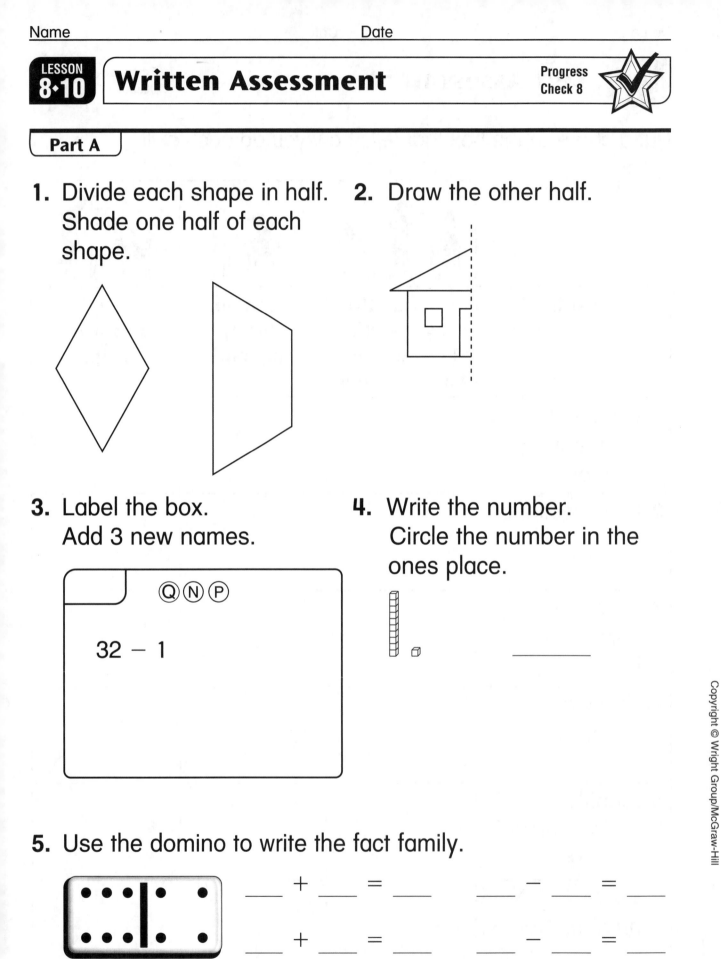

2. Draw the other half.

3. Label the box. Add 3 new names.

Q N P

32 – 1

4. Write the number. Circle the number in the ones place.

_____

5. Use the domino to write the fact family.

___ + ___ = ___   ___ – ___ = ___

___ + ___ = ___   ___ – ___ = ___

Written Assessment *continued*

6. Kimi bought 5 lollipops. Each lollipop costs 5¢.
How much did Kimi pay?

_____ ¢ or $_____._____

| **Part B** |

7. Label each equal part.

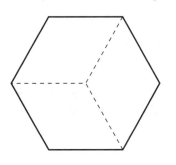

8. Draw a line to match each
face to the correct picture
of the 3-dimensional shape.

9. Fill in the fact triangle.
Write the fact family.

Column A   Column B

_____ + _____ = _____

_____ + _____ = _____

_____ − _____ = _____

_____ − _____ = _____

LESSON 8·10 Open Response

School Box

1. Draw different color crayons in the school box on this page. Use the clues to help you draw the crayons:

   $\frac{1}{2}$ of the crayons in the school box are blue.

   $\frac{1}{4}$ of the crayons in the school box are red.

   $\frac{1}{4}$ of the crayons in the school box are yellow.

SCHOOL BOX

2. How many blue crayons did you draw? _____ crayons

   How many red crayons did you draw? _____ crayons

   How many yellow crayons did you draw? _____ crayons

3. Explain how you know that half of the crayons you drew are blue. You may use words, numbers, and pictures to help you explain.

LESSON 9·9 | **Self Assessment** | Progress Check 9

Put a check in the box that tells how you do each skill.

Skills	I can do this by myself. I can explain how to do this.	I can do this by myself.	I can do this with help.
1. Draw hands on a clock face.			
2. Find fractions.			
3. Fill in rules and missing numbers on function machines.			
4. Know math facts.			
5. Count combinations of coins.			
6. Use base-10 blocks to count numbers.			

Written Assessment Progress Check 9

Part A

1. Write <, >, or =.

$1 + 9$ _____ $8 + 2$

$4 - 1$ _____ $6 - 3$

$7 - 0$ _____ $2 + 1$

2. 4 people share 12 cookies.

How many cookies does each person get?

_____ cookies

How many cookies do 3 people get altogether?

_____ cookies

3. Mia buys 2 flowers and 1 vase.

25¢   100¢

How much money does Mia spend?

_____ ¢ or $ _____

Show this amount with Ⓠ, Ⓓ, Ⓝ, and Ⓟ.

4. Draw the hands.

10:45

LESSON 9·9 | **Written Assessment** *continued*

5. Find the rule and the missing numbers.

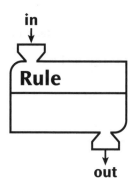

in
↓

| Rule |

↓
out

in	out
7	7
10	10
	12
	0

6. Write the numbers.

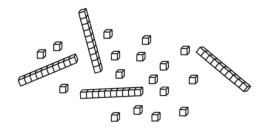

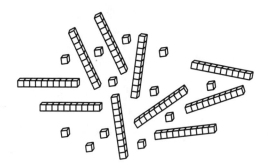

_____ _____

Part B

7. Solve.

11 − 1 = _____   4 + 6 = _____

21 − 1 = _____   40 + 60 = _____

111 − 1 = _____   400 + 600 = _____

8. Rene has Ⓓ Ⓓ Ⓓ Ⓓ Ⓓ Ⓓ Ⓓ Ⓓ Ⓓ Ⓓ.
How much money does she have? _____¢
Rene spent half of her money at the toy store.
How much money does she have now? _____¢
Show this amount with Ⓓs.

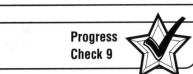

LESSON 9·9 | **Open Response** | Progress Check 9

Number-Grid Patterns

1. Deena filled in the number-grid puzzle. Finish the puzzle and find her mistake. Cross out her mistake and write the correct number.

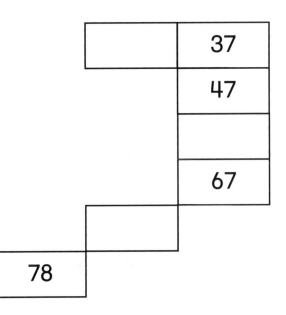

2. Explain how you used patterns in the number grid to correct Deena's mistake.

LESSON 10·8 Self Assessment

Put a check in the box that tells how you do each skill.

Skill	I can do this by myself. I can explain how to do this.	I can do this by myself.	I can do this with help.
1. Solve number-grid puzzles.			
2. Use +, −, and = to write number models.			
3. Solve easy addition and subtraction facts.			
4. Make change.			
5. Compare numbers larger than 100.			
6. Solve 2-digit by 1-digit number stories.			

Written Assessment

Progress
Check 10

Part A

1. Complete the number-grid puzzles.

186	187	
		198
	207	

		103
	112	
121		

2. I buy an apple for 15¢.
I pay 25¢.
How much change do I get?

_____ ¢

I buy gum for $0.72.
I pay $1.00.
How much change do I get?

$_____ . _____

3. Write $<$, $>$, or $=$.

154 ☐ 372

94 ☐ 149

406 ☐ 406

727 ☐ 272

233 ☐ 322

510 ☐ 501

4. Fill in the missing number.

6 + _____ = 10

_____ + 1 = 7

4 + 4 = _____

_____ − 6 = 6

3 − 0 = _____

10 − _____ = 9

LESSON 10·8 | Written Assessment *continued*

5. Write the number. _____

Write the number that is 10 less. _____

Write the number model to
show 10 less base-10 blocks. _____

6. Write the number. _____

Write the number that is 10 more. _____

Write the number model to
show 10 more base-10 blocks. _____

7. Circle the hundreds place

222	371	101
599	428	630

Circle the tens place.

390	45	200
810	167	333

Part B

8.

Dinner Times

Children
5
4
3
2
1
0
4:00 5:00 6:00 7:00
P.M.

Earliest Dinner Time: _____

Latest Dinner Time: _____

Range: _____ hours

9. Use the graph to answer the question.

What is the typical dinner time? _____

LESSON 10·8 | **Open Response**

Counting Books

Roel has 3 more books than Carol.
Together they have 9 books.

1. Find the number of books each one has.
Show your work.

2. Explain how you found your answer.

LESSON 1·14 | **Written Assessment**

Progress
Check 1

Part A

1. Count by 1s.

8, 9, 10, _11_ , _12_ , _13_ , _14_ , _15_

2. Write the numbers that come before and after.

_3_ 4 _5_   _8_ 9 _10_

3. Make tally marks for each number below.

7 = _⊬⊦⊦ //_   12 = _⊬⊦⊦ ⊬⊦⊦ //_

4. Write the numbers from 1 through 6.
Circle the number that you write best.

_____

_____

Part B

5. Count by 2s.

2, 4, _6_ , _8_ , _10_ , _12_ , _14_

Count by 5s.

5, 10, _15_ , 20, _25_ , _30_ , _35_ , _40_

6. Circle the winner of this round of *Top-It*.

| 12 | (13) |

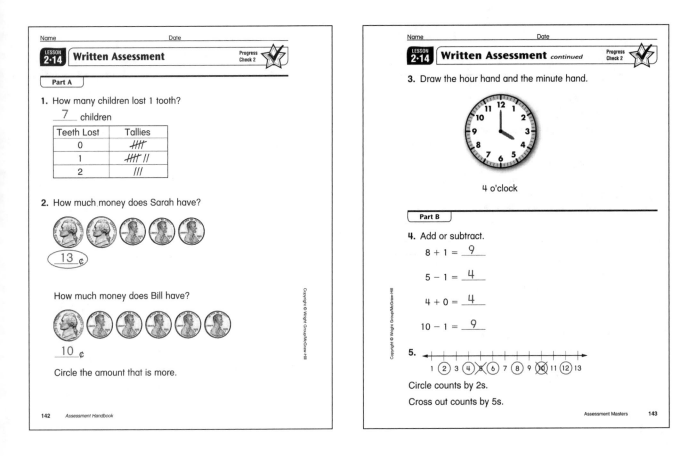

LESSON 2·14 **Written Assessment** Progress Check 2

Part A

1. How many children lost 1 tooth?

___7___ children

Teeth Lost	Tallies
0	∕∕∕∕
1	∕∕∕∕ ∕∕
2	∕∕∕

2. How much money does Sarah have?

(13) ¢

How much money does Bill have?

___10___ ¢

Circle the amount that is more.

LESSON 2·14 **Written Assessment** *continued* Progress Check 2

3. Draw the hour hand and the minute hand.

4 o'clock

Part B

4. Add or subtract.

$8 + 1 =$ ___9___

$5 - 1 =$ ___4___

$4 + 0 =$ ___4___

$10 - 1 =$ ___9___

5.

1 (2) 3 (4) ⊠ (6) 7 (8) 9 ⊠ 11 (12) 13

Circle counts by 2s.

Cross out counts by 5s.

LESSON
3·15 **Written Assessment**

Progress
Check 3 ✓

Part A

1. Make sums of 10 pennies.

Left Hand	Right Hand
2	8
1	9
4	6
Answers vary.	
Answers vary.	
Answers vary.	

Fill in the frames.

2. **Rule**
−1

| 26 | 25 | 24 | 23 | 22 | 21 |

3. **Rule**
5 more

| 10 | 15 | 20 | 25 | 30 | 35 |

How much money?

4. Ⓝ Ⓝ Ⓝ Ⓟ Ⓟ
___17___ ¢

5. Ⓓ Ⓓ Ⓝ Ⓟ Ⓟ Ⓟ
___28___ ¢

LESSON
3·15 **Written Assessment** *continued*

6. Draw the next four shapes.

□ ◇ □ ◇ □ ◇ □ ◇

Part B

7. Fill in the rule and the frames.

Rule
2 more

| 36 | 38 | 40 | 42 | 44 | 46 |

8. What time is it?

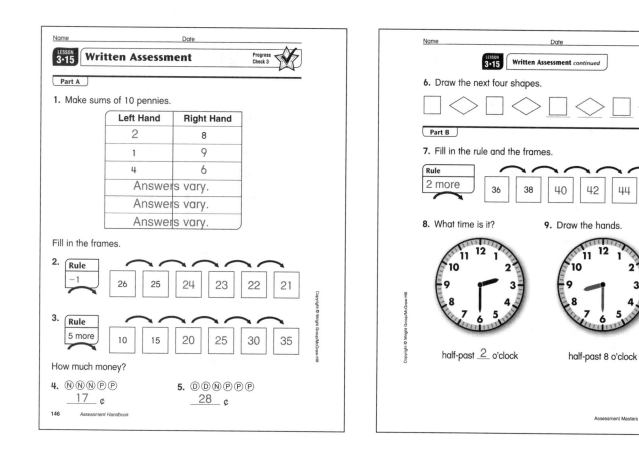

half-past _2_ o'clock

9. Draw the hands.

half-past 8 o'clock

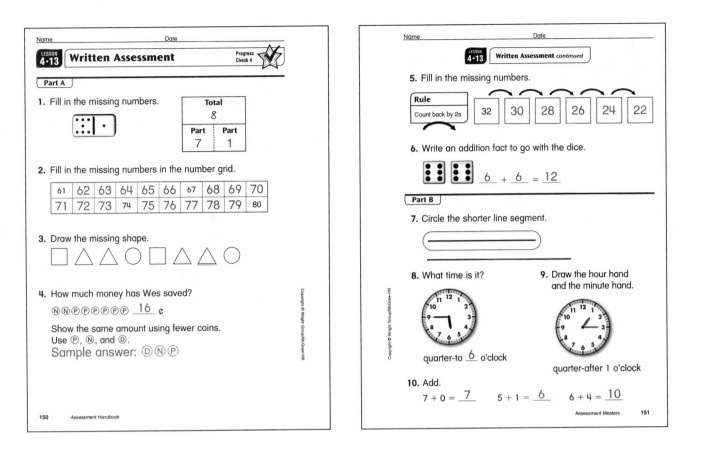

LESSON 4·13 | **Written Assessment** | Progress Check 4

Part A

1. Fill in the missing numbers.

Total	
8	
Part	**Part**
7	1

2. Fill in the missing numbers in the number grid.

61	62	63	64	65	66	67	68	69	70
71	72	73	74	75	76	77	78	79	80

3. Draw the missing shape.

□ △ △ ○ □ △ △ ○

4. How much money has Wes saved?

Ⓝ Ⓝ Ⓟ Ⓟ Ⓟ Ⓟ Ⓟ Ⓟ __16__ ¢

Show the same amount using fewer coins.
Use Ⓟ, Ⓝ, and Ⓓ.
Sample answer: Ⓓ Ⓝ Ⓟ

LESSON 4·13 | **Written Assessment** *continued*

5. Fill in the missing numbers.

Rule
Count back by 2s

32 30 28 26 24 22

6. Write an addition fact to go with the dice.

__6__ + __6__ = __12__

Part B

7. Circle the shorter line segment.

8. What time is it?

quarter-to __6__ o'clock

9. Draw the hour hand and the minute hand.

quarter-after 1 o'clock

10. Add.

$7 + 0 =$ __7__ $5 + 1 =$ __6__ $6 + 4 =$ __10__

LESSON 5·14 | **Written Assessment**

Progress Check 5

Part A

Write the numbers. Write <, >, or = in the circle.

1.

_37_ ⊘< _42_

Write <, >, or =.

2. 24 _=_ 24 **3.** 32 _>_ 23

4. Write how much money Tina and Elise each have.

Tina has ℗℗℗℗℗℗℗℗℗℗. _10_ ¢

Elise has ℗℗℗℗℗℗℗. _7_ ¢

Who has more money? _Tina_

How much more money? _3_ ¢

5. What comes out?

in
Rule
+2
out

in	out
3	5
12	14
9	11
25	27

6. Find the rule. Fill in the missing numbers.

in
Rule
+10
out

in	out
4	14
50	60
22	32
55	65
90	100

LESSON 5·14 | **Written Assessment** *continued*

Write addition facts.

7.

_4_ + _1_ = _5_

8.

_3_ + _3_ = _6_

Part B

9. Show each temperature. Color the warmer temperature yellow. Color the cooler temperature blue.

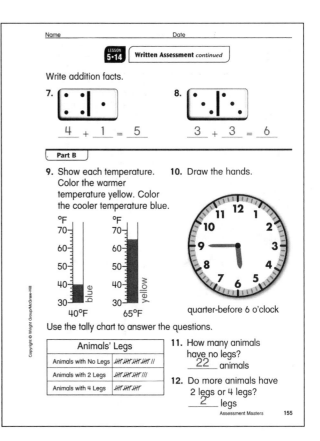

40°F (blue)   65°F (yellow)

10. Draw the hands.

quarter-before 6 o'clock

Use the tally chart to answer the questions.

Animals' Legs	
Animals with No Legs	JHT JHT JHT JHT //
Animals with 2 Legs	JHT JHT JHT ///
Animals with 4 Legs	JHT JHT JHT

11. How many animals have no legs?
_22_ animals

12. Do more animals have 2 legs or 4 legs?
_2_ legs

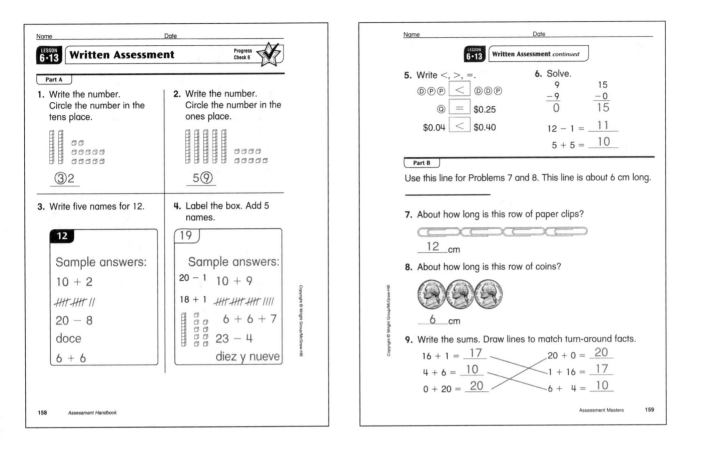

LESSON 6·13 **Written Assessment** Progress Check 6

Part A

1. Write the number.
Circle the number in the tens place.

③2

2. Write the number.
Circle the number in the ones place.

5⑨

3. Write five names for 12.

12

Sample answers:

10 + 2

~~HHT HHT~~ //

20 − 8

doce

6 + 6

4. Label the box. Add 5 names.

19

Sample answers:

20 − 1   10 + 9

18 + 1   ~~HHT HHT HHT~~ ////

6 + 6 + 7

23 − 4

diez y nueve

LESSON 6·13 **Written Assessment** continued

5. Write <, >, =.

D P P < D D P

Q = $0.25

$0.04 < $0.40

6. Solve.

$$\begin{array}{r} 9 \\ -9 \\ \hline 0 \end{array} \qquad \begin{array}{r} 15 \\ -0 \\ \hline 15 \end{array}$$

12 − 1 = 11

5 + 5 = 10

Part B

Use this line for Problems 7 and 8. This line is about 6 cm long.

7. About how long is this row of paper clips?

12 cm

8. About how long is this row of coins?

6 cm

9. Write the sums. Draw lines to match turn-around facts.

16 + 1 = 17   20 + 0 = 20

4 + 6 = 10   1 + 16 = 17

0 + 20 = 20   6 + 4 = 10

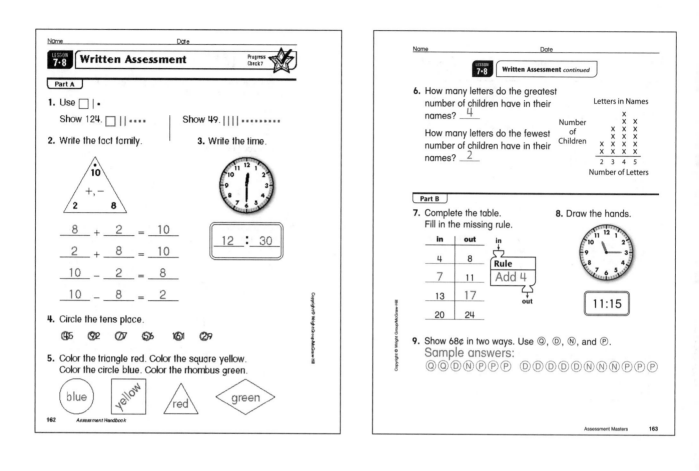

LESSON 7·8 **Written Assessment**

Progress Check 7

Part A

1. Use ☐ | •

Show 124. ☐ || •••• | Show 49. |||| •••••••••

2. Write the fact family. | **3.** Write the time.

$$8 + 2 = 10$$
$$2 + 8 = 10$$
$$10 - 2 = 8$$
$$10 - 8 = 2$$

12 : 30

4. Circle the tens place.

45   92   07   53   161   29

5. Color the triangle red. Color the square yellow.
Color the circle blue. Color the rhombus green.

blue   yellow   red   green

LESSON 7·8 **Written Assessment** *continued*

6. How many letters do the greatest number of children have in their names? __4__

How many letters do the fewest number of children have in their names? __2__

Letters in Names

	x		
	x	x	
x	x	x	
x	x	x	
x	x	x	x
x	x	x	x

Number of Children

2   3   4   5
Number of Letters

Part B

7. Complete the table.
Fill in the missing rule.

in	out
4	8
7	11
13	17
20	24

Rule
Add 4

8. Draw the hands.

11:15

9. Show 68¢ in two ways. Use Q, D, N, and P.
Sample answers:
Q Q D N P P P   D D D D D N N N P P P

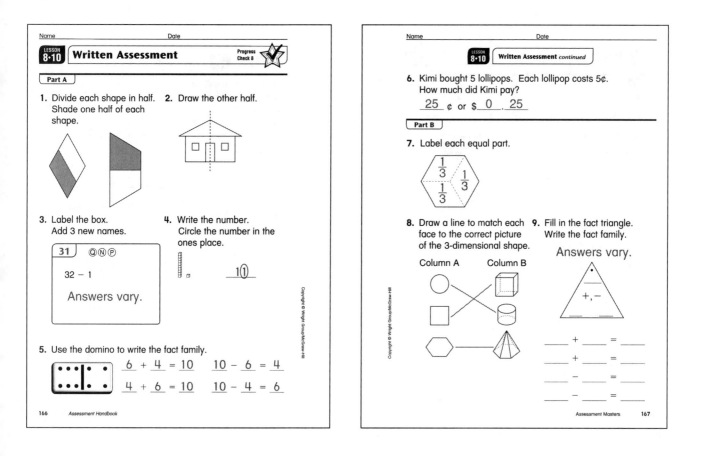

LESSON 8·10 | **Written Assessment** | Progress Check 8

Part A

1. Divide each shape in half. Shade one half of each shape.

2. Draw the other half.

3. Label the box. Add 3 new names.

31 Q N P

32 − 1

Answers vary.

4. Write the number. Circle the number in the ones place.

1(0)

5. Use the domino to write the fact family.

$6 + 4 = 10$ $10 − 6 = 4$

$4 + 6 = 10$ $10 − 4 = 6$

LESSON 8·10 | **Written Assessment** *continued*

6. Kimi bought 5 lollipops. Each lollipop costs 5¢. How much did Kimi pay?

__25__ ¢ or $__0__ . __25__

Part B

7. Label each equal part.

$\frac{1}{3}$ $\frac{1}{3}$ $\frac{1}{3}$

8. Draw a line to match each face to the correct picture of the 3-dimensional shape.

Column A   Column B

9. Fill in the fact triangle. Write the fact family.

Answers vary.

+,−

___ + ___ = ___

___ + ___ = ___

___ − ___ = ___

___ − ___ = ___

LESSON 9·9 | **Written Assessment** | Progress Check 9

Part A

1. Write $<$, $>$, or $=$.

$1 + 9 \underline{\ =\ } 8 + 2$

$4 - 1 \underline{\ =\ } 6 - 3$

$7 - 0 \underline{\ >\ } 2 + 1$

2. 4 people share 12 cookies.

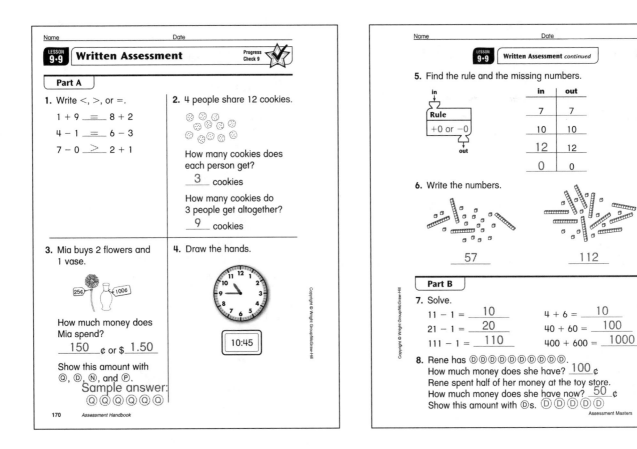

How many cookies does each person get?

__3__ cookies

How many cookies do 3 people get altogether?

__9__ cookies

3. Mia buys 2 flowers and 1 vase.

How much money does Mia spend?

__150__ ¢ or $ __1.50__

Show this amount with Ⓠ, Ⓓ, Ⓝ, and Ⓟ.

Sample answer:
Ⓠ Ⓠ Ⓠ Ⓠ Ⓠ Ⓠ

4. Draw the hands.

10:45

LESSON 9·9 | **Written Assessment** *continued*

5. Find the rule and the missing numbers.

in → **Rule** +0 or −0 → out

in	out
7	7
10	10
12	12
0	0

6. Write the numbers.

__57__   __112__

Part B

7. Solve.

$11 - 1 = \underline{\ 10\ }$ $4 + 6 = \underline{\ 10\ }$

$21 - 1 = \underline{\ 20\ }$ $40 + 60 = \underline{\ 100\ }$

$111 - 1 = \underline{\ 110\ }$ $400 + 600 = \underline{\ 1000\ }$

8. Rene has Ⓓ Ⓓ Ⓓ Ⓓ Ⓓ Ⓓ Ⓓ Ⓓ Ⓓ Ⓓ.
How much money does she have? __100__ ¢
Rene spent half of her money at the toy store.
How much money does she have now? __50__ ¢
Show this amount with Ⓓs. Ⓓ Ⓓ Ⓓ Ⓓ Ⓓ

LESSON 10·8 | **Written Assessment**   Progress Check 10 ✓

Part A

1. Complete the number-grid puzzles.

186	187	**188**
196	**197**	198
206	207	**208**

101	**102**	103
111	112	**113**
121	**122**	**123**

2. I buy an apple for 15¢.   I buy gum for $0.72.
   I pay 25¢.   I pay $1.00.
   How much change do I get?   How much change do I get?
   __10__ ¢ $ _0_ . _28_

3. Write <, >, or =.

   154 $\boxed{<}$ 372   727 $\boxed{>}$ 272

   94 $\boxed{<}$ 149   233 $\boxed{<}$ 322

   406 $\boxed{=}$ 406   510 $\boxed{>}$ 501

4. Fill in the missing number.

   6 + __4__ = 10   __12__ − 6 = 6

   __6__ + 1 = 7   3 − 0 = __3__

   4 + 4 = __8__   10 − __1__ = 9

LESSON 10·8 | **Written Assessment** *continued*

5. Write the number. __38__ ||| ····
   Write the number that is 10 less. __28__
   Write the number model to
   show 10 less base-10 blocks. __38 − 10 = 28__

6. Write the number. __52__ ||||| ··
   Write the number that is 10 more. __62__
   Write the number model to
   show 10 more base-10 blocks. __52 + 10 = 62__

7. Circle the hundreds place   Circle the tens place.

   ②22   ③71   ①01   3⑨0   ④5   2⓪0

   ⑤99   ④28   ⑥80   8①0   1⑥7   3③3

Part B

8.   **Dinner Times**   Earliest Dinner Time: __4:00__ P.M.

   | Children 5 4 3 2 1 | Latest Dinner Time: __7:00__ P.M.
   | 4:00 5:00 6:00 7:00 | Range: __3__ hours
   | P.M. |

9. Use the graph to answer the question.
   What is the typical dinner time? __5:00__ P.M.

LESSON 5·14 | **Mid-Year Assessment**

Part A

1.

How many ☐s? _____   How many ☐s? _____

Even or odd? _____   Even or odd? _____

2. Complete this part of the number grid.

		13		15					20
	22					27	28		
31			34		36			39	

3. Count by 2s.

2, _____, _____, _____, _____, _____

Count by 10s.

20, _____, _____, _____, _____, _____

4. Draw what comes next.

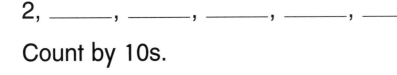

Mid-Year Assessment *continued*

5. Draw the hands.

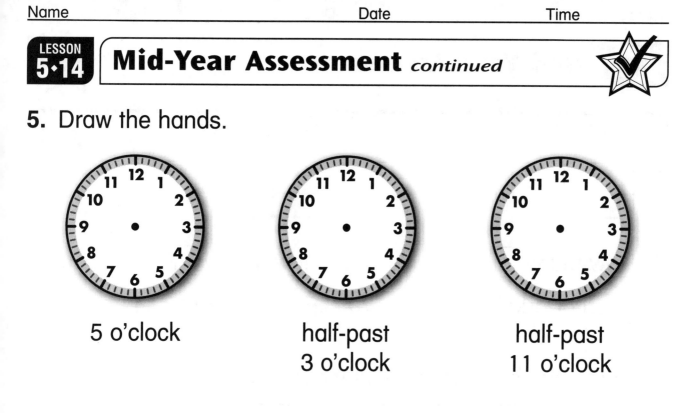

5 o'clock

half-past
3 o'clock

half-past
11 o'clock

6. Measure the line segment to the nearest inch.

_____ about _____ inches

7. Complete the tally chart.

Weather	Tallies	Total Days
Sunny	~~HHt~~ ~~HHt~~ ///	13
Cloudy	~~HHt~~ ~~HHt~~ ~~HHt~~	
Rainy		11
Snowy		8

How many sunny days? _____

How many more rainy days than snowy days?

_____

LESSON 5·14 **Mid-Year Assessment** *continued*

8. How much money? _____

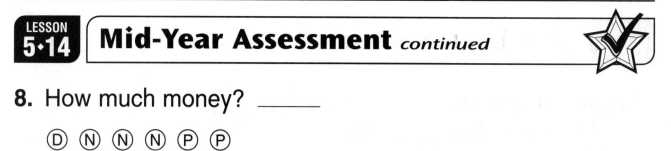

Ⓓ Ⓝ Ⓝ Ⓝ Ⓟ Ⓟ

Show 35¢. Use Ⓓ, Ⓝ, and Ⓟ.

Part B

9. Add.

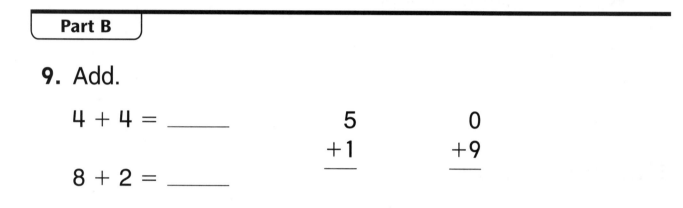

$4 + 4 =$ _____

$8 + 2 =$ _____

$$\begin{array}{r} 5 \\ +1 \\ \hline \end{array}$$

$$\begin{array}{r} 0 \\ +9 \\ \hline \end{array}$$

10. Fill in the frames.

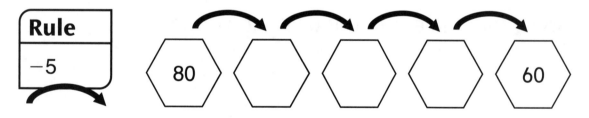

Rule

-5

80   60

Find the rule. Fill in the frames.

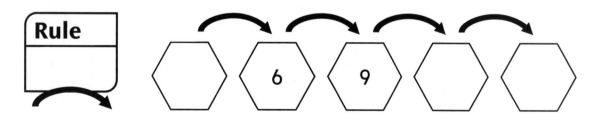

Rule

6   9

LESSON 5·14   **Mid-Year Assessment** *continued*

11. Draw and solve.
There are 12 eggs in a nest.
9 eggs hatch.

How many eggs are left?

_____ eggs

Write the number model.

_____

12. How much money?

Ⓓ Ⓓ Ⓝ Ⓝ Ⓝ Ⓝ Ⓟ Ⓟ

_____ ¢ or $_____ . _____

Show the same amount using fewer coins.

LESSON 10·8

End-Of-Year Assessment

Part A

1. Shade the fraction for each shape.

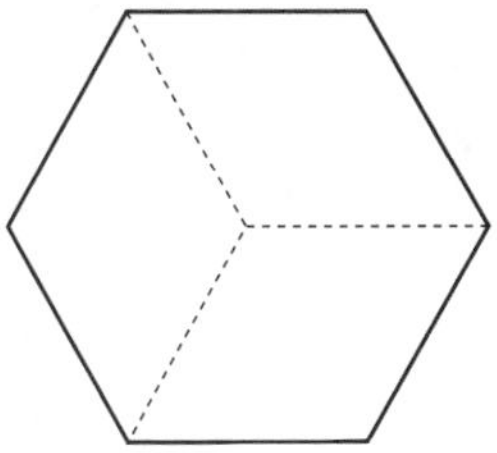

$\dfrac{1}{3}$ 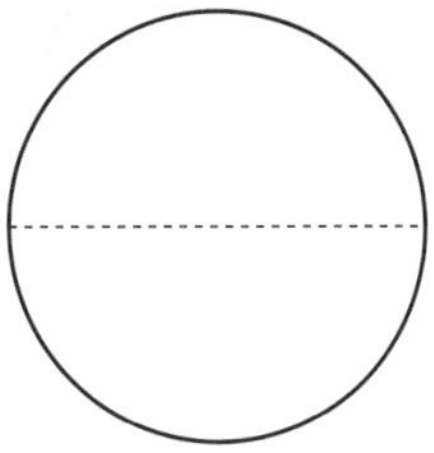 $\dfrac{1}{2}$ 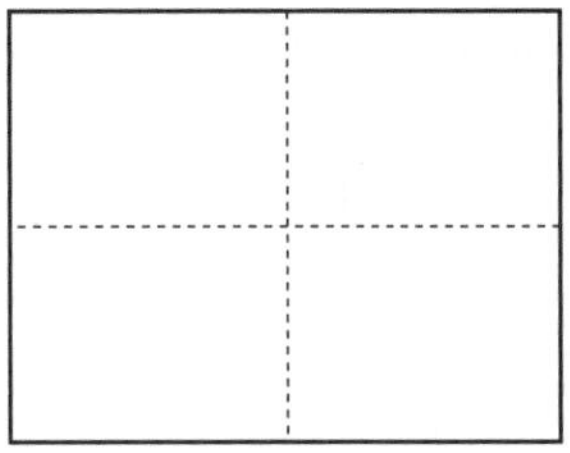 $\dfrac{3}{4}$

2. Use <, >, and =.

42 ☐ 24   4 + 6 ☐ 7 + 3

23 ☐ 20 + 10   78 ☐ 97

< is less than
> is more than
= is equal to

3. Use the word bank to help you write the name for each shape.

| rectangle | circle | pyramid | cone | square | cube | sphere |

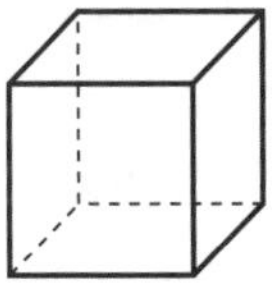

_____   _____   _____

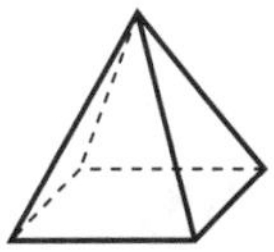

_____   _____   _____

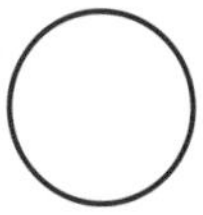

LESSON 10·8 | **End-Of-Year Assessment** *continued*

4. Add or subtract.

$3 + 3 =$ _____

$10 - 1 =$ _____

$7 +$ _____ $= 10$

_____ $= 8 - 4$

_____ $+ 0 = 17$

$0 +$ _____ $= 17$

$\begin{array}{r} 20 \\ -10 \\ \hline \end{array}$
$\begin{array}{r} 16 \\ -1 \\ \hline \end{array}$
$\begin{array}{r} 2 \\ -2 \\ \hline \end{array}$

5. What is your favorite flavor of ice cream?
Add your vote to the graph.

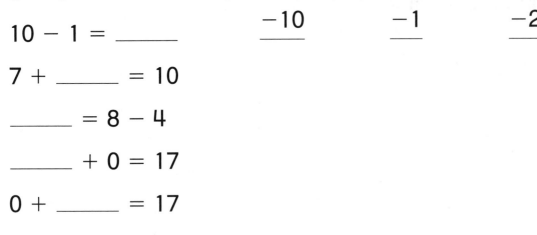

Favorite Ice Cream Flavors

Number of Children

What flavor is least

popular? _____

What flavor is most

popular? _____

How many children like vanilla ice cream? _____

6. Circle the symmetrical picture.

LESSON 10·8 | **End-Of-Year Assessment** *continued*

7. What letter are you most likely to spin? _____

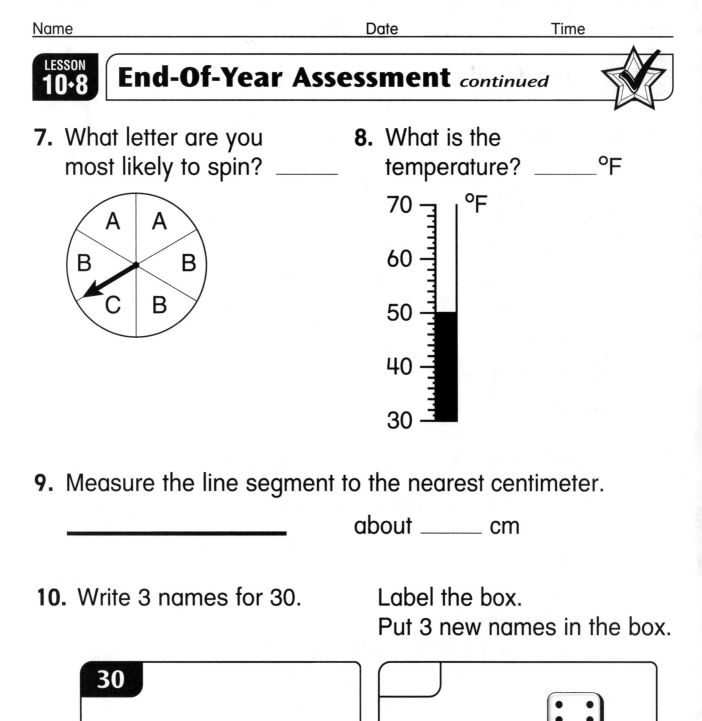

8. What is the temperature? _____ °F

9. Measure the line segment to the nearest centimeter.

_____ about _____ cm

10. Write 3 names for 30.

30

Label the box.
Put 3 new names in the box.

12 − 0

End-Of-Year Assessment *continued*

11. Draw the hands.

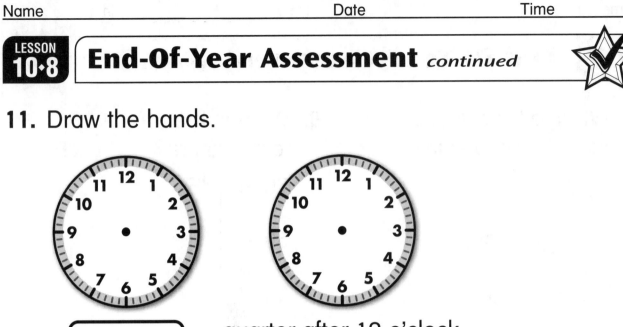

4:45

quarter after 12 o'clock

12. Ⓠ Ⓠ Ⓓ Ⓓ Ⓝ Ⓝ Ⓝ Ⓟ   How much money?   _____¢

Show this amount with fewer coins.

13. Find the rule. Fill in the table.

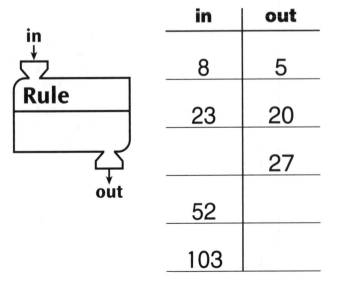

in	out
8	5
23	20
	27
52	
103	

in

Rule

out

LESSON 10·8 End-Of-Year Assessment *continued*

14. Write the numbers shown by the base-10 blocks.

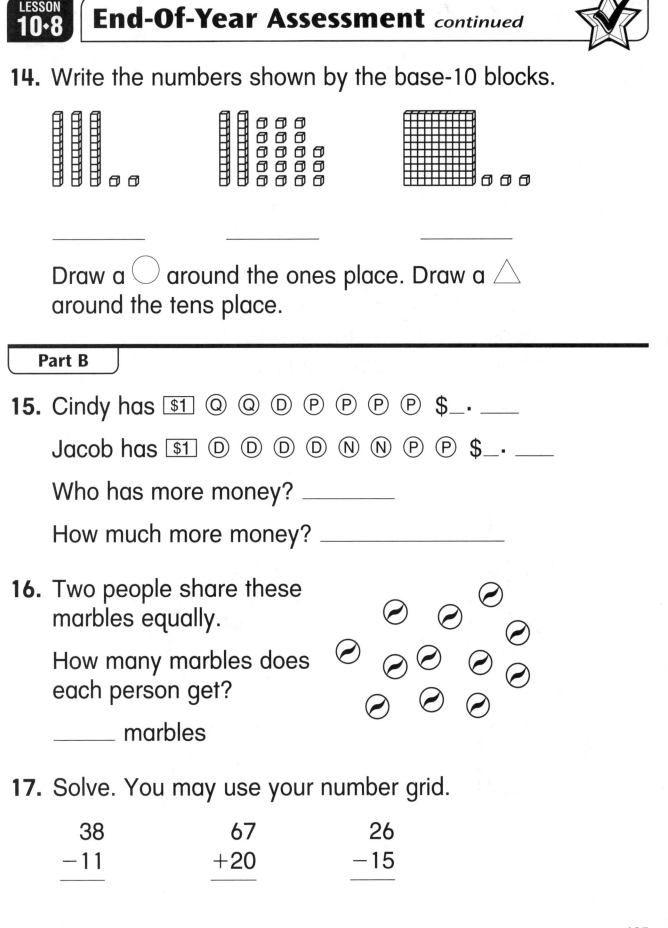

_____   _____   _____

Draw a ◯ around the ones place. Draw a △ around the tens place.

Part B

15. Cindy has $1 Q Q D P P P P $__.___

Jacob has $1 D D D D N N P P $__.___

Who has more money? _____

How much more money? _____

16. Two people share these marbles equally.

How many marbles does each person get?

_____ marbles

17. Solve. You may use your number grid.

$$\begin{array}{r} 38 \\ -11 \\ \hline \end{array} \qquad \begin{array}{r} 67 \\ +20 \\ \hline \end{array} \qquad \begin{array}{r} 26 \\ -15 \\ \hline \end{array}$$

LESSON 10·8 **End-Of-Year Assessment** *continued*

18. Add.

2 + 5 = _____   10 + 4 = _____

20 + 50 = _____   20 + 4 = _____

200 + 500 = _____   30 + 4 = _____

19. Solve.
Zack found 17 shells at the beach.
Miles found 20 shells at the beach.
How many shells did Zack and Miles find in all?

_____ shells

Write a number model. _____

20. What time is it?

LESSON 5·14 Mid-Year Assessment

Part A

1.

How many ☐s? __6__   How many ☐s? __9__
Even or odd? __even__   Even or odd? __odd__

2. Complete this part of the number grid.

11	12	13	14	15	16	17	18	19	20
21	22	23	24	25	26	27	28	29	30
31	32	33	34	35	36	37	38	39	40

3. Count by 2s.
2, __4__, __6__, __8__, __10__, __12__

Count by 10s.
20, __30__, __40__, __50__, __60__, __70__

4. Draw what comes next.

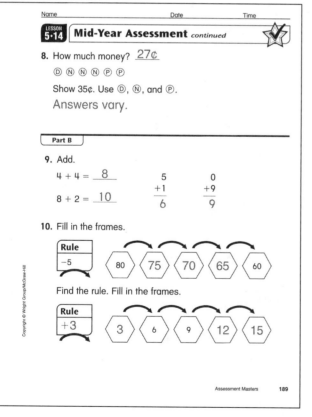

LESSON 5·14 Mid-Year Assessment *continued*

5. Draw the hands.

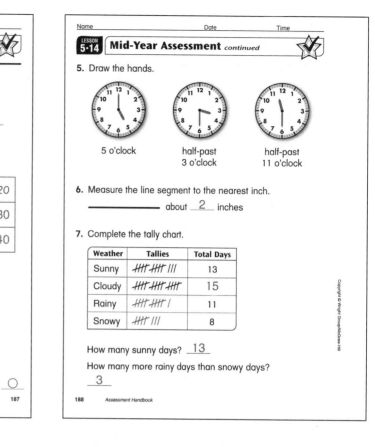

5 o'clock   half-past 3 o'clock   half-past 11 o'clock

6. Measure the line segment to the nearest inch.
——————— about __2__ inches

7. Complete the tally chart.

Weather	Tallies	Total Days
Sunny	HHT HHT ///	13
Cloudy	HHT HHT HHT	15
Rainy	HHT HHT /	11
Snowy	HHT ///	8

How many sunny days? __13__

How many more rainy days than snowy days?
__3__

LESSON 5·14 Mid-Year Assessment *continued*

8. How much money? __27¢__

Ⓓ Ⓝ Ⓝ Ⓝ Ⓟ Ⓟ

Show 35¢. Use Ⓓ, Ⓝ, and Ⓟ.
Answers vary.

Part B

9. Add.
4 + 4 = __8__

8 + 2 = __10__

```
  5        0
 +1       +9
 ———      ———
  6        9
```

10. Fill in the frames.

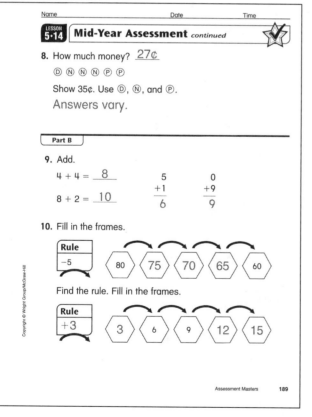

Rule −5

80   75   70   65   60

Find the rule. Fill in the frames.

Rule +3

3   6   9   12   15

LESSON 5·14 Mid-Year Assessment *continued*

11. Draw and solve.
There are 12 eggs in a nest.
9 eggs hatch.

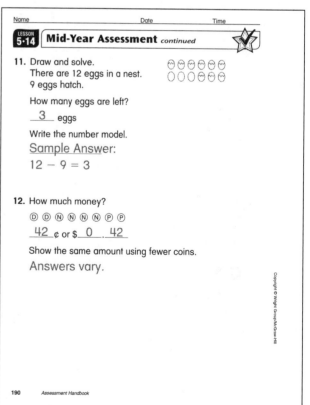

How many eggs are left?
__3__ eggs

Write the number model.
Sample Answer:
12 − 9 = 3

12. How much money?

Ⓓ Ⓓ Ⓝ Ⓝ Ⓝ Ⓟ Ⓟ

__42__ ¢ or $ __0__ . __42__

Show the same amount using fewer coins.
Answers vary.

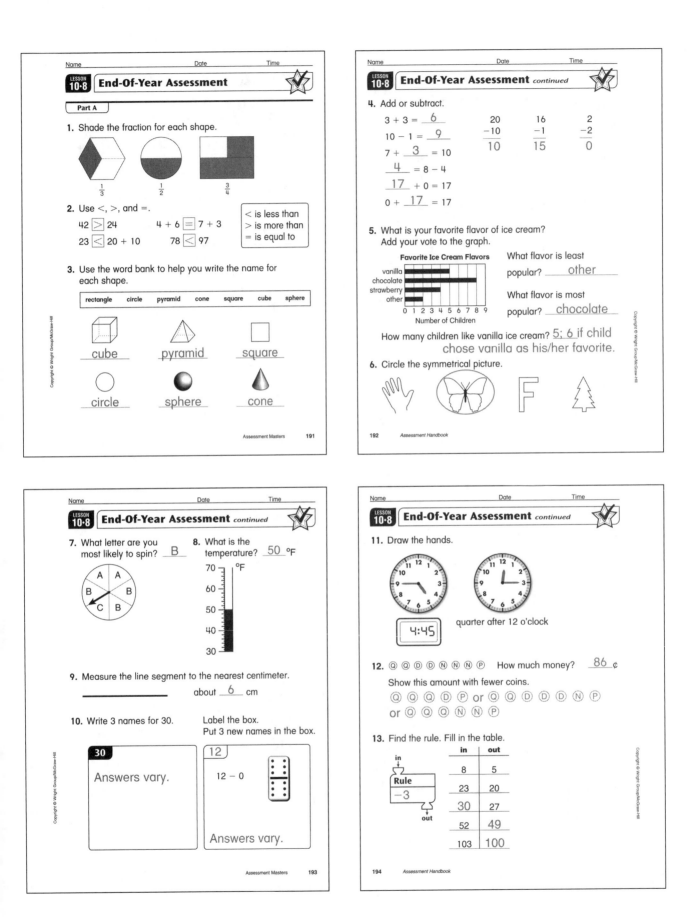

Part A

1. Shade the fraction for each shape.

   $\frac{1}{3}$ $\frac{1}{2}$ $\frac{3}{4}$

2. Use <, >, and =.

   42 $>$ 24   4 + 6 $=$ 7 + 3

   23 $<$ 20 + 10   78 $<$ 97

   | < is less than |
   | > is more than |
   | = is equal to |

3. Use the word bank to help you write the name for each shape.

   | rectangle | circle | pyramid | cone | square | cube | sphere |

   cube   pyramid   square

   circle   sphere   cone

4. Add or subtract.

   3 + 3 = __6__   20   16   2
   10 − 1 = __9__   −10   −1   −2
   7 + __3__ = 10   __10__ __15__ __0__
   __4__ = 8 − 4
   __17__ + 0 = 17
   0 + __17__ = 17

5. What is your favorite flavor of ice cream? Add your vote to the graph.

   Favorite Ice Cream Flavors

   What flavor is least popular? __other__

   What flavor is most popular? __chocolate__

   How many children like vanilla ice cream? _5; 6 if child chose vanilla as his/her favorite._

6. Circle the symmetrical picture.

7. What letter are you most likely to spin? __B__

8. What is the temperature? __50__ °F

9. Measure the line segment to the nearest centimeter.

   about __6__ cm

10. Write 3 names for 30.   Label the box.
    Put 3 new names in the box.

    30
    Answers vary.

    12
    12 − 0
    Answers vary.

11. Draw the hands.

    4:45   quarter after 12 o'clock

12. Q Q D D N N N P   How much money? __86__ ¢

    Show this amount with fewer coins.

    Q Q Q D P or Q Q D D N P
    or Q Q Q N N P

13. Find the rule. Fill in the table.

in	out
8	5
23	20
30	27
52	49
103	100

    Rule
    −3

LESSON 10·8 **End-Of-Year Assessment** *continued*

14. Write the numbers shown by the base-10 blocks.

32   38   103

Draw a ○ around the ones place. Draw a △ around the tens place.

Part B

15. Cindy has $1 Q Q D P P P P $1. 64

Jacob has $1 D D D N N P P $1. 52

Who has more money? Cindy

How much more money? 12¢ or $0.12

16. Two people share these marbles equally.

How many marbles does each person get?

6 marbles

17. Solve. You may use your number grid.

38	67	26
−11	+20	−15
27	87	11

LESSON 10·8 **End-Of-Year Assessment** *continued*

18. Add.

2 + 5 = 7   10 + 4 = 14

20 + 50 = 70   20 + 4 = 24

200 + 500 = 700   30 + 4 = 34

19. Solve.
Zack found 17 shells at the beach.
Miles found 20 shells at the beach.
How many shells did Zack and Miles find in all?

37 shells

Write a number model. Sample Answer: 17 + 20 = 37

20. What time is it?

7:10   1:55

Individual Profile of Progress

Name _____ Date _____

Lesson	Recognizing Student Achievement	A.P.*	Comments
1◆1	**Count by 1s.** [Number and Numeration Goal 1]		
1◆2	**Count by 1s and 5s.** [Number and Numeration Goal 1]		
1◆3	**Compare numbers.** [Number and Numeration Goal 7]		
1◆4	**Write the numbers 1 and 2.** [Number and Numeration Goal 3]		
1◆5	**Name numbers that come before and after a given number.** [Number and Numeration Goal 7]		
1◆6	**Tell the number that is *one more* or *one less*.** [Number and Numeration Goal 7]		
1◆7	**Write the numbers 3 and 4.** [Number and Numeration Goal 3]		
1◆8	**Make tally marks for a number.** [Number and Numeration Goal 6]		
1◆9	**Write the numbers 5 and 6.** [Number and Numeration Goal 3]		
1◆10	**Count hops on a number line.** [Operations and Computation Goal 2]		
1◆11	**Compare numbers.** [Number and Numeration Goal 7]		
1◆12	**Count by 2s.** [Number and Numeration Goal 1]		
1◆13	**Solve simple number stories.** [Operations and Computation Goal 4]		

*Assess Progress: **A** = adequate progress **N** = not adequate progress **N/A** = not assessed

Name _____   Date _____

Problem(s)	Progress Check 1	A.P.*	Comments
Oral/Slate Assessment			
1	**Ask children to count backward by 1s and forward by 5s orally.** [Number and Numeration Goal 1]		
2	**Ask what number comes before 1; 5; 8; 11; 13; 20.** [Number and Numeration Goal 7]		
3	**Ask children to write the numerals 3, 5, 10, 14, and 16.** [Number and Numeration Goal 3]		
4	**State a number and ask children to draw the tally marks for 2, 6, 9, and 12.** [Number and Numeration Goal 6]		
Written Assessment Part A			
1	**Count forward by 1s.** [Number and Numeration Goal 1]		
2	**Write the numbers that come before and after a given number.** [Number and Numeration Goal 7]		
3	**Write tally marks for numbers.** [Number and Numeration Goal 6]		
4	**Write the numbers 1–6.** [Number and Numeration Goal 3]		
Written Assessment Part B			
5	**Count forward by 2s and 5s.** [Number and Numeration Goal 1]		
6	**Compare pairs of numbers.** [Number and Numeration Goal 7]		

*Assess Progress: **A** = adequate progress   **N** = not adequate progress   **N/A** = not assessed   **Formative Assessments**

Class Checklist:
Recognizing Student Achievement

Class _____

Date _____

Names	Count by 1s. [Number and Numeration Goal 1] 1•1	Count by 1s and 5s. [Number and Numeration Goal 1] 1•2	Compare numbers. [Number and Numeration Goal 7] 1•3	Write the numbers 1 and 2. [Number and Numeration Goal 7] 1•4	Name numbers that come before and after a given number. [Number and Numeration Goal 3] 1•5	Tell the number that is one more or one less. [Number and Numeration Goal 7] 1•6	Write the numbers 3 and 4. [Number and Numeration Goal 7] 1•7	Make tally marks for a number. [Number and Numeration Goal 3] 1•8	Write the numbers 5 and 6. [Number and Numeration Goal 6] 1•9	Count hops on a number line. [Number and Numeration Goal 3] 1•10	Compare numbers. [Operations and Computation Goal 2] 1•11	Count by 2s. [Number and Numeration Goal 7] 1•12	Solve simple number stories. [Operations and Computation Goal 4] 1•13
1.													
2.													
3.													
4.													
5.													
6.													
7.													
8.													
9.													
10.													
11.													
12.													
13.													
14.													
15.													
16.													
17.													
18.													
19.													
20.													
21.													
22.													
23.													
24.													
25.													

Assess Progress: **A** = adequate progress   **N** = not adequate progress   **N/A** = not assessed

Class Checklist:
Progress Check 1

Names	Oral/Slate				Written					
					Part A				Part B	
	1. Ask children to count backward by 1s and forward by 5s orally. [Number and Numeration Goal 1]	2. Ask what number comes before 1; 5; 8; 11; 13; 20. [Number and Numeration Goal 7]	3. Ask children to write the numeral 3; 5; 10; 14; 16. [Number and Numeration Goal 3]	4. State a number and ask children to draw the tally marks: 2; 6; 9; 12. [Number and Numeration Goal 6]	1. Count forward by 1s. [Number and Numeration Goal 1]	2. Write the numbers that come before and after a given number. [Number and Numeration Goal 7]	3. Write tally marks for numbers. [Number and Numeration Goal 6]	4. Write the numbers 1–6. [Number and Numeration Goal 3]	5. Count forward by 2s and 5s. [Number and Numeration Goal 1]	6. Compare pairs of numbers. [Number and Numeration Goal 7]
1.										
2.										
3.										
4.										
5.										
6.										
7.										
8.										
9.										
10.										
11.										
12.										
13.										
14.										
15.										
16.										
17.										
18.										
19.										
20.										
21.										
22.										
23.										
24.										
25.										

Class _____

Date _____

Assess Progress: **A** = adequate progress   **N** = not adequate progress   **N/A** = not assessed   **Formative Assessments**

Individual Profile of Progress

Unit 2

Name _____ Date _____

Lesson	Recognizing Student Achievement	A.P.*	Comments
2◆1	**Compare numbers.** [Number and Numeration Goal 7]		
2◆2	**Write the numbers 7 and 8.** [Number and Numeration Goal 3]		
2◆3	**Find sums of 10.** [Operations and Computation Goal 1]		
2◆4	**Write the numbers 9 and 0.** [Number and Numeration Goal 3]		
2◆5	**Order numbers.** [Number and Numeration Goal 7]		
2◆6	**Find equivalent names for numbers.** [Number and Numeration Goal 6]		
2◆7	**Count on a number grid.** [Operations and Computation Goal 2]		
2◆8	**Compare quantities.** [Number and Numeration Goal 7]		
2◆9	**Count by 5s.** [Number and Numeration Goal 1]		
2◆10	**Count nickels and pennies.** [Operations and Computation Goal 2]		
2◆11	**Tell time to the hour.** [Measurement and Reference Frames Goal 4]		
2◆12	**Find sums of 1-digit numbers.** [Operations and Computation Goal 2]		
2◆13	**Count nickels and pennies.** [Operations and Computation Goal 2]		

*Assess Progress: **A** = adequate progress   **N** = not adequate progress   **N/A** = not assessed

Individual Profile of Progress

Name _____ Date _____

Problem(s)	Progress Check 2	A.P.*	Comments
Oral/Slate Assessment			
1	**Do "stop-and-start" counting.** [Number and Numeration Goal 1]		
2	**Tell the time shown on a demonstration clock.** [Measurement and Reference Frames Goal 4]		
3	**Use a number grid to count spaces.** [Operations and Computation Goal 2]		
4	**Play *Penny Plate* to find sums of 10.** [Operations and Computation Goal 1]		
Written Assessment Part A			
1	**Use a tally chart to answer questions.** [Data and Chance Goal 2]		
2	**Calculate and compare the value of penny and nickel coin collections.** [Operations and Computation Goal 2]		
3	**Show time to the hour on an analog clock.** [Measurement and Reference Frames Goal 4]		
Written Assessment Part B			
4	**Know easy addition facts.** [Operations and Computation Goal 1]		
5	**Count forward by 2s and 5s.** [Number and Numeration Goal 1]		

*Assess Progress: **A** = adequate progress   **N** = not adequate progress   **N/A** = not assessed   Formative Assessments

Class _____

Date _____

Names	Compare numbers. [Number and Numeration Goal 7] 2•1	Write the numbers 7 and 8. [Number and Numeration Goal 3] 2•2	Find sums of 10. [Operations and Computation Goal 1] 2•3	Write the numbers 9 and 0. [Number and Numeration Goal 3] 2•4	Order numbers. [Number and Numeration Goal 7] 2•5	Find equivalent names for numbers. [Number and Numeration Goal 6] 2•6	Count on a number grid. [Operations and Computation Goal 2] 2•7	Compare quantities. [Number and Numeration Goal 7] 2•8	Count by 5s. [Number and Numeration Goal 1] 2•9	Count nickels and pennies. [Operations and Computation Goal 2] 2•10	Tell time to the hour. [Measurement and Reference Frames Goal 4] 2•11	Find sums of 1-digit numbers. [Operations and Computation Goal 2] 2•12	Count nickels and pennies. [Operations and Computation Goal 2] 2•13
1.													
2.													
3.													
4.													
5.													
6.													
7.													
8.													
9.													
10.													
11.													
12.													
13.													
14.													
15.													
16.													
17.													
18.													
19.													
20.													
21.													
22.													
23.													
24.													
25.													

Assess Progress: **A** = adequate progress   **N** = not adequate progress   **N/A** = not assessed

Class Checklist:
Progress Check 2

Unit 2

Class _____

Date _____

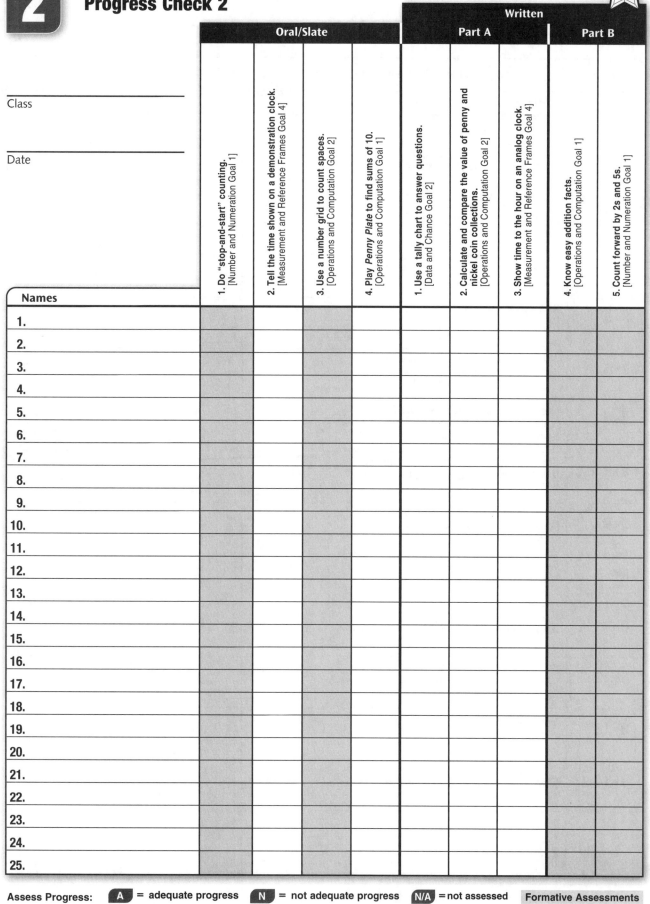

Names	Oral/Slate				Written Part A			Part B	
	1. Do "stop-and-start" counting. [Number and Numeration Goal 1]	2. Tell the time shown on a demonstration clock. [Measurement and Reference Frames Goal 4]	3. Use a number grid to count spaces. [Operations and Computation Goal 2]	4. Play *Penny Plate* to find sums of 10. [Operations and Computation Goal 1]	1. Use a tally chart to answer questions. [Data and Chance Goal 2]	2. Calculate and compare the value of penny and nickel coin collections. [Operations and Computation Goal 2]	3. Show time to the hour on an analog clock. [Measurement and Reference Frames Goal 4]	4. Know easy addition facts. [Operations and Computation Goal 1]	5. Count forward by 2s and 5s. [Number and Numeration Goal 1]
1.									
2.									
3.									
4.									
5.									
6.									
7.									
8.									
9.									
10.									
11.									
12.									
13.									
14.									
15.									
16.									
17.									
18.									
19.									
20.									
21.									
22.									
23.									
24.									
25.									

Assess Progress: **A** = adequate progress   **N** = not adequate progress   **N/A** = not assessed   **Formative Assessments**

Individual Profile of Progress

Name _____ Date _____

Lesson	Recognizing Student Achievement	A.P.*	Comments
3•1	**Create and extend patterns.** [Patterns, Functions, and Algebra Goal 1]		
3•2	**Distinguish between even and odd numbers.** [Number and Numeration Goal 5]		
3•3	**Compare numbers.** [Number and Numeration Goal 7]		
3•4	**Count spaces on a number grid.** [Operations and Computation Goal 2]		
3•5	**Skip count.** [Number and Numeration Goal 1]		
3•6	**Write number models for subtraction.** [Patterns, Functions, and Algebra Goal 2]		
3•7	**Use a tally chart to answer questions.** [Data and Chance Goal 2]		
3•8	**Count up and back from a given number.** [Number and Numeration Goal 1]		
3•9	**Solve Frames-and-Arrows problems.** [Patterns, Functions, and Algebra Goal 1]		
3•10	**Count by 5s and then by 1s.** [Number and Numeration Goal 1]		
3•11	**Make exchanges between coins.** [Measurement and Reference Frames Goal 2]		
3•12	**Solve parts-and-total number stories.** [Operations and Computation Goal 4]		
3•13	**Make sums of 10.** [Operations and Computation Goal 1]		
3•14	**Find dice sums.** [Operations and Computation Goal 2]		

*Assess Progress: A = adequate progress   N = not adequate progress   N/A = not assessed

Individual Profile of Progress

Name _____   Date _____

Problem(s)	Progress Check 3	A.P.*	Comments
Oral/Slate Assessment			
1	**Describe how to continue patterns.** [Patterns, Functions, and Algebra Goal 1]		
2	**Use a number grid to count hops.** [Operations and Computation Goal 2]		
3	**Write the values of coin combinations using cent notation.** [Measurement and Reference Frames Goal 2]		
4	**Write the rules for Frames-and-Arrows problems.** [Patterns, Functions, and Algebra Goal 1]		
Written Assessment Part A			
1	**Know sums of 10.** [Operations and Computation Goal 1]		
2, 3	**Count forward by 5s and backward by 1s; solve problems involving simple functions represented in Frames-and-Arrows problems.** [Number and Numeration Goal 1; Patterns, Functions, and Algebra Goal 1]		
4, 5	**Know the value of a penny, nickel, and dime; calculate the value of a combination of coins.** [Measurement and Reference Frames Goal 2]		
6	**Continue non-numeric patterns.** [Patterns, Functions, and Algebra Goal 1]		
Written Assessment Part B			
7	**Count forward by 2s to 100; solve problems involving simple functions represented in Frames-and-Arrows problems.** [Number and Numeration Goal 1; [Patterns, Functions, and Algebra Goal 1]		
8, 9	**Show and tell time on an analog clock to the nearest half-hour.** [Measurement and Reference Frames Goal 4]		

*Assess Progress: **A** = adequate progress   **N** = not adequate progress   **N/A** = not assessed   **Formative Assessments**

Class Checklist:
Recognizing Student Achievement

Class _____

Date _____

Names	**Create and extend patterns.** [Patterns, Functions, and Algebra Goal 1]	**Distinguish between even and odd numbers.** [Number and Numeration Goal 5]	**Compare numbers.** [Number and Numeration Goal 7]	**Count spaces on a number grid.** [Operations and Computation Goal 2]	**Skip count.** [Number and Numeration Goal 1]	**Write number models for subtraction.** [Patterns, Functions, and Algebra Goal 2]	**Use a tally chart to answer questions.** [Data and Chance Goal 2]	**Count up and back from a given number.** [Number and Numeration Goal 1]	**Solve Frames-and-Arrows problems.** [Patterns, Functions, and Algebra Goal 1]	**Count by 5s and then by 1s.** [Number and Numeration Goal 1]	**Make exchanges between coins.** [Measurement and Reference Frames Goal 2]	**Solve parts-and-total number stories.** [Operations and Computation Goal 4]	**Make sums of 10.** [Operations and Computation Goal 1]	**Find dice sums.** [Operations and Computation Goal 2]
	3•1	3•2	3•3	3•4	3•5	3•6	3•7	3•8	3•9	3•10	3•11	3•12	3•13	3•14
1.														
2.														
3.														
4.														
5.														
6.														
7.														
8.														
9.														
10.														
11.														
12.														
13.														
14.														
15.														
16.														
17.														
18.														
19.														
20.														
21.														
22.														
23.														
24.														
25.														

Assess Progress: **A** = adequate progress   **N** = not adequate progress   **N/A** = not assessed

Class Checklist:
Progress Check 3

Class _____

Date _____

Names	Oral/Slate				Written Part A				Written Part B	
	1. Describe how to continue patterns. [Patterns, Functions, and Algebra Goal 1]	2. Use a number grid to count hops. [Operations and Computation Goal 2]	3. Write the values of coin combinations using cent notation. [Measurement and Reference Frames Goal 2]	4. Write the rules for Frames-and-Arrows problems. [Patterns, Functions, and Algebra Goal 1]	1. Know sums of 10. [Operations and Computation Goal 1]	2, 3. Count forward by 5s and backward by 1s; solve problems involving simple functions represented in Frame-and-Arrows problems. [Number and Numeration Goal 1; Patterns, Functions, and Algebra Goal 1]	4, 5. Know the value of a penny, nickel, and dime; calculate the value of a combination of coins. [Measurement and Reference Frames Goal 2]	6. Continue non-numeric patterns. [Patterns, Functions, and Algebra Goal 1]	7. Count forward by 2s to 100; solve problems involving simple functions represented in Frames-and-Arrows problems. [Number and Numeration Goal 1; Patterns, Functions, and Algebra Goal 1]	8, 9. Show and tell time on an analog clock to the nearest half-hour. [Measurement and Reference Frames Goal 4]
1.										
2.										
3.										
4.										
5.										
6.										
7.										
8.										
9.										
10.										
11.										
12.										
13.										
14.										
15.										
16.										
17.										
18.										
19.										
20.										
21.										
22.										
23.										
24.										
25.										

Assess Progress: **A** = adequate progress **N** = not adequate progress **N/A** = not assessed **Formative Assessments**

Individual Profile of Progress

Name _____ Date _____

Lesson	Recognizing Student Achievement	A.P.*	Comments
4◆1	**Skip count by 2s.** [Number and Numeration Goal 1]		
4◆2	**Find complements of numbers.** [Operations and Computation Goal 2]		
4◆3	**Solve Frames-and-Arrows problems.** [Patterns, Functions, and Algebra Goal 1]		
4◆4	**Measure in feet.** [Measurement and Reference Frames Goal 1]		
4◆5	**Find domino sums and compare quantities.** [Number and Numeration Goal 7]		
4◆6	**Solve parts-and-total number stories.** [Operations and Computation Goal 4]		
4◆7	**Solve easy dice sums.** [Operations and Computation Goal 2]		
4◆8	**Tell time.** [Measurement and Reference Frames Goal 4]		
4◆9	**Measure to the nearest inch.** [Measurement and Reference Frames Goal 1]		
4◆10	**Answer probability questions.** [Data and Chance Goal 3]		
4◆11	**Tell time to the quarter-hour.** [Measurement and Reference Frames Goal 4]		
4◆12	**Write easy addition facts.** [Operations and Computation Goal 1]		

*Assess Progress: **A** = adequate progress   **N** = not adequate progress   **N/A** = not assessed

Name _____ Date _____

Problem(s)	Progress Check 4	A.P.*	Comments
Oral/Slate Assessment			
1	**Estimate whether various objects are shorter, longer, or the same length as a 6-inch line.** [Measurement and Reference Frames Goal 1]		
2	**Show various times using tool-kit clocks.** [Measurement and Reference Frames Goal 4]		
3	**Write the three numbers that go with each domino.** [Operations and Computation Goals 1 and 4]		
4	**Write numbers that come before and after various numbers.** [Number and Numeration Goal 7]		
Written Assessment Part A			
1	**Know easy addition facts including + 0, + 1, and sums of 10; demonstrate parts-and-total situations.** [Operations and Computation Goals 1 and 4]		
2	**Order whole numbers through 100s.** [Number and Numeration Goal 7]		
3	**Continue simple non-numeric patterns.** [Patterns, Functions, and Algebra Goal 1]		
4	**Make exchanges between coins.** [Measurement and Reference Frames Goal 2]		
5	**Solve problems involving simple functions represented in Frames and Arrows; count back by 2s.** [Number and Numeration Goal 1; Patterns, Functions, and Algebra Goal 1]		
6	**Know easy addition facts including + 0, + 1, doubles, and sums of 10.** [Operations and Computation Goal 1]		
Written Assessment Part B			
7	**Compare lengths of objects.** [Measurement and Reference Frames Goal 1]		·
8	**Show and tell time on an analog clock to the nearest quarter-hour.** [Measurement and Reference Frames Goal 4]		
9	**Know easy addition facts including + 0, + 1, and sums of 10.** [Operations and Computation Goal 1]		

*Assess Progress: **A** = adequate progress   **N** = not adequate progress   **N/A** = not assessed   **Formative Assessments**

Class Checklist:
Recognizing Student Achievement

Class _____

Date _____

Names	**Skip count by 2s.** [Number and Numeration Goal 1] 4·1	**Find complements of numbers.** [Operations and Computation Goal 2] 4·2	**Solve Frames-and-Arrows problems.** [Patterns, Functions, and Algebra Goal 1] 4·3	**Measure in feet.** [Measurement and Reference Frames Goal 1] 4·4	**Find domino sums and compare quantities.** [Number and Numeration Goal 7] 4·5	**Solve parts-and-total number stories.** [Operations and Computation Goal 4] 4·6	**Solve easy dice sums.** [Operations and Computation Goal 4] 4·7	**Tell time.** [Measurement and Reference Frames Goal 2] 4·8	**Measure to the nearest inch.** [Measurement and Reference Frames Goal 4] 4·9	**Answer probability questions.** [Data and Chance Goal 3] 4·10	**Tell time to the quarter-hour.** [Measurement and Reference Frames Goal 1] 4·11	**Write easy addition facts.** [Operations and Computation Goal 1] 4·12
1.												
2.												
3.												
4.												
5.												
6.												
7.												
8.												
9.												
10.												
11.												
12.												
13.												
14.												
15.												
16.												
17.												
18.												
19.												
20.												
21.												
22.												
23.												
24.												
25.												

Assess Progress: **A** = adequate progress   **N** = not adequate progress   **N/A** = not assessed

Class Checklist:
Progress Check 4

Class _____

Date _____

Names	**Oral/Slate**				**Written** Part A						**Written** Part B		
	1. Estimate whether various objects are shorter, longer, or the same length as a 6-inch line. [Measurement and Reference Frames Goal 1]	2. Show various times using tool-kit clocks. [Measurement and Reference Frames Goal 4]	3. Write the three numerals that go with each domino. [Operations and Computation Goals 1 and 4]	4. Write numbers that come before and after various numbers. [Number and Numeration Goal 7]	1. Know easy addition facts including + 0, + 1, and sums of 10; demonstrate parts-and-total situations. [Operations and Computation Goal 1]	2. Order whole numbers through 100s. [Number and Numeration Goal 7]	3. Continue simple non-numeric patterns. [Patterns, Functions, and Algebra Goal 1]	4. Make exchanges between coins. [Measurement and Reference Frames Goal 2]	5. Solve problems involving simple functions represented in Frames and Arrows; count back by 2s. [Number and Numeration Goal 1; Patterns, Functions, and Algebra Goal 2]	6. Know easy addition facts including + 0, + 1, doubles, and sums of 10. [Operations and Computation Goal 1]	7. Compare lengths of objects. [Measurement and Reference Frames Goal 1]	8, 9. Show and tell time on an analog clock to the nearest quarter-hour. [Measurement and Reference Frames Goal 4]	10. Know easy addition facts including + 0, + 1, and sums of 10. [Operations and Computation Goal 1]
1.													
2.													
3.													
4.													
5.													
6.													
7.													
8.													
9.													
10.													
11.													
12.													
13.													
14.													
15.													
16.													
17.													
18.													
19.													
20.													
21.													
22.													
23.													
24.													
25.													

Assess Progress: **A** = adequate progress   **N** = not adequate progress   **N/A** = not assessed   **Formative Assessments**

Individual Profile of Progress

Name _____ Date _____

Lesson	Recognizing Student Achievement	A.P.*	Comments
5◆1	**Name numbers represented by base-10 blocks.** [Number and Numeration Goal 3]		
5◆2	**Find complements of numbers.** [Operations and Computation Goal 2]		
5◆3	**Solve Frames-and-Arrows problems.** [Patterns, Functions, and Algebra Goal 1]		
5◆4	**Find equivalent names for numbers.** [Number and Numeration Goal 6]		
5◆5	**Compare lengths of objects.** [Measurement and Reference Frames Goal 1]		
5◆6	**Compare numbers through hundreds using < and >.** [Patterns, Functions, and Algebra Goal 2]		
5◆7	**Compare numbers of pennies.** [Number and Numeration Goal 7]		
5◆8	**Identify digits in numbers.** [Number and Numeration Goal 3]		
5◆9	**Show time to the quarter-hour on a clock.** [Measurement and Reference Frames Goal 4]		
5◆10	**Solve simple number stories.** [Operations and Computation Goal 4]		
5◆11	**Write turn-around facts.** [Patterns, Functions, and Algebra Goal 3]		
5◆12	**Use thermometers to record temperature.** [Measurement and Reference Frames Goal 3]		
5◆13	**Compare the values of coin combinations.** [Operations and Computation Goal 2]		

*****Assess Progress:**   **A** = adequate progress   **N** = not adequate progress   **N/A** = not assessed

Individual Profile of Progress

Name _____ Date _____

Problem(s)	Progress Check 5	A.P.*	Comments
Oral/Slate Assessment			
1	Find the answers to various math facts mentally, and then state verbally. [Operations and Computation Goal 1]		
2	Write the amounts of combinations of coins on slates. [Operations and Computation Goal 2]		
3	Record a number model and answers to number stories on slates. [Operations and Computation Goals 2 and 4; Patterns, Functions, and Algebra Goal 2]		
4	Record various temperatures shown on the Class Thermometer Poster. [Measurement and Reference Frames Goal 3]		
Written Assessment Part A			
1	Read, write, and represent with base-10 blocks whole numbers through hundreds. [Number and Numeration Goal 3]		
1–3	Compare whole numbers through 100. [Number and Numeration Goal 7] Calculate and compare the values of combinations of coins. [Operations and Computation of Goal 2]		
5, 6	Solve problems involving simple functions represented as Function Machines. [Patterns, Functions, and Algebra Goal 1]		
7, 8	Know easy addition facts. [Operations and Computation Goal 1]		
Written Assessment Part B			
9	Recognize appropriate range of temperatures as hot or cold. [Measurement and Reference Frames Goal 3]		
10	Show and tell time on an analog clock to the nearest quarter-hour. [Measurement and Reference Frames Goal 4]		
11, 12	Answer questions and draw conclusions based on data representations; compare numbers. [Number and Numeration Goal 7; Data and Chance Goal 2]		

*Assess Progress: **A** = adequate progress   **N** = not adequate progress   **N/A** = not assessed   Formative Assessments

Class Checklist:
Recognizing Student Achievement

Class _____

Date _____

Names	Name numbers represented by base-10 blocks. [Number and Numeration Goal 3] 5·1	Find complements of numbers. [Operations and Computation Goal 2] 5·2	Solve Frames-and-Arrows problems. [Patterns, Functions, and Algebra Goal 1] 5·3	Find equivalent names for numbers. [Number and Numeration Goal 6] 5·4	Compare lengths of objects. [Measurement and Reference Frames Goal 1] 5·5	Compare numbers through hundreds using < and >. [Patterns, Functions, and Algebra Goal 2] 5·6	Compare numbers of pennies. [Number and Numeration Goal 7] 5·7	Identify digits in numbers. [Number and Numeration Goal 3] 5·8	Show time to the quarter-hour on a clock. [Measurement and Reference Frames Goal 4] 5·9	Solve simple number stories. [Operations and Computation Goal 4] 5·10	Write turn-around facts. [Patterns, Functions, and Algebra Goal 3] 5·11	Use thermometers to record temperature. [Measurement and Reference Frames Goal 3] 5·12	Compare the values of coin combinations. [Operations and Computation Goal 2] 5·13
1.													
2.													
3.													
4.													
5.													
6.													
7.													
8.													
9.													
10.													
11.													
12.													
13.													
14.													
15.													
16.													
17.													
18.													
19.													
20.													
21.													
22.													
23.													
24.													
25.													

Assess Progress: **A** = adequate progress   **N** = not adequate progress   **N/A** = not assessed

Unit 5

Class Checklist:
Progress Check 5

Class _____

Date _____

Names	Oral/Slate				Written				Part A		Part B		
	1. Find the answers to various math facts mentally, and then state verbally. [Operations and Computation Goal 1]	**2.** Write the amounts of combinations of coins on slates. [Operations and Computation Goal 2]	**3.** Record a number model and answers to number stories on slates. [Operations and Computation Goals 2 and 4; Patterns, Functions, and Algebra Goal 2]	**4.** Record various temperatures shown on the Class Thermometer Poster. [Measurement and Reference Frames Goal 3]	**1.** Read, write, and represent with base-10 blocks whole numbers through hundreds. [Number and Numeration Goal 3]	**1–3.** Compare whole numbers through 100. [Number and Numeration Goal 7] Calculate and compare values of combinations of coins. [Operations and Computation Goal 2]	**5, 6.** Solve problems involving simple functions represented as Function Machines. [Patterns, Functions, and Algebra Goal 1]	**7, 8.** Know easy addition facts. [Operations and Computation Goal 1]	**9.** Recognize appropriate range of temperatures as hot or cold. [Measurement and Reference Frames Goal 3]	**10** Show and tell time on an analog clock to the nearest quarter-hour. [Measurement and Reference Frames Goal 4]	**11, 12.** Answer questions and draw conclusions based on data representations; compare numbers. [Number and Numeration Goal 7; Data and Chance Goal 2]		
1.													
2.													
3.													
4.													
5.													
6.													
7.													
8.													
9.													
10.													
11.													
12.													
13.													
14.													
15.													
16.													
17.													
18.													
19.													
20.													
21.													
22.													
23.													
24.													
25.													

Assess Progress: **A** = adequate progress   **N** = not adequate progress   **N/A** = not assessed   **Formative Assessments**

Copyright © Wright Group/McGraw-Hill

Class Checklist   **219**

Individual Profile of Progress

Name _____ Date _____

Lesson	Recognizing Student Achievement	A.P.*	Comments
6◆1	**Find a number between two numbers.** [Number and Numeration Goal 7]		
6◆2	**Write addition problems with a sum of 7.** [Operations and Computation Goal 2]		
6◆3	**Solve parts-and-total problems.** [Operations and Computation Goal 4]		
6◆4	**Do "stop-and-start" counting.** [Number and Numeration Goal 1]		
6◆5	**Use the Addition/Subtraction Facts Table to solve addition problems.** [Operations and Computation Goal 2]		
6◆6	**Analyze and interpret data.** [Data and Chance Goal 2]		
6◆7	**Solve easy addition facts.** [Operations and Computation Goal 1]		
6◆8	**Find the rule in "What's My Rule?" problems.** [Patterns, Functions, and Algebra Goal 1]		
6◆9	**Answer probability questions.** [Data and Chance Goal 3]		
6◆10	**Solve number stories.** [Operations and Computation Goal 4]		
6◆11	**Show and tell time.** [Measurement and Reference Frames Goal 4]		
6◆12	**Solve and record addition problems.** [Operations and Computation Goal 2]		

*Assess Progress: **A** = adequate progress   **N** = not adequate progress   **N/A** = not assessed

Individual Profile of Progress

Name _____ Date _____

Problem(s)	Progress Check 6	A.P.*	Comments
Oral/Slate Assessment			
1	Tell which number is greater: 10 or 15; 42 or 24; 37 or 22. [Number and Numeration Goal 7]		
2	Tell which number is less: 33 or 13; 9 or 10; 60 or 70. [Number and Numeration Goal 7]		
3	Solve number stories and record number models on slates. [Operations and Computation Goal 4]		
4	Write the sum and the turn-around fact for addition problems. [Operations and Computation Goal 1; Patterns, Functions, and Algebra Goal 3]		
Written Assessment Part A			
1, 2	Read, write, and represent with base-10 blocks whole numbers through hundreds; identify digits and express their values in such numbers. [Number and Numeration Goal 3]		
3, 4	Use concrete materials and pictures to find equivalent names for numbers; use tally marks and numerical expressions involving addition and subtraction of 1-digit and 2-digit whole numbers to represent equivalent names for numbers. [Number and Numeration Goal 6]		
5	Know and compare the value of a penny, nickel, dime, and quarter; calculate and compare the values of combinations of coins. [Operations and Computation Goal 2; Measurement and Reference Frames Goal 2]		
6	Know easy addition and subtraction facts including −0, −1, doubles, and sums of 10. [Operations and Computation Goal 1]		
Written Assessment Part B			
7, 8	Estimate and compare the lengths of objects. [Measurement and Reference Frames Goal 1]		
9	Use the Commutative Property of Addition (the turn-around rule) to solve basic addition facts. [Operations and Computation Goal 1; Patterns, Functions, and Algebra Goal 3]		

*Assess Progress: **A** = adequate progress **N** = not adequate progress **N/A** = not assessed **Formative Assessments**

Class _____

Date _____

Names	Find a number between two numbers. [Number and Numeration Goal 7] 6•1	Write addition problems with a sum of 7. [Operations and Computation Goal 2] 6•2	Solve parts-and-total problems. [Operations and Computation Goal 4] 6•3	Do "stop-and-start" counting. [Number and Numeration Goal 1] 6•4	Use the Addition/Subtraction Facts Table to solve addition problems. [Operations and Computation Goal 2] 6•5	Analyze and interpret data. [Data and Chance Goal 2] 6•6	Solve easy addition facts. [Operations and Computation Goal 1] 6•7	Find the rule in "What's My Rule?" problems. [Patterns, Functions, and Algebra Goal 1] 6•8	Answer probability questions. [Data and Chance Goal 3] 6•9	Solve number stories. [Operations and Computation Goal 4] 6•10	Show and tell time. [Measurement and Reference Frames Goal 4] 6•11	Solve and record addition problems. [Operations and Computation Goal 2] 6•12
1.												
2.												
3.												
4.												
5.												
6.												
7.												
8.												
9.												
10.												
11.												
12.												
13.												
14.												
15.												
16.												
17.												
18.												
19.												
20.												
21.												
22.												
23.												
24.												
25.												

Assess Progress:　**A** = adequate progress　**N** = not adequate progress　**N/A** = not assessed

Class Checklist:
Progress Check 6

Unit 6

Class _____

Date _____

Names	Oral/Slate				Written Part A					Part B	
	1. Tell which number is greater: 10 or 15; 42 or 24; 37 or 22. [Number and Numeration Goal 7]	2. Tell which number is less: 33 or 13; 9 or 10; 60 or 70. [Number and Numeration Goal 7]	3. Solve number stories and record number models on slates. [Operations and Computation Goal 4]	4. Write the sum and the turn-around fact for addition problems. [Operations and Computation Goal 1; Patterns, Functions, and Algebra Goal 3]	1, 2. Read, write, and represent with base-10 blocks whole numbers through hundreds; identify digits and express their values in such numbers. [Number and Numeration Goal 3]	3, 4. Use concrete materials and pictures to find equivalent names for numbers; use tally marks and numerical expressions involving addition and subtraction of 1-digit and 2-digit whole numbers to represent equivalent names for numbers. [Number and Numeration Goal 6]	5. Know and compare the value of a penny, nickel, dime, and quarter; calculate and compare the values of combinations of coins. [Operations and Computation Goal 2; Measurement and Reference Frames Goal 2]	6. Know easy addition and subtraction facts including −0, −1, doubles, and sums of 10. [Operations and Computation Goal 1]	7, 8. Estimate and compare the lengths of objects. [Measurement and Reference Frames Goal 1]	9. Use the Commutative Property of Addition (the turn-around rule) to solve basic addition facts. [Operations and Computation Goal 1; Patterns, Functions, and Algebra Goal 3]
1.										
2.										
3.										
4.										
5.										
6.										
7.										
8.										
9.										
10.										
11.										
12.										
13.										
14.										
15.										
16.										
17.										
18.										
19.										
20.										
21.										
22.										
23.										
24.										
25.										

Assess Progress: **A** = adequate progress   **N** = not adequate progress   **N/A** = not assessed   **Formative Assessments**

Individual Profile of Progress

Name _____   Date _____

Lesson	Recognizing Student Achievement	A.P.*	Comments
7◆1	**Solve change-to-less problems.** [Operations and Computation Goal 4]		
7◆2	**Write fact families.** [Patterns, Functions, and Algebra Goal 3]		
7◆3	**Identify 2-dimensional shapes.** [Geometry Goal 1]		
7◆4	**Count the value of quarters.** [Measurement and Reference Frames Goal 2]		
7◆5	**Name numbers represented by base-10 blocks.** [Number and Numeration Goal 3]		
7◆6	**Identify attributes of attribute blocks.** [Geometry Goal 1]		
7◆7	**Identify cylinders.** [Geometry Goal 1]		

*Assess Progress: **A** = adequate progress   **N** = not adequate progress   **N/A** = not assessed

Individual Profile of Progress

Name _____   Date _____

Problem(s)	Progress Check 7	A.P.*	Comments
Oral/Slate Assessment			
1	**Look around the room to find and point to a triangle, a square, a rectangle, a hexagon, a circle, a trapezoid, and a rhombus.** [Geometry Goal 1]		
2	**Tell the times shown on the demonstration clock. 4:45, 1:15, 11:45.** [Measurement and Reference Frames Goal 4]		
3	**Know easy addition and subtraction facts.** [Operations and Computation Goal 1]		
4	**Write the numbers and fact families that go with the Fact Triangles on slates.** [Patterns, Functions, and Algebra Goal 3]		
Written Assessment Part A			
1, 4	**Read, write, and represent with base-10 blocks whole numbers; identify digits.** [Number and Numeration Goal 3]		
2	**Use the Commutative Property of Addition.** [Patterns, Functions, and Algebra Goal 3]		
3	**Tell time on an analog clock.** [Measurement and Reference Frames Goal 4]		
5	**Identify and describe plane figures.** [Geometry Goal 1]		
6	**Answer questions based on data representations.** [Data and Chance Goal 2]		
Written Assessment Part B			
7	**Solve problems involving Function Machines.** [Patterns, Functions, and Algebra Goal 1]		
8	**Show time on an analog clock.** [Measurement and Reference Frames Goal 4]		
9	**Calculate the values of combinations of coins.** [Operations and Computation Frames Goal 2]		

*Assess Progress: **A** = adequate progress   **N** = not adequate progress   **N/A** = not assessed   Formative Assessments

Class _____

Date _____

Names	Solve change-to-less problems. [Operations and Computation Goal 4] 7•1	Write fact families. [Patterns, Functions, and Algebra Goal 3] 7•2	Identify 2-dimensional shapes. [Geometry Goal 1] 7•3	Count the value of quarters. [Measurement and Reference Frames Goal 2] 7•4	Name numbers represented by base-10 blocks. [Number and Numeration Goal 3] 7•5	Identify attributes of attribute blocks. [Geometry Goal 1] 7•6	Identify cylinders. [Geometry Goal 1] 7•7
1.							
2.							
3.							
4.							
5.							
6.							
7.							
8.							
9.							
10.							
11.							
12.							
13.							
14.							
15.							
16.							
17.							
18.							
19.							
20.							
21.							
22.							
23.							
24.							
25.							

Assess Progress: **A** = adequate progress   **N** = not adequate progress   **N/A** = not assessed

Class Checklist:
Progress Check 7

Class _____

Date _____

	Oral/Slate				Written Part A					Part B		
Names	1. Look around the room to find and point to a triangle, a square, a rectangle, a hexagon, a circle, a trapezoid, and a rhombus. [Geometry Goal 1]	2. Tell the times shown on the demonstration clock. 4:45, 1:15, 11:45. [Measurement and Reference Frames Goal 4]	3. Know easy addition and subtraction facts. [Operations and Computation Goal 1]	4. Write the numbers and fact families that go with the Fact Triangles on slates. [Patterns, Functions, and Algebra Goal 3]	1, 4. Read, write, and represent with base-10 blocks whole numbers; identify digits. [Number and Numeration Goal 3]	2. Use the Commutative Property of Addition. [Patterns, Functions, and Algebra Goal 3]	3. Tell time on an analog clock. [Measurement and Reference Frames Goal 4]	5. Identify and describe plane figures. [Geometry Goal 1]	6. Answer questions based on data representations. [Data and Chance Goal 2]	7. Solve problems involving Function Machines. [Patterns, Functions, and Algebra Goal 1]	8. Show time on an analog clock. [Measurement and Reference Frames Goal 4]	9. Calculate the values of combinations of coins. [Operations and Computation Goal 2]
1.												
2.												
3.												
4.												
5.												
6.												
7.												
8.												
9.												
10.												
11.												
12.												
13.												
14.												
15.												
16.												
17.												
18.												
19.												
20.												
21.												
22.												
23.												
24.												
25.												

Assess Progress: **A** = adequate progress   **N** = not adequate progress   **N/A** = not assessed   **Formative Assessments**

Individual Profile of Progress

Name _____   Date _____

Lesson	Recognizing Student Achievement	A.P.*	Comments
8◆1	**Count money.** [Operations and Computation Goal 2]		
8◆2	**Compare numbers using <, >, and =.** [Patterns, Functions, and Algebra Goal 2]		
8◆3	**Model numbers with base-10 blocks.** [Number and Numeration Goal 3]		
8◆4	**Solve subtraction facts.** [Operations and Computation Goal 1]		
8◆5	**Find 10 more and 10 less than numbers and circle the tens digits.** [Number and Numeration Goal 3]		
8◆6	**Divide a region into halves.** [Number and Numeration Goal 4]		
8◆7	**Draw the missing half of a symmetrical figure.** [Geometry Goal 2]		
8◆8	**Determine the likelihood of spinning a certain number.** [Data and Chance Goal 3]		
8◆9	**Name 2-dimensional shapes.** [Geometry Goal 1]		

*Assess Progress: **A** = adequate progress   **N** = not adequate progress   **N/A** = not assessed

Individual Profile of Progress

Name _____ Date _____

Problem(s)	Progress Check 8	A.P.*	Comments
Oral/Slate Assessment			
1	**State an equivalent of a given number.** [Number and Numeration Goal 6]		
2	**Determine whether there would be two equal parts if the shape were folded on the dotted line.** [Number and Numeration Goal 4]		
3	**Draw given shapes using the Pattern-Block Template, divide the shape into equal parts, and label the equal parts with fractions.** [Number and Numeration Goal 4]		
4	**Write a given number on slates and circle the digit in the specified place.** [Number and Numeration Goal 3]		
Written Assessment Part A			
1, 2	**Use drawings to represent and explain simple fractions (halves) as equal parts of a region.** [Number and Numeration Goal 4]		
2	**Complete simple 2-dimensional symmetric shapes or designs.** [Geometry Goal 2]		
3	**Use pictures to find equivalent names for numbers; use tally marks and numerical expressions involving addition and subtraction of 1-digit and 2-digit whole numbers to represent equivalent names for numbers.** [Number and Numeration Goal 6]		
4	**Read, write, and represent with base-10 blocks whole numbers through hundreds; identify digits and express their values in such numbers.** [Number and Numeration Goal 3]		
5	**Know easy addition and subtraction facts including sums to 10; use +, −, and = to write number sentences; use the Commutative Property of Addition to solve basic addition facts.** [Operations and Computation Goal 1; Patterns, Functions, and Algebra Goals 2 and 3]		
6	**Know the value of a penny, nickel, dime, quarter. Calculate and compare the values of combinations of coins. Solve number stories.** [Operations and Computation Goal 2]		
Written Assessment Part B			
7	**Use drawings to represent and explain simple fractions (thirds) as equal parts of a region.** [Number and Numeration Goal 4]		
8	**Identify and describe solid figures such as pyramids, cubes, and cylinders.** [Geometry Goal 1]		
9	**Know addition facts; use +, −, and = to write number sentences; use the Commutative Property of Addition to solve basic addition facts.** [Operations and Computation Goal 1; Patterns, Functions, and Algebra Goals 2 and 3]		

*Assess Progress: **A** = adequate progress **N** = not adequate progress **N/A** = not assessed **Formative Assessments**

Class Checklist:

Recognizing Student Achievement

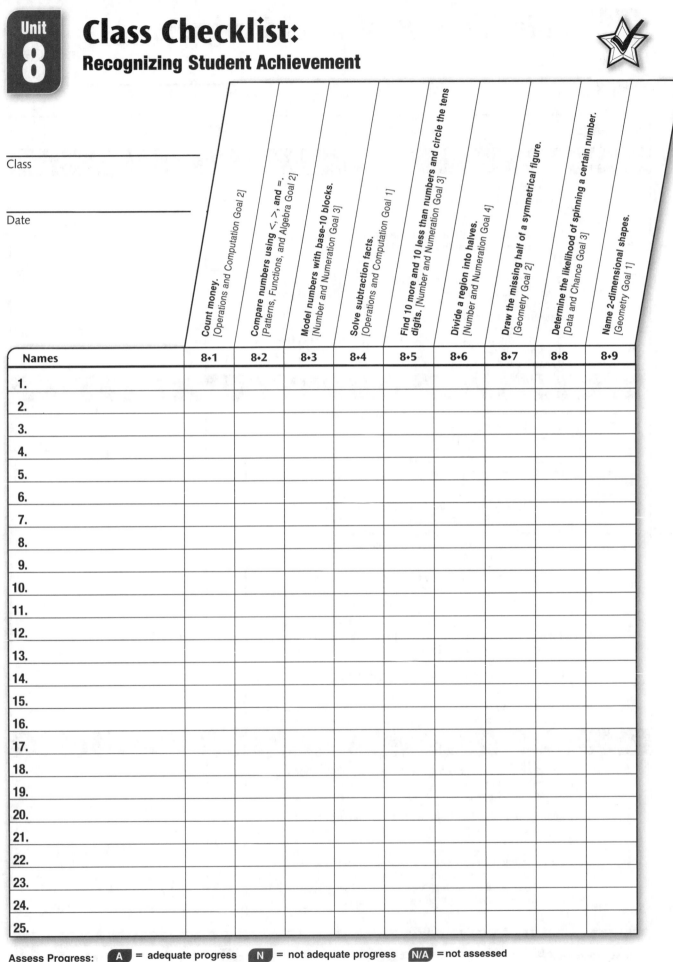

Class _____

Date _____

Names	Count money. [Operations and Computation Goal 2] 8·1	Compare numbers using <, >, and =. [Patterns, Functions, and Algebra Goal 2] 8·2	Model numbers with base-10 blocks. [Number and Numeration Goal 3] 8·3	Solve subtraction facts. [Operations and Computation Goal 1] 8·4	Find 10 more and 10 less than numbers and circle the tens digits. [Number and Numeration Goal 3] 8·5	Divide a region into halves. [Number and Numeration Goal 4] 8·6	Draw the missing half of a symmetrical figure. [Geometry Goal 2] 8·7	Determine the likelihood of spinning a certain number. [Data and Chance Goal 3] 8·8	Name 2-dimensional shapes. [Geometry Goal 1] 8·9
1.									
2.									
3.									
4.									
5.									
6.									
7.									
8.									
9.									
10.									
11.									
12.									
13.									
14.									
15.									
16.									
17.									
18.									
19.									
20.									
21.									
22.									
23.									
24.									
25.									

Assess Progress: **A** = adequate progress **N** = not adequate progress **N/A** = not assessed

Unit 8

Class Checklist:
Progress Check 8

Class _____

Date _____

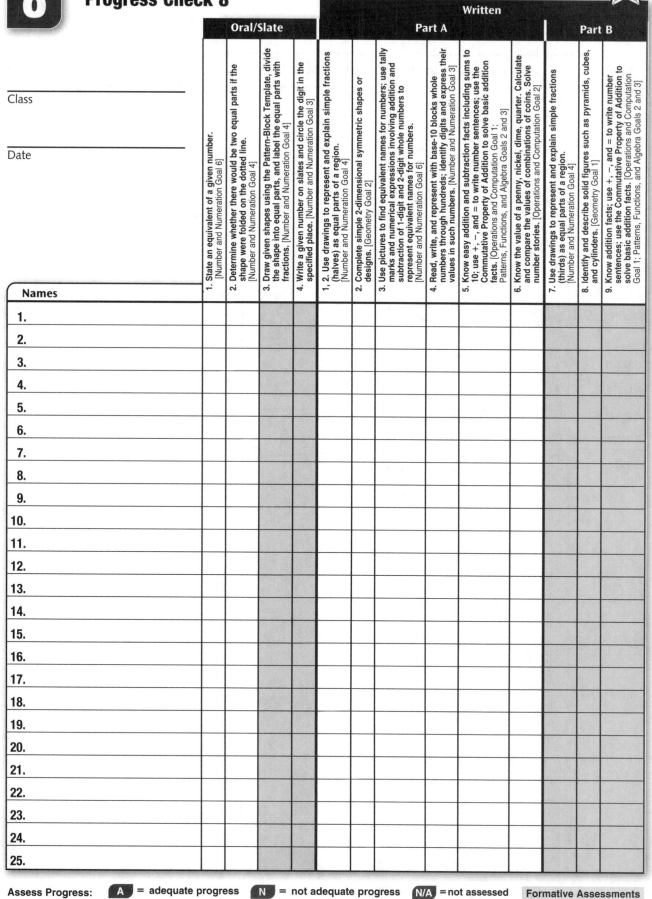

	Oral/Slate				Written Part A						Part B		
Names	1. State an equivalent of a given number. [Number and Numeration Goal 6]	2. Determine whether there would be two equal parts if the shape were folded on the dotted line. [Number and Numeration Goal 4]	3. Draw given shapes using the Pattern-Block Template, divide the shape into equal parts, and label the equal parts with fractions. [Number and Numeration Goal 4]	4. Write a given number on slates and circle the digit in the specified place. [Number and Numeration Goal 3]	1, 2. Use drawings to represent and explain simple fractions (halves) as equal parts of a region. [Number and Numeration Goal 4]	2. Complete simple 2-dimensional symmetric shapes or designs. [Geometry Goal 2]	3. Use pictures to find equivalent names for numbers; use tally marks and numerical expressions involving addition and subtraction of 1-digit and 2-digit whole numbers to represent equivalent names for numbers. [Number and Numeration Goal 6]	4. Read, write, and represent with base-10 blocks whole numbers through hundreds; identify digits and express their values in such numbers. [Number and Numeration Goal 3]	5. Know easy addition and subtraction facts including sums to 10; use +, −, and = to write number sentences; use the Commutative Property of Addition to solve basic addition facts. [Operations and Computation Goal 1; Patterns, Functions, and Algebra Goals 2 and 3]	6. Know the value of a penny, nickel, dime, quarter. Calculate and compare the values of combinations of coins. Solve number stories. [Operations and Computation Goal 2]	7. Use drawings to represent and explain simple fractions (thirds) as equal parts of a region. [Number and Numeration Goal 4]	8. Identify and describe solid figures such as pyramids, cubes, and cylinders. [Geometry Goal 1]	9. Know addition facts; use +, −, and = to write number sentences; use the Commutative Property of Addition to solve basic addition facts. [Operations and Computation Goal 1; Patterns, Functions, and Algebra Goals 2 and 3]
1.													
2.													
3.													
4.													
5.													
6.													
7.													
8.													
9.													
10.													
11.													
12.													
13.													
14.													
15.													
16.													
17.													
18.													
19.													
20.													
21.													
22.													
23.													
24.													
25.													

Assess Progress: **A** = adequate progress   **N** = not adequate progress   **N/A** = not assessed   **Formative Assessments**

Individual Profile of Progress

Name _____   Date _____

Lesson	Recognizing Student Achievement	A.P.*	Comments
9◆1	**Order numbers to 110.** [Number and Numeration Goal 7]		
9◆2	**Use a number grid to add and subtract.** [Operations and Computation Goal 2]		
9◆3	**Name 2-dimensional shapes.** [Geometry Goal 1]		
9◆4	**Find fractions of a collection.** [Number and Numeration Goal 4]		
9◆5	**Create numbers using specified digits.** [Number and Numeration Goal 3]		
9◆6	**Divide shapes into equal parts.** [Number and Numeration Goal 4]		
9◆7	**Solve number-grid puzzles.** [Patterns, Functions, and Algebra Goal 1]		
9◆8	**Estimate sums.** [Operations and Computation Goal 3]		

*Assess Progress: **A** = adequate progress   **N** = not adequate progress   **N/A** = not assessed

Name _____   Date _____

Problem(s)	Progress Check 9	A.P.*	Comments
Oral/Slate Assessment			
1	**Tell time on an analog clock.** [Measurement and Reference Frames Goal 4]		
2	**Find the rule in function machines.** [Patterns, Functions, and Algebra Goal 1]		
3	**Write the number represented by the base-10 blocks and the new number.** [Number and Numeration Goal 3]		
4	**Show amounts of money by drawing symbols on slates.** [Operations and Computation Goal 2; Measurement and Reference Frames Goal 2]		
Written Assessment Part A			
1	**Know easy addition and subtraction facts including +/−1, −0, and sums of 10. Compare sums.** [Number and Numeration Goal 7; Operations and Computation Goal 1]		
2	**Use drawings to represent and explain simple fractions (fourths) as equal parts of a collection.** [Number and Numeration Goal 4]		
3	**Know the value of a penny, nickel, dime, quarter and dollar bill; make exchanges between coins; calculate and compare the values of combinations of coins.** [Operations and Computation Goal 2; Measurement and Reference Frames Goal 2]		
4	**Show and tell the time on an analog clock to the nearest quarter-hour.** [Measurement and Reference Frames Goal 4]		
5	**Know easy addition and subtraction facts including +/−0; solve problems represented as function machines.** [Operations and Computation Goal 1; Patterns, Functions, and Algebra Goal 1]		
6	**Read, write, and represent with base-10 blocks whole numbers through hundreds.** [Number and Numeration Goal 3]		
Written Assessment Part B			
7	**Know easy addition and subtraction facts including −1.** [Operations and Computation Goal 1]		
8	**Use drawings to represent and explain simple fractions (halves) as equal parts of a region. Know the value of a dime; calculate and compare the values of combinations of coins.** [Number and Numeration Goal 4; Operations and Computation Goal 2; Measurement and Reference Frames Goal 2]		

*Assess Progress: **A** = adequate progress   **N** = not adequate progress   **N/A** = not assessed   **Formative Assessments**

Class _____

Date _____

Names	Order numbers to 110. [Number and Numeration Goal 7] 9•1	Use a number grid to add and subtract. [Operations and Computation Goal 2] 9•2	Name 2-dimensional shapes. [Geometry Goal 1] 9•3	Find fractions of a collection. [Number and Numeration Goal 4] 9•4	Create numbers using specified digits. [Number and Numeration Goal 3] 9•5	Divide shapes into equal parts. [Number and Numeration Goal 4] 9•6	Solve number-grid puzzles. [Patterns, Functions, and Algebra Goal 1] 9•7	Estimate sums. [Operations and Computation Goal 3] 9•8
1.								
2.								
3.								
4.								
5.								
6.								
7.								
8.								
9.								
10.								
11.								
12.								
13.								
14.								
15.								
16.								
17.								
18.								
19.								
20.								
21.								
22.								
23.								
24.								
25.								

Assess Progress: **A** = adequate progress   **N** = not adequate progress   **N/A** = not assessed

Class Checklist:
Progress Check 9

Class _____

Date _____

	Oral/Slate				Written Part A							Written Part B	
Names	1. Tell time on an analog clock. [Measurement and Reference Frames Goal 4]	2. Find the rule in function machines. [Patterns, Functions, and Algebra Goal 1]	3. Write the number represented by the base-10 blocks and the new number. [Number and Numeration Goal 3]	4. Show amounts of money by drawing symbols on slates. [Operations and Computation Goal 2; Measurement and Reference Frames Goal 2]	1. Know easy addition and subtraction facts including +/−1, −0, and sums of 10. Compare sums. [Number and Numeration Goal 7; Operations and Computation Goal 1]	2. Use drawings to represent and explain simple fractions (fourths) as equal parts of a collection. [Number and Numeration Goal 4]	3. Know the value of a penny, nickel, dime, quarter, and dollar bill; make exchanges between coins; calculate and compare the values of combinations of coins. [Operations and Computation Goal 2; Measurement and Reference Frames Goal 2]	4. Show and tell the time on an analog clock to the nearest quarter-hour. [Measurement and Reference Frames Goal 4]	5. Know easy addition and subtraction facts including +/−0; solve problems represented as function machines. [Operations and Computation Goal 1; Patterns, Functions, and Algebra Goal 1]	6. Read, write, and represent with base-10 blocks whole numbers through hundreds. [Number and Numeration Goal 3]		7. Know easy addition and subtraction facts including −1. [Operations and Computation Goal 1]	8. Use drawings to represent and explain simple fractions (halves) as equal parts of a region. Know the value of a dime; calculate and compare the values of combinations of coins. [Number and Numeration Goal 4; Operations and Computation Goal 2; Measurement and Reference Frames Goal 2]
1.													
2.													
3.													
4.													
5.													
6.													
7.													
8.													
9.													
10.													
11.													
12.													
13.													
14.													
15.													
16.													
17.													
18.													
19.													
20.													
21.													
22.													
23.													
24.													
25.													

Assess Progress: **A** = adequate progress **N** = not adequate progress **N/A** = not assessed **Formative Assessments**

Name _____ Date _____

Lesson	Recognizing Student Achievement	A.P.*	Comments
10◆1	**Find data landmarks.** [Data and Chance Goal 2]		
10◆2	**Identify the number of minutes in movements of the minute hand.** [Measurement and Reference Frames Goal 4]		
10◆3	**Compare numbers.** [Number and Numeration Goal 7]		
10◆4	**Find the difference between two money amounts.** [Operations and Computation Goal 2]		
10◆5	**Estimate sums.** [Operations and Computation Goal 3]		
10◆6	**Compare temperatures.** [Measurement and Reference Frames Goal 3]		
10◆7	**Solve number-grid puzzles.** [Patterns, Functions, and Algebra Goal 1]		

*Assess Progress: **A** = adequate progress   **N** = not adequate progress   **N/A** = not assessed

Name _____ Date _____

Problem(s)	Progress Check 10	A.P.*	Comments
Oral/Slate Assessment			
1	**Solve coin riddles using tool-kit coins.** [Operations and Computation Goal 2; Measurement and Reference Frames Goal 2]		
2	**Play *Beat the Calculator* with easy addition and subtraction facts.** [Operations and Computation Goal 1]		
3	**Write the number that is 10 more or 10 less than a given number and circle the digit in the specified place.** [Number and Numeration Goals 1 and 3]		
4	**Record a number model and the answers to number stories on slates.** [Operations and Computation Goal 4]		
Written Assessment Part A			
1	**Solve number-grid puzzles.** [Patterns, Functions, and Algebra Goal 2]		
2	**Know and compare the value of pennies, nickels, dimes, and quarters.** [Operations and Computation Goal 2; Measurement and Reference Frames Goal 2]		
3	**Compare whole numbers up to 1,000 using >, <, and =.** [Number and Numeration Goal 7; Patterns, Functions, and Algebra Goal 2]		
4	**Demonstrate proficiency with +/−0, +/−1, doubles, and sum-equals-ten addition and subtraction facts.** [Operations and Computation Goal 1]		
5, 6	**Write number sentences using the symbols +, −, and =.** [Patterns, Functions, and Algebra Goal 2]		
5–7	**Identify places in given numbers and the values of the digits in those places.** [Number and Numeration Goal 3]		
Written Assessment Part B			
8	**Find the maximum and minimum of a data set.** [Data and Chance Goal 2]		
9	**Use graphs to answer simple questions and draw conclusions.** [Data and Chance Goal 2]		

*Assess Progress: **A** = adequate progress **N** = not adequate progress **N/A** = not assessed **Formative Assessments**

Class _____

Date _____

Names	Find data landmarks. [Data and Chance Goal 2] 10·1	Identify the number of minutes in movements of the minute hand. [Measurement and Reference Frames Goal 4] 10·2	Compare numbers. [Number and Numeration Goal 7] 10·3	Find the difference between two money amounts. [Operations and Computation Goal 2] 10·4	Estimate sums. [Operations and Computation Goal 3] 10·5	Compare temperatures. [Measurement and Reference Frames Goal 3] 10·6	Solve number-grid puzzles. [Patterns, Functions, and Algebra Goal 1] 10·7
1.							
2.							
3.							
4.							
5.							
6.							
7.							
8.							
9.							
10.							
11.							
12.							
13.							
14.							
15.							
16.							
17.							
18.							
19.							
20.							
21.							
22.							
23.							
24.							
25.							

Assess Progress: **A** = adequate progress **N** = not adequate progress **N/A** = not assessed

Class _____

Date _____

	Oral/Slate				Written Part A						Part B	
Names	1. Solve coin riddles using tool-kit coins. [Operations and Computation Goal 2; Measurement and Reference Frames Goal 2]	2. Play *Beat the Calculator* with easy addition and subtraction facts. [Operations and Computation Goal 1]	3. Write the number that is 10 more or 10 less than a given number and circle the digit in the specified place. [Number and Numeration Goals 1 and 3]	4. Record a number model and the answers to number stories on slates. [Operations and Computation Goal 4]	1. Solve number-grid puzzles. [Patterns, Functions, and Algebra Goal 2]	2. Know and compare the value of pennies, nickels, dimes, and quarters. [Operations and Computation Goal 2; Measurement and Reference Frames Goal 2]	3. Compare whole numbers up to 1,000 using >, <, and =. [Number and Numeration Goal 7; Patterns, Functions, and Algebra Goal 2]	4. Demonstrate proficiency with +/−0, +/−1, doubles, and sum-equals-ten addition and subtraction facts. [Operations and Computation Goal 1]	5, 6. Write number sentences using the symbols +, −, and =. [Patterns, Functions, and Algebra Goal 2]	5–7. Identify places in given numbers and the values of the digits in those places. [Number and Numeration Goal 3]	8. Find the maximum and minimum of a data set. [Data and Chance Goal 2]	9. Use graphs to answer simple questions and draw conclusions. [Data and Chance Goal 2]
1.												
2.												
3.												
4.												
5.												
6.												
7.												
8.												
9.												
10.												
11.												
12.												
13.												
14.												
15.												
16.												
17.												
18.												
19.												
20.												
21.												
22.												
23.												
24.												
25.												

Assess Progress: **A** = adequate progress   **N** = not adequate progress   **N/A** = not assessed   **Formative Assessments**

Quarterly Checklist: Quarter 1

Goal	1	1	7	3	7	3	6	3	7	1	7	3	3	7	6	7	1
Number and Numeration																	
Lesson	1·1	1·2	1·3	1·4	1·5	1·6	1·7	1·8	1·9	1·11	1·12	2·1	2·2	2·4	2·5	2·6	2·8	2·9
Names / Date																		
1.																		
2.																		
3.																		
4.																		
5.																		
6.																		
7.																		
8.																		
9.																		
10.																		
11.																		
12.																		
13.																		
14.																		
15.																		
16.																		
17.																		
18.																		
19.																		
20.																		
21.																		
22.																		

Quarterly Checklist: Quarter 1

Names	Operations and Computation							Data and Chance			Measurement and Reference Frames			Geometry			Patterns, Functions, and Algebra		
Goal	2	4	1	2	2	2	2				4								
Lesson	1·10	1·13	2·3	2·7	2·10	2·12	2·13				2·11								
Date																			
1.																			
2.																			
3.																			
4.																			
5.																			
6.																			
7.																			
8.																			
9.																			
10.																			
11.																			
12.																			
13.																			
14.																			
15.																			
16.																			
17.																			
18.																			
19.																			
20.																			
21.																			
22.																			

Quarterly Checklist: Quarter 2

Names	Number and Numeration											Operations and Computation										
Goal	5	7	1	1	1	1	7	3	6	7	3	2	4	1	2	2	4	2	1	2	4	2
Lesson	3•2	3•3	3•5	3•8	3•10	4•1	4•5	5•1	5•4	5•7	5•8	3•4	3•12	3•13	3•14	4•2	4•6	4•7	4•12	5•2	5•10	5•13
Date																						
1.																						
2.																						
3.																						
4.																						
5.																						
6.																						
7.																						
8.																						
9.																						
10.																						
11.																						
12.																						
13.																						
14.																						
15.																						
16.																						
17.																						
18.																						
19.																						
20.																						
21.																						
22.																						

Quarterly Checklist: Quarter 2

Names	Goal																				
	Data and Chance				Measurement and Reference Frames								Geometry				Patterns, Functions, and Algebra				
	2	3		2	1	4	4	1	4	1	3				1	2	1	1	1	2	3
Lesson	3•7	4•10		3•11	4•4	4•8	4•11	4•9	5•5	5•9	5•12				3•1	3•6	3•9	4•3	5•3	5•6	5•11
Date																					
1.																					
2.																					
3.																					
4.																					
5.																					
6.																					
7.																					
8.																					
9.																					
10.																					
11.																					
12.																					
13.																					
14.																					
15.																					
16.																					
17.																					
18.																					
19.																					
20.																					
21.																					
22.																					

Quarterly Checklist: Quarter 3

Names	Number and Numeration						Operations and Computation									Data and Chance		
Goal	7	1	3	3	3	4	2	4	2	1	4	2	4	2	1	2	3	3
Lesson	6·1	6·4	7·5	8·3	8·5	8·6	6·2	6·3	6·5	6·7	6·10	6·12	7·1	8·1	8·4	6·6	6·9	8·8
Date																		
1.																		
2.																		
3.																		
4.																		
5.																		
6.																		
7.																		
8.																		
9.																		
10.																		
11.																		
12.																		
13.																		
14.																		
15.																		
16.																		
17.																		
18.																		
19.																		
20.																		
21.																		
22.																		

Quarterly Checklist: Quarter 3

Names	Measurement and Reference Frames			Geometry				Patterns, Functions, and Algebra		
Goal	4	2	2	1	1	2	1	1	3	2
Lesson	6·11	7·4	8·2	7·3	7·6	7·7	8·7	8·9	6·8	7·2	8·2
Date											
1.											
2.											
3.											
4.											
5.											
6.											
7.											
8.											
9.											
10.											
11.											
12.											
13.											
14.											
15.											
16.											
17.											
18.											
19.											
20.											
21.											
22.											

Quarterly Checklist: Quarter 4

Names	Goal										
	Number and Numeration					**Operations and Computation**				**Data and Chance**
	7	4	3	4	7	2	3	2	3	2
Lesson	9·1	9·4	9·5	9·6	10·3	9·2	9·8	10·4	10·5	10·1
Date										
1.										
2.										
3.										
4.										
5.										
6.										
7.										
8.										
9.										
10.										
11.										
12.										
13.										
14.										
15.										
16.										
17.										
18.										
19.										
20.										
21.										
22.										

Quarterly Checklist: Quarter 4

Names		Measurement and Reference Frames				Geometry			Patterns, Functions, and Algebra					
Goal		4	3			1			1	1				
Lesson		10·2	10·6			9·3			9·7	10·7					
Date														
1.														
2.														
3.														
4.														
5.														
6.														
7.														
8.														
9.														
10.														
11.														
12.														
13.														
14.														
15.														
16.														
17.														
18.														
19.														
20.														
21.														
22.														

Individual Profile of Progress

Name _____   Date _____

Lesson	Recognizing Student Achievement	A.P.*	Comments

*Assess Progress: **A** = adequate progress   **N** = not adequate progress   **N/A** = not assessed

Class Checklist:
Recognizing Student Achievement

Class _____

Date _____

Names								
1.								
2.								
3.								
4.								
5.								
6.								
7.								
8.								
9.								
10.								
11.								
12.								
13.								
14.								
15.								
16.								
17.								
18.								
19.								
20.								
21.								
22.								
23.								
24.								
25.								

Assess Progress: **A** = adequate progress   **N** = not adequate progress   **N/A** = not assessed

Parent Reflections

Use some of the following questions (or your own) and tell us how you see your child progressing in mathematics.

Do you see evidence of your child using mathematics at home?

What do you think are your child's strengths and challenges in mathematics?

Does your child demonstrate responsibility for completing Home Links?

What thoughts do you have about your child's progress in mathematics?

_____

_____

_____

_____

_____

_____

_____

_____

_____

_____

_____

_____

_____

_____

_____

_____

My Exit Slip

251

- -

Name   Date   Time

My Exit Slip

About My Math Class A

Draw a face or write the words that show how you feel.

☺ 😐 ☹
Good   OK   Not so good

1. This is how I feel about math:	**2.** This is how I feel about working with a partner or in a group:	**3.** This is how I feel about working by myself:
4. This is how I feel about solving number stories:	**5.** This is how I feel about doing Home Links with my family:	**6.** This is how I feel about finding new ways to solve problems:

Circle **yes, sometimes**, or **no**.

7. I like to figure things out. I am curious.

yes   sometimes   no

8. I keep trying even when I don't understand something right away.

yes   sometimes   no

About My Math Class B

Circle the word that best describes how you feel.

1. I enjoy mathematics class.   **yes   sometimes   no**

2. I like to work with a partner   **yes   sometimes   no**
or in a group.

3. I like to work by myself.   **yes   sometimes   no**

4. I like to solve problems   **yes   sometimes   no**
in mathematics.

5. I enjoy doing Home Links   **yes   sometimes   no**
with my family.

6. In mathematics, I am good at _____

_____

_____

7. One thing I like about mathematics is _____

_____

_____

8. One thing I find difficult in mathematics is _____

_____

_____

Math Log A

What did you learn in mathematics this week?

Math Log B

Question:

Math Log C

Work Box	Tell how you solved this problem.
	_____
	_____
	_____
	_____
	_____

256

✂

Math Log C

Work Box	Tell how you solved this problem.
	_____
	_____
	_____
	_____
	_____

Good Work!

I have chosen this work for my portfolio because

_____

_____

_____

_____

_____

_____

_____

_____

_____

_____

_____

_____

_____

_____

_____

_____

_____

My Work

This work shows that I can _____

_____

_____

I am still learning to _____

_____

_____

_____

258

--✂

My Work

This work shows that I can _____

_____

_____

I am still learning to _____

_____

_____

_____

Name-Collection Boxes

1.

2.

3.

4.

Glossary

Assessment Management System An online management system designed to track student, class, school, and district progress toward Grade-Level Goals.

Class Checklists Recording tools that can be used to keep track of a class's progress on specific Grade-Level Goals.

Content for Assessment Material that is important for children to learn and is the focus of assessment. *Everyday Mathematics* highlights this content through Grade-Level Goals.

Contexts for Assessment Ongoing, periodic, and external assessments based on products or observations.

Enrichment activities Optional activities that apply or deepen children's understanding.

Evidence from Assessment Information about children's knowledge, skills, and dispositions collected from observations or products.

External Assessments Assessments that are independent of the curriculum, for example, standardized tests.

Formative Assessments Assessments that provide information about children's current knowledge and abilities so that teachers can plan future instruction more effectively and so that children can identify their own areas of weakness or strength.

Grade-Level Goals Mathematical goals organized by content strand and articulated across grade levels from Kindergarten through Grade 6.

Individual Profile of Progress A recording tool that can be used to keep track of children's progress on specific Grade-Level Goals.

Informing Instruction note These notes in the *Teacher's Lesson Guide* suggest how to use observations of children's work to adapt instruction by describing common errors and misconceptions in children's thinking and alerting the teacher to multiple solution strategies or unique insights children might offer.

Making Adequate Progress On a trajectory to meet a Grade-Level Goal.

Math Boxes Collections of problems designed to provide distributed practice. Math Boxes revisit content from prior units to build and maintain important concepts and skills. One or two problems on each page preview content from the next unit.

Mental Math and Reflexes Exercises at three levels of difficulty that prepare children for the lesson, build mental-arithmetic skills, and help teachers quickly assess individual strengths and weaknesses.

Observational Assessments Assessments based on observing children during daily activities or periodic assessments.

Ongoing Assessments Assessments based on children's everyday work during regular classroom instruction.

Open Response task An extended response assessment included in the Progress Check lesson of each unit.

Periodic Assessments Formal assessments that are built into a curriculum such as the end-of-unit Progress Checks.

Portfolios Collections of student products and observations that provide opportunities for children to reflect on their mathematical growth and for teachers to understand and document that growth.

Product Assessments Assessments based on children's work from daily activities or from periodic assessments.

Program Evaluation Assessment intended to reveal how well a program of instruction is working. A school district, for example, might carry out program evaluation to identify schools with strong mathematics programs so that their success can be replicated.

Program Goals The fifteen cross-grade goals in *Everyday Mathematics* that weave the program together across grade levels. They form an organizing framework that supports both curriculum and assessment. Every Grade-Level Goal is linked to a Program Goal.

Progress Check lesson The last lesson in every unit. Progress Check lessons include a student Self Assessment, an Oral and Slate Assessment, a Written Assessment, and an Open Response task.

Purposes of Assessment The reasons for assessment, which include providing information that can be used to plan future instruction, identifying what students have achieved during a period of time, and evaluating the quality of the mathematics program.

Readiness Activities Optional activities in many lessons that preview lesson content or provide alternative routes of access for learning concepts and skills.

Recognizing Student Achievement note A feature in many lessons that highlights specific tasks used to monitor children's progress toward Grade-Level Goals. The notes identify the expectations for a child who is making adequate progress and point to skills or strategies that some children might be able to demonstrate.

Rubric A set of suggested guidelines for scoring assessment activities.

Student Self Assessment The individual reflection included in the Progress Check lesson of each unit.

Summative Assessments Assessments that aim to measure children's growth and achievement, for example, an assessment to determine whether children have learned certain material by the end of a fixed period of study such as a semester or a course.

Writing/Reasoning Prompt A question linked to a specific Math Boxes problem. Writing/Reasoning Prompts provide children with opportunities to respond to questions that extend and deepen their mathematical thinking.

Written Progress Check The Written Assessment included in the Progress Check lesson of each unit.

Index

A

Adequate progress. *See* Making adequate progress
Assessment. *See* Balanced Assessment; Content Assessed; Contexts for Assessment; External Assessment; Formative Assessment; Ongoing Assessment; Periodic Assessment; Purposes of Assessment; and Sources of Evidence for Assessment; Summative Assessment
Assessment Management System, 28–30
Assessment Masters, 137–176. *See* Open Response task, assessment masters; Self Assessment masters; Written Assessment, masters.
Assessment Overviews, 51–133

B

Balanced Assessment, 2–6, 7, 8, 16, 18, 20–21, 28, 30
    creating a plan, 4, 7

C

Checklists. *See* Class Checklists; Individual Profiles of Progress
    using checklists, 25–27
Class Checklists, 25–27
    general master, 249
    masters, Unit 1: 202–203, Unit 2: 206–207,
        Unit 3: 210–211, Unit 4: 214–215,
        Unit 5: 218–219, Unit 6: 222–223,
        Unit 7: 226–227, Unit 8: 230–231,
        Unit 9: 234–235, Unit 10: 238–239
    quarterly checklists, 26, 240–247
Content Assessed, 5–6
Contexts for Assessment 3–4

E

End-of-Year Assessment Answers, 197–199
End-of-Year Assessment Goals, 134–135
End-of-Year Assessment Masters, 191–196
End-of-Year written assessment, 4, 18, 20, 28
Enrichment activities, 12–14
Exit Slips, 4, 8, 10–11, 15
    master, 251
External Assessment, 3–4, 8, 18, 24

F

Formative Assessment, 2, 7, 19, 20
Frequently asked questions, 31–35

G

Game record sheets, 4, 8, 10, 12
General Masters, 248–259
    About My Math Class A, 17, 252
    About My Math Class B, 17, 253
    Class Checklist, 25–27, 249
    Good Work!, 16, 257
    Individual Profile of Progress, 25–26, 248
    Math Log A, 17, 254
    Math Log B, 17, 255
    Math Log C, 17, 256
    My Exit Slip, 251
    My Work, 16, 258
    Name-Collection Boxes, 259
    Parent Reflections, 17, 250
Grade-Level Goals, 6, 7, 10–14, 19–22, 25, 27–34, 37–50
    adequate progress toward, 10–14, 19, 20, 25, 27–30,
        32–34
    definition of, 6, 32
    exposure to versus mastery of, 6, 32, 34–35
    table list, 37–50
Grading, 30, 34

I

Informing Instruction notes, 4, 8, 9, 19
Individual Profiles of Progress, 25–26, 248
    general master, 248
    masters, Unit 1: 200–201, Unit 2: 204–205,
        Unit 3: 208–209, Unit 4: 212–213,
        Unit 5: 216–217, Unit 6: 220–221,
        Unit 7: 224–225, Unit 8: 228–229,
        Unit 9: 232–233, Unit 10: 236–237

J

Journal pages, 4, 8, 10

K

Kid Watching 4, 8

Making adequate progress
    based on a rubric, 27
    definition of, 12, 27, 32–33
    in Recognizing Student Achievement notes, 10–14, 27,
        29, 32–33
    in Written Assessments, 19
Math Boxes, 4, 8, 10, 12, 15, 24, 33
Math Logs, 15, 17, 254–256
Mental Math and Reflexes, 4, 8, 10–11, 20
Mid-Year Assessment Answers, 197–199
Mid-Year Assessment Goals, 92–93, 187
Mid-Year Assessment masters, 187–190
Mid-Year written assessment, 4, 18, 20, 28

Observations, 4, 8, 18, 26, 30
Ongoing Assessment, 3–4, 8–17, 25–26, 28
    by unit, Unit 1: 52–53, Unit 2: 60–61, Unit 3: 68,
        Unit 4: 76, Unit 5: 84, Unit 6: 94, Unit 7: 102,
        Unit 8: 110, Unit 9: 118, Unit 10: 126
Open Response tasks, 4, 18, 21–22, 24, 28
    assessment masters,140, 144, 148, 152, 156, 160, 164,
        168, 172
    by unit, Unit 1: 55–59, Unit 2: 63–67, Unit 3: 71–75
        Unit 4: 79–83, Unit 5: 87–91, Unit 6: 97–101,
        Unit 7: 105–109, Unit 8: 113–117,
        Unit 9: 121–125, Unit 10: 129–133
Oral and Slate Assessments, 20
Outside tests, 24

Parent Reflections, 17, 250
Performance-based assessments, 24, 32–33
Periodic Assessment, 3, 4, 18–23, 25–26
    by unit, Unit 1: 54–59, Unit 2: 62–67, Unit 3: 70–75,
        Unit 4: 78–83, Unit 5: 86–91, Unit 6: 96–101,
        Unit 7: 104–109, Unit 8: 112–117,
        Unit 9: 119–125, Unit 10: 128–133
Planning tips, 7
Portfolios, 4, 8, 15, 16–17, 26
Product Assessment, 16–17, 26
Products 4, 8, 18
Program Goals, 5–6, 29, 32, 37–50
    definition of, 5–6
    table list, 37–50
        Data and Chance, 5, 44–45
        Geometry, 5, 48
        Measurement and Reference Frames, 5, 46–47
        Number and Numeration, 5, 37–39
        Operations and Computation, 5, 40–43
        Patterns, Functions, and Algebra, 5, 49–50
    track progress toward, 32
Program Evaluation, 2
Progress Check Oral/Slate Assessments, 4, 18, 20, 28,
    33, 34
Progress Check Written Assessments, 4, 18, 19, 20, 28, 33,
    34, 138–176, 177–186
Purposes of Assessment, 2

Readiness activities, 12–14, 21
Recognizing Student Achievement notes, 4, 8, 10–14,
    25–29, 32–34
Record-Keeping, 25–28, 34
    Assessment Management System, 28–30
    options for recording data on checklists, 27
Rubrics, 22–23, 27, 29

Self Assessment Masters, 21, 138, 141, 145, 149, 153, 157,
    161, 165, 169, 173
Student Reports, 29
Student Self Assessment, 4, 21
Sources of Evidence for Assessment, 4
Summative Assessment, 2, 7, 19–20

Written Assessments, 4, 18, 19–20
    masters, 139, 142–143, 146–147, 150–151, 154–155,
        158–159, 162–163, 166–167, 170–171, 174–175
Writing/Reasoning Prompts for Math Boxes, 4, 8, 15